Preface ........................  .............o

Introduction ................................................................7

1.  Abbreviated Autobiography (1941-2010) ...........................9

2.  Life In Philadelphia (1941-1951) .....................................21

3.  Move to Kentucky (1951) ...........................................35

4.  Breathitt County, Kentucky (1952-1956) ............................43

5.  Perry County, Kentucky (1956-1959) ...............................53

6.  Back to Philadelphia (1959-1963) .................................71

7.  An Unexpected Reunion in Kentucky (1963) .......................93

8.  Back to Philadelphia, Again (1963-1964) .........................101

9.  Marriage and Move to Melrose Park, Pennsylvania (1964) ....113

10. Prefield Experiences (1965-1966) ................................123

11. Bonaire, Netherlands Antilles (1966-1975) ......................139

12. Guam, Western Pacific (1975-1984) .............................159

13. TWR - Chatham, New Jersey (1984-1987) ......................181

14. SLM - Madison, Georgia (1987-2004) ...........................203

15. NGM - Lexington, Georgia (2005-2011) .........................227

16. God's Faithfulness (Eternally) ..................................249

End Notes ...........................................................263

# Preface

## Myopia

Myopia is a condition of the eye in which parallel rays are focused in front of the retina, objects being seen distinctly only when near to the eye; nearsightedness (Random House Webster's College Dictionary).

## Zone

Zone refers to an area that differs in some respect, or is distinguished for some purpose, from adjoining areas, or within which distinctive circumstances exist or are established (Random House Webster's College Dictionary).

The Myopic Zone fittingly describes the basic characteristics in my journey of life. Also, my extremely nearsighted vision has resulted in many distinct circumstances that have affected and influenced how I have had to respond and react in my life's journey.

Certainly, my journey is one that has been continually affected by the Myopic Zone. And I would like to share my journey with you.

# Introduction

Life is a journey, a very brief earthly journey compared to eternity. The journey begins at birth and generally ends with death (or with the Lord's return for His saints).

It is very interesting to reflect on what has happened in the journey from its beginning to the present time. Some events are very significant, while others are extremely unimportant. Some of life's experiences are joyful; others are unhappy and sad. Many situations are unbelievable, and others are predictable.

No matter what our reactions are to specific events which take place in the journey, it is true that time is rapidly passing away. It is another reminder of the brevity of life.

James 4:14b describes it this way: "For what is your life? It is even a vapor, that appeareth for a little time, and then vanisheth away." What a picture! It's like a jet plane *just passing through* the atmosphere leaving a trail of vapor that is so unstable it will be dispersed by the wind and disappear. Sometimes the vapor trail can be an awesome sight when seen from the ground. It may last for several minutes, or even hours, but then it disappears. It's gone.

The old song is a reminder that "this world is not my home; I'm *just a passing through.* My treasures are laid up somewhere beyond the blue."

All of us are *just passing through.* Our stay may be for a good many years, or it may be very brief, but we can be very sure it will be according to God's perfect timetable. Some of the experiences that God allows to come into our lives may not be the most pleasant, but He has a purpose for them. We can take comfort from God's Word in Isaiah 32:21a: "When thou *passest through* the waters, they shall not overflow thee." These difficulties are just temporary.

What happens when someone *just passes through?* How will it have an influence on others? It may be great, or it may be small. It may be for good, or it may be for evil. The results may be momentary, or they may last for a good long time.

Whenever I travel overseas, I carry a Travel Cup with me. This cup contains a small but effective filter that will remove contaminants and impurities from water. The water *just passes through* the filter, making it safe to drink. It takes only seconds, but what a difference that brief time makes in purifying the water! The water must be flowing. Water that is not moving tends to become stagnant. The filter must be unclogged, otherwise, no pure water will be available.

God desires to remove impurities from our spiritual lives. He may use a variety of preliminary steps to begin accomplishing this, but the only filter that will provide power for cleansing is the blood of the Lord Jesus Christ. I am so glad that this "spiritual filter" is more than adequate to remove sin from the very largest to the most minute.

It is my prayer that God would allow my life to be an inspiration to others as I share the journey of my life through the Myopic Zone. I'm just *passing through,* but pray that my heritage will honor and glorify God from now through eternity.

And remember, your life is being watched by others and will have an influence on them. May it be a heritage that will bring honor and glory to our heavenly Father.

Rev. David E. Newell
Lexington, Georgia
2011

## 1

## ABBREVIATED AUTOBIOGRAPHY (1941-2010)

---

*I will instruct thee and teach thee in the way which thou shalt go: I will guide thee with mine eye.* Psalm 32:8

### Part 1

My journey through the Myopic Zone began when I was born on March 17, 1941. At that time, I apparently had long eyes and nearsighted vision. However, it was not until I was in the first grade, that my parents realized that something was wrong with my eyes and that I needed help. I was bringing weird-spelled words home from school because I could not clearly see the blackboard. I was continually bumping into things, and then I fell down the basement steps. On my first visit to the eye doctor, he determined that I was very nearsighted and needed to have corrective lenses. In 1947, I began wearing my first glasses at the age of six. This same year, I prayed to receive the Lord Jesus Christ as my Savior on June 14 (Father's Day). That evening, after returning home from church, my dad explained to me the plan of salvation. As we knelt beside my bed, I asked Jesus to come into my heart, and I was born again into the family of God.

Every year my eyes were checked by the eye doctor, and with each visit I needed stronger lenses to correct my vision to bring it to 20/20. My myopic vision was getting so bad that by the time I was in high school, I had to wear glasses with bifocal lenses. This gave me the ability to see distance, and it gave me better vision for reading and writing. I am thankful that even though my eyeglasses had to be made thicker and thicker, I was able to function quite well.

I have had my fair share of accidents on many occasions, resulting in glasses that were broken with cracked lenses and bent ear pieces. I have worn glasses that were patched together with scotch tape, adhesive tape, and duct tape with ear pieces held together by pieces of wire or paper clips. Without my glasses and the thick lenses, I could not see and had a hard time functioning because everything was so out of focus due to my myopic vision.

When I was in the second grade, one of my "friends" got mad at me for some reason and, I guess since I wore glasses, hollered, "You look like a Jap!" I ran home crying. The old adage, "Sticks and stones will break my bones, but names will never hurt me" is not quite true. That incident in the Myopic Zone made a lasting impression, one that I have never forgotten.

In 1952, my family (dad, mom, and younger brother) moved from Philadelphia to the mountains in southeastern Kentucky. My parents were following God's plan for them to be involved in missionary work, serving under the Rural Evangel Mission.

In 1953, I was baptized (without my glasses) by my dad and another missionary in a swimming hole in Lost Creek at the mouth of Cockrell's Fork in Breathitt County, Kentucky. That same year, I dedicated my life to the Lord for full-time missionary service.

Because of the thick lenses and my natural ability to perspire, my glasses were always sliding down my nose. They were so heavy that by 1960, they almost looked like the bottoms of Coke bottles. I admit that is a bit of an exaggeration, but needless to say, my lenses were extremely thick.

In 1963, I graduated from Philadelphia College of Bible with a B.S. in Bible with an emphasis in Missions. Then, I studied radio electronics for two years at Philadelphia Wireless Technical Institute in preparation for service in missionary radio. Meanwhile, the lenses for my glasses had to be made thicker and thicker.

The Lord brought Anna Gay Chapman from Huntington, West Virginia, into my life while we were spending the summer of 1960 as counselors at Camp Nathanael, a Christian camp located in Kentucky not far from where I was raised. At the time, she was attending Appalachian Bible Institute, and I was attending Philadelphia College of Bible. We met again in Kentucky in 1963. Very quickly we developed an understanding that the Lord was calling both of us into missionary service. It also became quite evident as we got to know each other better that our unplanned meeting in Kentucky that summer was no accident. It was God's divine appointment.

On July 11, 1964, Anna Gay and I were married at her home church, Grace Gospel Church, in Huntington, West Virginia. It was a very hot day, and my glasses kept steaming up and sliding down my nose, but we made it. At that time, Anna Gay joined me in journeying through the Myopic Zone "for better or for worse."

Anna Gay and I began our missionary service with Trans World Radio on the island of Bonaire in the Southern Caribbean in 1966. By this time, contact lenses were gaining in popularity, and the suggestion was made to me at various times that I should try to use contact lenses and give up the glasses. Some of our co-workers on the island did use contact lenses. However, because of the constant trade winds blowing and the dust that was prevalent in these winds, I noticed that those who wore contact lenses spent a lot of time either taking their contacts out to clean them, or they were continually experiencing watery eyes. This did not appeal to me, and so I continued my journey through the Myopic Zone with the super-thick lenses in my eyeglasses.

Our first child, Gaylene Anne, was born on Bonaire in January 1971. Two years later, in March 1973, our second child, Philip David, was born on Bonaire.

When our schedules permitted, Anna Gay and I, and the kids, enjoyed swimming and snorkeling in the crystal clear waters of the Caribbean Sea. Of course, I could not see anything clearly without my trusty glasses. I had a bright idea of how to correct that situation! I removed the ear pieces from a spare pair of glasses and wedged the plastic frame with the thick lenses inside the swimming mask. It gave me the ability to see fairly well under water.

One time, though, things appeared to be farther away when looking through the mask. Then, I discovered that I had put the frame in the mask backwards, and I was actually looking through the front side of the glasses. No wonder! Eventually, I was able to get my prescription ground into lenses that were glued to the front of the swimming mask. That sure was better than trying to see through the eyeglasses with the frames jammed inside the mask.

### Part 2

It was not until 1975, when our family of four was transferred to the island of Guam in the Western Pacific to continue our service with Trans World Radio, that I began to rethink the matter of contact lenses. On Guam, there was not the constant wind blowing sand and grit all over the place. The living conditions there were better from the standpoint of using contact lenses. Due to the intense heat and humidity, my glasses were constantly steaming up and sliding off my face! In 1982, my decision was finalized after some friends on Guam offered to cover the cost of the eye examination and the initial cost of contact lenses. That first visit to the eye doctor to be fit with contact lenses was very traumatic and somewhat scary.

The thought of having an object placed on my eyeball made me queasy. I almost passed out the first time a lens was placed on my eyeball. Soft contact lenses could not be made strong enough for my super-myopic prescription, so the only choice was to use hard contact lenses.

For the first few weeks, it would take me over forty-five minutes to get my contact lenses in place on my eyeballs. A real frustration! After finally getting used to the hard contact lenses, I was amazed to see the vast difference and the improvement in my vision compared to eyeglasses. Of course, the contacts had their own set of advantages and disadvantages, but now I could see much better without looking through the thick lenses that caused a considerable amount of distorted and bowed peripheral vision. Everything I saw was its correct size, and proportions were normal.

Our third child, Holly Beth, was born on Guam in March 1979. And now we had an international family – two children were Bonairians and one was a Guamanian. Of course, they were and are citizens of the United States of America.

In 1984, our family of five was transferred from Guam to continue our missionary service with Trans World Radio at the headquarters located in Chatham, New Jersey. Then, in 1987, we changed mission organizations and moved to Madison, Georgia, to serve in the headquarters of Source of Light Ministries.

In December of 1987, without any warning, I began seeing inky spots in my right eye along with flashes of light in the corner of my vision. My eye doctor diagnosed the problem as a tear in the retina. He immediately made arrangements for me to see a retina specialist at Piedmont Hospital in Atlanta. There, Dr. Jarrett (Eye Consultants of Atlanta) performed cryosurgery to prevent the retina from detaching. Thank the Lord, this surgery was successful, the retina remained attached, and my vision was restored to "normal."

The same thing happened to my left eye in October 1992. Again, cryosurgery was successfully performed by Dr. Jarrett. This prevented the retina from detaching, and my vision was restored to "normal." I was told that tears in the retinas were to be expected because of the extreme nearsightedness of my eyes.

I actually wore the very same pair of hard contact lenses for thirteen years from 1982 to 1995. The hard lenses helped stabilize my vision, and for that period of time, each annual eye checkup showed no change was needed in my prescription. I came close to losing my contact lenses from time to time, but I always managed to find the missing lens.

One problem sometimes happened with the contact in my right eye. If I sneezed unusually hard or if I suddenly flicked my eye, the contact would disappear. It would move from the center of my eye and lodge way back in the corner under the eyelid. It felt like it was up inside my head close to my ear! To retrieve the contact lens, Anna Gay would have to use a tiny suction device, snag the contact, and pull it out of my eye. After cleaning it, I would put it back into my eye in the correct position. What a job! There was always the danger of dropping the contact in the sink or on the floor during this rather delicate procedure.

It was always a challenge with my myopic condition when traveling overseas and having to switch between my contacts and glasses. When traveling by plane, for example, I would begin the flight with the contacts in place. After several hours, I would have to remove the contacts and use my glasses. Then, as the plane got close to landing, I would have to go to the lavoratory and replace the glasses with the contacts. On one occasion, I was waiting to board my flight at the airport in Hong Kong. Without warning, I sneezed and, you guessed it, my right contact lens disappeared. Anna Gay was not with me, and I almost panicked! I asked the Lord to help me with this situation. I immediately headed to the restroom and looked in the mirror. I managed to see the edge of the contact in the corner of my eye and was able to slide it back into its correct position with the little plunger tool. A real answer to prayer! I boarded the plane in great relief as if nothing unusual had happened with my eye.

I used hard contact lenses until the end of 1999. By that time, cataracts had fully formed on both my eyes. Contact lenses could no longer be made with the strength that was needed to counteract the cataracts in both eyes. In order to see correctly in the Myopic Zone, I had to revert back to eyeglasses, now with extra super-thick lenses, so that I could have at least some vision. At this point, I was almost legally blind and was unable to drive at night. I depended on Anna Gay to handle all the night time driving. After a month or so, I was not able to drive at all, even in daylight, and this really frustrated me.

## Part 3

In February of 2000, I had an appointment with the Laser and Cataract Institute in Tarpon Springs, Florida, to have the cataracts removed from both eyes and have lenses implanted. Prior to the surgeries, my eyes were checked and mapped by several technicians using a variety of unusual instruments. I kept hearing the comment, "He has long eyes, very long eyes." I did not understand what the term "long eye" meant. I learned the "normal" shape of the eye is round, but mine were oblong shaped, kind of like a football. The retina is in the back part of the oblong shape. Between my long eyes and my extremely thick lenses in my glasses, I was somewhat of a celebrity at the clinic. When I first met the surgeon, Dr. James Gills, he commented that he had to see the glasses that I was wearing. He had heard that they had the thickest lenses this side of the Mississippi River. He may have been right. Dr. Gills assured me that all would go well with the cataract removal and lens implants. The day of the first surgery, as usually is done, Dr. Gills prayed for successful procedures as he performed these operations. I was really impressed with that. Also, in some of our discussions, he commented that God had given doctors tremendous skills and knowledge in how to do very delicate and intricate surgeries in areas of the eye, for example. But ultimately it is God who does the healing, and that gave me reassurance knowing that God was in control of the procedures that I was about to experience. Surgery was done first on my right eye, and the left eye was done the next day.

After successful surgeries with the cataracts removed and lenses implanted, during the post-op checks, Dr. Gills said we are going to sing "Amazing Grace" to commemorate the fact that I had been blind, but now I could see. After several weeks of recovery and after hundreds of drops in my eyes, I could see 20/20 in both eyes without corrective lenses, and I had no need to use glasses. Wow! And I could see true colors. As an artist, this was amazing! Eventually, I did get a pair of glasses to make reading and oil-painting a bit easier on my eyes. I could look out across a field into a wooded area and see individual leaves on a tree, and I could look in the yard and almost see a blade of grass growing. This was the best vision that I ever had in my life!

In January 2005, Anna Gay and I began a new missionary assignment. We were seconded to Neighborhood Gospel Missions

(NGM) and moved to Lexington, Georgia. Our assignment was to establish the NGM Home Office and to help develop the NGM Camp and Conference Center at the newly acquired property in Oglethorpe County.

After a few years, I discovered my distance vision was not as sharp, but it was still within the legal limits for a driver's license. In 2006, I did begin wearing glasses again which helped me see things a bit clearer in the distance. At that time, I had bifocals put into the lenses to improve my vision for reading and for working on projects close up. The lenses of my glasses were really thin compared to what I needed before the cataracts were removed and the lenses implanted.

## Part 4

In the spring of 2010, I was suddenly reminded that I was still journeying through the Myopic Zone when I began to notice distorted vision in my right eye. In a few weeks I was scheduled to have my annual eye check up and at that time told my eye doctor what I was seeing. With my glasses I was seeing 20/20 in both eyes, but the distortion in my right eye was a problem. The eye doctor immediately scheduled me to see Dr. Mohan Iyer, a retina specialist at the Athens Retina Center in Athens, Georgia. I was diagnosed with a macular hole in my right eye, and surgery (vitrectomy) was scheduled at Athens Regional Medical Center on June 10, 2010, to remove the vitreous gel that was pulling on the macula.

Little did I realize then that this was going to be the first of several surgeries on my right eye. Following this first surgery, Dr. Mohan Iyar, spoke to Anna Gay and explained to her what he had done and what he had attempted to do. He told her that my eyes were extremely long, and it was like working with the delicate instruments in the bottom of a pit. Here again was a reference to my long eyes. The post-op appointment the following day showed that the gas bubble that was inserted during the surgery was pressing against the retina and that I must keep my head in a face-down position for the next couple of weeks. However, a few days later, I noticed a black shroud coming across the vision of my right eye, and I called the doctor's office concerning this new development. Dr. Iyer wanted to see me in his office immediately, and he determined the retina had detached. Surgery would be done the next day. So, I found myself back in Athens Regional Medical Center to have a second surgery on June 24. A scleral buckle (a permanent synthetic band) was placed around the right eye to hold it against the retina to aid in the healing process and to keep the retina attached.

Unfortunately, this was followed by another setback when fluid began leaking inside the eye, indicating that the retina was trying to detach again. On June 30, Dr. Iyer did cryosurgery on the eye in his office in an attempt to seal the area where the fluid was leaking.

However, on July 6, a third surgery (vitrectomy) had to be performed at Athens Regional Medical Center to seal another tear that was allowing fluid to form under the retina. At this time, another gas bubble was placed in my right eye, and I had to maintain my head in a face-down position fifty per-cent of the time.

The July 14 post-op checkup showed yet another tear was forming. This was checked again on July 21, and at that time, through a very painful surgical procedure in his office, Dr. Iyer refilled my eye with the gas bubble. The next day, the doctor did additional laser surgery in an attempt to seal the area where fluid was still leaking.

My checkup on July 26 showed the leakage area was sealed. There was no fluid, and the retina remained attached. I had to continue to maintain my head in a face-down position seventy-five percent of the time so the gas bubble would press the eye against the correct area of the retina during the healing process. However, I experienced another setback when Dr. Iyer checked my eye on July 30. Fluid was again leaking, an indication that the retina was trying again to detach.

The next day (Saturday), a fourth surgery (vitrectomy) was done at Athens Regional Medical Center. During this surgery, Dr. Iyer removed the gas bubble, repaired the leaking area with stitches and laser, and placed silicone oil in my eye instead of the gas bubble. Later on, another surgery would be required at Athens Regional Medical Center to remove the oil bubble after the retina is completely attached and healed.

After the July 31 surgery, with my right eye filled with the silicone oil bubble, I finally could keep my head in a normal face-up position. The oil stays in place and does not dissolve like the gas bubble. I can see better through the oil, but my vision is not clearly focused, and it is very distorted. I was seeing double vision for a week or so, but that basically has cleared. My eye continues to be very sensitive to light since one of the eye drops keeps my pupil dilated.

Five weeks after my last surgery at Athens Regional Medical Center the retina remained attached. My right eye has not felt this good since before the first surgery on June 10, and I am indeed thankful. The bloodshot color, watering, and swelling have almost completely cleared.

I had no idea that I was going to experience these problems with my right eye and that the healing process would take so long. All this began with my annual eye checkup on May 11 and with my first visit to Dr. Iyar on May 17, 2010. From June 8 through July 31, I had a total of eight surgeries in my eye. Four of these surgeries were performed by Dr. Iyer at Athens Regional Medical Center, and four surgeries were done in his office. The procedures done in the doctor's office included cryosurgery to seal tears in the retina, two separate laser surgeries to assure the retina remained attached and to seal the areas where fluid had been leaking, and a surgery to inject more gas in my eye to increase the gas bubble.

I received a good report from Dr. Iyer on August 17, and he did not need to see me again for four weeks unless something unusual occurred with the vision in my right eye. He cautioned me to be very careful about quick head movements and to avoid heavy lifting. A check on September 14, showed the retina was still attached, but there was some swelling. So another series of eye drops was begun (eight drops daily in the right eye for at least another four weeks).

Throughout the weeks of limited activity from June 10 through July 31, I had to keep my head in a face-down position. I had to be extremely careful not to do anything that would tend to detach the retina or let the gas bubble move away from the back area of the retina. I have had plenty of time to meditate, pray, quote Scripture, think, and try to understand what this means in my present and future missionary service. It certainly has been apparent that I needed to modify my current responsibilities in Neighborhood Gospel Missions and to see what changes should be made in ministry. I am not interested in retiring, and I am trusting the Lord to sufficiently restore my vision so that I can continue my journey through the Myopic Zone in missionary service.

Anna Gay had to do all the driving from June 10 through the end of August because of my inability to see clearly. Thankfully, she loves to drive and is an excellent driver.

## Part 5

During one of my quiet times as I thought about journeying through the Myopic Zone, I remembered the words in Scripture written by the Psalmist David: "I will praise thee; for I am fearfully and wonderfully made. . ." (Psalm 139:14a).

God, the Master Creator, made my eyes just the way He wanted them to be. He purposely made them extra long with their myopic features. They were made according to His perfect design. That goes for every part of my body. Another verse states: "My substance was not hid from thee when I was made in secret. . ." (Psalm 139:15a).

I was especially blessed when I read the next verse: "Thine eyes did see my substance, yet being unperfect; and in thy book all my members were written, which in continuance were fashioned, when as yet there was none of them" (Psalm 139:16). Wow! God is good; He does all things well; He created me just the way I was supposed to be! In fact, this verse states that God has a special book that has His master designs of every part of me, including my long, nearsighted eyes. This is all recorded in His Book of Design. I have nothing to complain about and everything to rejoice about, having the assurance that God knows all about my eyes and the challenges that I would experience after the macular hole was diagnosed in mid-May 2010.

I am also encouraged when I think about a couple of other books that God is keeping. Not only does He keep a Book of Design, but God keeps a Book of Remembrance. Malachi 3:16 states: "Then they that feared the Lord spake often one to another: and the Lord harkened, and heard it, and a book of remembrance was written before him for them that feared the Lord, and that thought upon his name." Here is another verse: "Thou tellest my wanderings: put thou my tears into thy bottle: are they not in thy book?" (Psalm 56:8).

During the weeks of surgeries and healings, Anna Gay and I have prayed much and thought much about the Lord and His goodness. Anna Gay has read many Scripture passages to me when I could not read myself. We have shed tears together – tears of pain, tears of frustration, tears of joy, and tears of blessing.

Psalm 23 has been especially meaningful, knowing that "the Lord is my Shepherd." He is with me as I walk through the valley of the Myopic Zone. Surely His "goodness and mercy" has sustained me to this point, and I know He will continue to sustain me in the valleys and in the storms.

The Book of Life is the third book that God is keeping. This is the Lamb's Book of Life as found in Revelation 20:12: ". . . the books were opened and another book was opened, which is the book of life. . ." and Revelation 20:15 states: "And whosoever was not found written in the book of life was cast into the lake of fire."

Praise God, I know my name is written on the Book of Life. God is my Father; I am His child! He knows all about me and my circumstances, and I take great comfort and confidence in that fact. I have the blessed hope of spending eternity in Heaven because I have received Jesus Christ as my Savior. I have the Holy Spirit dwelling within me, and I rejoice in the guidance and the comfort He gives.

Anna Gay and I have been blessed and encouraged by many cards, e-mails, and letters from friends, former Trans World Radio co-workers, and Source of Light missionaries who had prayed for us.

Many friends and supporting churches have shared words of comfort and financial gifts with us to help during this time of need. Some from local churches have brought in food, and two men have kept the grass cut at our house.

I do not know what the future holds with my eye filled with silicone oil, but I know Who holds my future. Whatever the outcome, my desire is to be conformed to the image of God's Son and to honor and glorify Him in all things, especially through the vision of my right eye.

My journey through the Myopic Zone will continue according to God's perfect plan for my life. The old hymn, "Be Thou My Vision," sums up my situation and testimony now and in the days ahead.

### *Be Thou My Vision*

*Be Thou my Vision, O Lord of my heart; Naught be all else to me save that Thou art;*
*Thou my best thought by day or by night, Waking or sleeping, Thy presence my light.*

*Be Thou my wisdom, be Thou my true word; I ever with Thee and Thou with me, Lord;*
*Thou my great Father and I Thy true son, Thou in me dwelling, and I with Thee one.*

19

*Be Thou my shield and my sword for the fight;  Be Thou my dignity, be Thou my might;*
*Thou my soul's shelter and Thou my high tow'r,  Raise Thou me heavenward, O pow'r of my pow'r.*

*Riches I heed not nor man's empty praise,  Thou mine inheritance now and always;*
*Thou and Thou only be first in my heart,  High King of heaven, my treasure Thou art.*

*High King of heaven, when vict'ry is won,  May I reach heaven's joys, O bright heav'n's Sun!*
*Heart of my own heart, whatever befall,  Still by my Vision, O Ruler of all.*

**(August 31, 2010)**

## 2

## LIFE IN PHILADELPHIA (1941-1951)

*For the ways of man are before the eyes of the Lord, and he pondereth all his goings.* Proverbs 5:21

I was born on March 17, 1941, to Earl Foster Newell and LaVerne Florence Newell. My mother's maiden name was Foote. I made my entry into the world, and the Myopic Zone, in the Germantown Hospital, Philadelphia, Pennsylvania, on a very special day, Saint Patrick's Day.

My dad recounts the event while he and another soon-to-be father were in the waiting room. The man was nervously pacing back and forth. He asked my dad, "If it's a boy, are you going to name him Patrick?" More pacing and another question, "If it's a girl, are you going to name her Patricia?" My dad's answer to both questions was, "No." Even though it was Saint Patrick's Day, my parents had already determined that a boy would be named after King David in the Bible.

I was the healthy baby boy who was born at 6:08 am, weighing in at 5 pounds 6 ounces, with dark blue eyes (that later turned brown) and brown hair. I was named David Earl. My middle name Earl was for my dad's first name, Earl. My son's name is Philip David Newell, and his first-born son is named Isaiah Philip Newell. One day, if Isaiah has a son, I would hope his middle name would be Isaiah to keep this tradition alive for another generation by giving the middle name for the father's first name.

Earl Foster Newell
David Earl Newell
Philip David Newell
Isaiah Philip Newell
__?__ Isaiah Newell

March 17, 1941, was also the date that I began my journey through the Myopic Zone. However, my parents did not recognize my nearsighted condition until I was six years old and in school. That is when I began wearing eyeglasses which dramatically changed my outlook on life. (No pun intended!) I could see things clearly and in focus. I have been thankful for corrective lenses ever since getting my first pair of glasses in 1947.

I am also thankful for godly parents who instilled in me spiritual truths and stories from the Bible. I have truly been blessed with a "goodly heritage" as David the psalmist states in Psalm 16:16. At 13 ½ months old, my dad taught me to kneel at the lowered side of my crib and fold my hands while he prayed.

Some of my first words were, "da da" and "ma ma." I also would say "gock" (sock), "cook cook" (cookie), "guck" (duck), and "cack cack" (cracker).

We lived at 6426 North Norwood Street, Philadelphia 38, Pennsylvania. Our house was a two-story row house with a basement that opened into a small fenced-in back yard with an alley behind that ran the length of the block between houses and yards. Norwood Street ran into Chelten Avenue. Chelten Avenue made a turn a couple of blocks past our street and continued for several blocks to Germantown Avenue and beyond. The number 52 trolley car ran on Chelten Avenue, and this was our major mode of transportation since my parents did not own an automobile.

In 1942, my little baby brother Paul Richard was born. There are just a few pictures of Paul and me together. I am sorry that I never got to know him because he died about a year and five months later of kidney failure. This was a hard time for my parents, but they took comfort in knowing that their second-born son was in heaven, safe in the arms of Jesus.

My parents were members of a Conservative Baptist Church, named Chelten Avenue Baptist Church. They were faithful in their church attendance and had me in tow from my birth. Sometimes we walked the eight blocks to and from church, and other times we rode on the trolley car. They pushed me in a stroller until I was old enough to walk the distance on my own. Walking was all right, but I always preferred to ride the trolley. It was fascinating to watch the motorman operate the controls and to listen to the roar of the motor and the clatter of the steel wheels on the tracks.

In late 1944, my mom was very pregnant with my brother Richard James. By then, I was a very active three-year-old. My dad was very actively serving in the U.S. Army, and he was overseas at this time. During a service at Chelten Avenue Baptist Church, while a hymn was being sung by the congregation, I managed to get out of the pew and away from my mom's grasp. I toddled up to the pipe organ at the front of the church being played so beautifully by Margaret Steigner. Without any hesitation, I proceeded to "help" her play the hymn. At that moment I was having "fun!" This was short-lived, though, because my very embarrassed mom waddled up the aisle to the front of the auditorium and onto the platform, and she dragged me back to her seat. I cannot remember what my punishment was, but I am sure it was not "fun." Some of the older members of the church still talk about this now-funny incident.

My brother Richard James was born on March 7, 1945. My parents called him Dickie Jim. I was called David Earl or, sometimes, David, or at other times, simply Dave (which I preferred). When I was in trouble with my parents, I was always sternly called David Earl Newell!

I must have been a real handful for my mom during the time that my dad was away from home in the service. My dad wrote letters to my mom, and he even wrote some letters to me! I have two of those letters today, dated May 3, 1945, and June 3, 1945, addressed to Master David E. Newell. In the May letter he wrote:

"Hija David; how are you doing? Were you a good boy last week? Did you get to Sunday school and learn your memory verse? Do you like the picture book Daddy sent you? When I come home, you can tell me the story all about Jesus. Mummy tells me you go out into the alley now. You must be a big boy now that you go out by yourself. When you are out of the yard you must not fight with anybody unless they hit you first.

"Daddy is proud of his big boy. I was just showing your picture to some of the men that are in the same hut daddy is in. Ask Mummy what a hut is. Do not forget to save some kisses for me. I am going to look for a nice big hug and a kiss when I get home. As soon as you hear me come in the door and yell 'Yo Ho' you come running.

"Here is a dollar for you and Dickie Jim to buy something for Mummy for Mother's Day. Be a good boy and take care of Dickie Jim and help Mummy all you can for Daddy. Tell Grandma to behave herself or I will start writing to her. You mind Grandma, too. Good bye now. Daddy.

"P.S. Here is another dollar for you to buy some defense stamps for Dickie Jim and yourself. If you have any money left, buy some ice cream for Mummy, Grandma, and yourself. Daddy."

Following are some excepts from the June letter written by my dad to me:

"Whenever Mummy tells you to do something, you do it and do it right away so she will not have to holler at you. Mummy and Daddy love you and do not like to holler at our nice big boy.

"I was glad to hear that you do not fight much. Remember, never hit first. Never hit a boy who is smaller than yourself. Never, never hit a little girl. Big boys never hit girls.

"You know sometimes Phillip is not such a good boy. Daddy does not want you to do the bad things that other boys do. You tell them that Jesus wants boys and girls to be good all the time.

"I am glad you like your bicycle so much. Be careful you do not hit anything, or any boys and girls with your bike. Don't you think you ought only to ride your bike outside of the house? When you ride indoors be careful not to bump into anything.

"How is baby brother? You will have to help Mummy take care of Dickie Jim until Daddy is there to help. Don't forget to put your toys and books away when you finish playing with them. Now do not forget to help Mummy all you can. Your loving Daddy."

Even though my dad was not physically present during the time he was in the service, he was concerned about me and gave his wise advice in those early formative years of my life. It sure was great to have my dad home after he returned from the Philippines and was honorably discharged from the Army. One Sunday evening, after getting home from church, my dad talked with me at length, reading John 3:16 from my own little Bible. He explained the plan of salvation in simple terms that a six-year-old could understand. I did not want to go to hell; I wanted to go to heaven when I died. That evening, June 14, 1947, I gave my heart to Jesus and was born into the family of God. That was a Father's Day I will never forget! As I grew older, I learned more and more truths from God's Word. I am so thankful that I was saved at an early age and that the Lord was my Shepherd, guiding my journey through the Myopic Zone.

At the age of five, I experienced my first hospital stay since being born. I had to have my tonsils removed, a rather unpleasant and scary event. I can still remember being wheeled down the hospital hallway and into the operating room. A nurse tried to calm my nerves just before covering my face with the ether mask. The next thing I knew, I was jumping on top of hundreds of empty milk bottles. Then, as I became fully awake, I had an almost unbearable sore throat, and I vomited a basin full of blood! I tried to be brave, though, and was rewarded with a neat toy steam shovel that I played with for years after this rough and very unpleasant incident.

By 1947, at the age of six, I was wearing glasses and learning how to deal with them continuously parked on my nose, in addition to the earpieces hanging around my ears. My friend Phillip did not need to wear glasses. Most of the time, we played well together and wandered around the neighborhood since he also was allowed to go out in the alley from his yard just like me. We were even permitted to play in the alley and on the sidewalks if we were careful to stay out of the streets. Sometimes we squabbled about this, that, or the other thing. On one occasion, Phillip got very mad at me for some reason and yelled in my face, "You look like a Jap!" Wow! That really hurt my feelings, and I ran home crying. I was comforted by my mom, but it was a rude reminder that I was just beginning my journey through the Myopic Zone.

My mom used to sing choruses to me, as well as other tunes and ditties. I still remember one crazy song that didn't make much sense because the words were all run together. It goes something like this:

"Mairsey dotes and dosey dotes, and liddle lans edivey,
Aunt Kiddle edivey doo, wooden chew?"

Sung with more clarity and distinction, it makes sense like this:

"Mares eat oats, and does eat oats,
And kids will eat ivy, too, wouldn't you?"

Mares are horses, does are deer, and they all eat oats. Kids are baby goats, and they eat ivy. Simple.

Not only did my mom like to sing, she really enjoyed playing the old piano that we had in our house. She got the bright idea that I should learn how to play the piano, too. Could that have come from my eagerness to hit a few keys on the church organ a couple of years back? I'll never know. So, I began taking piano lessons for a period of time, straining to see the music notes through my glasses. I had nice little stickers put in my music book as I advanced from one page to another, playing with one hand. I guess I never got to the place where I learned to play with both hands. I could play "Jingle Bells" without making a single mistake. I can still play "Jingle Bells" with my right index finger at almost 70 years-of-age. How 'bout that accomplishment! Many times, I wish I would have applied myself more to the piano lessons, but through various circumstances that occurred in 1951 at the age of ten, I was not able or encouraged to proceed any farther with the lessons.

While not showing overwhelming enthusiasm for playing the piano, I did have a great interest in doodling and drawing. My dad liked to doodle, too. He would draw pictures of trains and trolleys, cars and trucks, and people and cartoons. Then, I would try to copy what he drew. Ever since I could hold a pencil or crayon, I was forever trying to draw something. I was thankful to have glasses that helped me see more clearly what I was drawing.

As I grew older, I realized that my mom was journeying through her own Myopic Zone. She was extremely nearsighted and had to have her eyeglasses on all the time in order to function as a wife and mother.

I attended grades one through three at the Kinsey Elementary School, located just a few blocks from our house. I remember damaging and breaking my glasses on several occasions during my early days in school. One time I was running at school, tripped over something, and crashed headfirst into the black iron fence that surrounded the schoolyard. The results were not good – broken glasses, bent frames, blood splatters all over the place, a black eye, and a pump-knot on my forehead. This was just one of many bumps and bruises that I would experience in the Myopic Zone.

My parents arranged for me to attend the fourth grade at a Christian Day School in a Presbyterian Church in the Germantown section of Philadelphia. The church was located off Chelten Avenue on past Germantown Avenue. By this time, I was old enough to travel to and from this school on the number 52 trolley car. I was responsible for taking my younger brother Richard, who was in the first grade, with me to and from the school.

A small grocery store was located on the corner of Norwood Street and Chelten Avenue. It was called Ben and Jen's Delicatessen, named after the store owners. They were Jewish and very nice people and were good friends with our family. It was really a great convenience to have this small store right there in the neighborhood just a short walk from our house.

I remember a big wooden barrel in the store that was filled with what we called "Jewish pickles." They were delicious, and it was a treat to get one of these every once in a while. You could grab the pickle of your choice with tongs and place it in a little waxed-covered bag. I liked to watch Ben and Jen slice and package lunchmeats. They had a special way of wrapping the meats, first in wax paper, and then in white butcher paper. They folded the white paper from the bottom, and then folded in both sides, leaving a top flap. They folded the top flap down and tucked the end inside the bottom of the folded two sides. Really neat packaging! At home, I practiced how to do the same thing, and believe it or not, I can do that same special packaging even today.

There was a small bake shop located on Chelten Avenue just around the corner from Ben and Jen's. This was called Schneider's Bakery. They made the best cakes with the best icing. Sometimes I would wander into the bakery, hold out my arm hand-down, and ask Mr. Schneider if he had any extra icing. If he did, he would put a bird or some other design made out of icing on the back of my hand. I would look at the design for a while and then lick off the icing little-by-little. This special treat sure tasted good!

When I was a bit older, around the age of eight or nine, my parents started giving me a very small weekly allowance. I was taught to save this money and use it to buy something special and to use some of it for my Sunday school offering. I am thankful that the principle of giving a tithe to the Lord was taught to me at a very early age. I found some ways to add to my savings by collecting discarded bottles and newspapers from the neighbors and selling them at a small scrap yard not far from our house. Sometimes I found old chunks of metal and steel that I could also sell for a few cents.

The saying, "keep looking up" is good, but I learned by do-ing just the opposite, "keep looking down" could be pretty rewarding. I remember finding all kinds of interesting stuff on the sidewalks, in the streets, and along the curbs. I found discarded colorful paper transfers and tokens used by the PTC (Philadelphia Transportation Company) on trolleys, busses, and subways. I also found coins, matchbooks (sometimes even with unused matches inside), and bottle caps. If I was careful, I could pry out the cork from inside the bottle cap and use it to hold the bottle cap to my shirt like a badge. My mom was probably not too happy to see my shirts with all the impressions and perforations in the material made by the bottle caps.

It was fun playing with matches, something I knew I was not permitted to do. I was very careful, in my way of thinking, and nothing bad was going to happen. I tried burning little piles of leaves in the gutter. If I didn't have any matches, occasionally I tried to get leaves to burn with my little magnifying glass. But I could never get the sunlight focused quite right, and I only generated some black smoldering smoke. Somehow, my parents always found out what I was doing, and I paid the consequences.

As I grew older, I was permitted to venture two or three blocks away from the house. There was a 5 and 10 Cent Store a little farther down Chelten Avenue close to Chew Street. I liked to go inside and look at all the interesting things that were for sale in the store. One time, I saw a neat pocket knife that I felt that I really needed. I had saved enough money to buy it, and that is what I proudly did. Somehow, that evening my parents discovered what I had done, and they were not pleased with my purchase. "You are too young to have your own pocket knife," they said as they confiscated the knife. The next day, my dad marched me back to the store and made me return my prized pocket knife. Boy, that was a very embarrassing experience, but I learned my lesson to ask before acting on my own, especially when it came to something like a knife that could cause me and others injury.

It seemed like there was always something of interest taking place around 6426 North Norwood Street. I liked to watch the milkman deliver milk along the block with his horse-drawn milk wagon. The milk was in glass bottles at that time, and I can still hear the clank of bottles being taken in and out of the metal carriers. The horse pulling the wagon would patiently wait while the milkman made his deliveries of fresh milk and picked up the empty bottles. It then clopped down the street, happily pulling the milk wagon.

The deliveries of other commodities were fun to watch. Big blocks of ice were delivered to some of the houses that still had ice boxes and not refrigerators. The iceman carried the chunk of ice on his shoulder over a heavy protective piece of leather. He carried the ice using heavy-duty tongs with sharp points that bit into and held the block of ice.

Unloading coal from trucks was another activity I liked to watch. The coal trucks usually had to be driven partway up onto the sidewalk to be positioned in front of the house where the delivery was to be made. A basement window was opened so the end of the coal chute could be put inside and into the coal bin close to the furnace. After the coal chute was in place and attached to the back of the truck, the truck bed was raised to a dump position. The little door was carefully opened, and coal began to cascade down the chute and into the coal bin. The small chunks of coal going down the chute made a very loud noise, and there was no mistaking the fact that a neighbor was getting a load of coal.

Then, there were the trash trucks. Men would go up and down the back alley shouting, "Trash man!" as they collected trash and garbage in huge metal cans. They took these out to the street and dumped them into the trash truck. This was another noisy activity as trash cans were banged around and crashed to the ground. The driver was up in the back of the truck trying to distribute the trash and garbage evenly so it could be loaded as full as possible. Even though the trash might be spilling over the sides, the men kept dumping in more. It seemed to be a pretty neat job, particularly for the one tramping through the trash in the back of the truck.

In the summertime, men selling produce would come down the alley, shouting things like, "Fresh Jersey tomatoes; buy your Jersey tomatoes here!" Or they would holler out that they had fresh corn or fresh asparagus, all grown on farms in New Jersey. Then, there were the men wanting to grind your scissors and sharpen knives at the most reasonable expense. They had their grinding machines strapped onto their backs ready for business.

When I was smaller, I had a tricycle (which my dad called a bicycle or bike). As I grew older, I really wanted and felt I needed a real bicycle to replace my tricycle. Even though I learned how to ride a regular two-wheeler, my parents could not afford to buy one for me. So, my friend Phillip let me ride his bike every once in a while.

Most of us boys did have our own roller skates. They were noisy things with steel wheels. The skates were made of metal with two parts that could be adjusted and bolted together. They had adjustable clips in the front that clamped to the sides of your shoes. The strap in the back part held the heel of your shoes to the back of the skates. These skates could be used to make what we called a "skate-o." One time my dad made a real neat skate-o for me. He took one skate apart. The front part of the roller skate was attached to the front of a 2x4 board about three feet long. The back part of the roller skate was attached to the back end of the board. A wooden orange crate was attached to the top front of the board. A couple of pieces of wood were attached to the top of the orange crate to be used as handles. And there you have it, a skate-o!

You rode with one foot on the board and used the other foot to propel the skate-o forward. With increasing speed, you could put both feet on the board, and away you go! This was the forerunner of what we call today a "skateboard." We had more fun on those skate-os than you can imagine. They sure made a lot of noise on the streets and sidewalks, and many times we had races, and sometimes even crashes. I always had to be very careful not to jar my eyeglasses off my face when bouncing along on my skate-o.

One fine day, I was walking along Chelten Avenue checking out some of the stores and just looking around to see if anything interesting was happening in the neighborhood. I approached the corner of Chew Street and had to cross Chelten Avenue as I headed for home. There were two sets of trolley car tracks running down the middle of Chelten Avenue which was a very wide street. As I began crossing to the other side of Chelten Avenue, I noticed a trolley coming on my left. Very good. Then, I saw another trolley approaching from the opposite direction on my right. I figured I could get at least halfway across, so I stopped between the two sets of tracks to let the trolley cars pass on either side of me. I guess I was not looking through my glasses well enough to judge the space between the two trolleys as they would pass each other.

At about the same instant, both motormen saw what I was up to, and they brought their trolleys to a screeching stop as the braking plates made contact with the rails. The motormen knew there was not enough room for a person, even a small guy like me, to stand between those trolley cars without being crushed to death. The motormen proceeded to clang the warning bells on the trolleys, adding to the sudden excitement and confusion. I quickly ran on across the street as angry shouts from the trolleys erupted, "Are you crazy kid; get outa' the street!" "Hey kid, quit showin' off, and go home!" And that is exactly what I did! I ran down Chelten Avenue, up the alley, into my backyard, and sat down on the back steps while I caught my breath and tried to stop shaking. I was really scared as it dawned on me how foolish I had been and that I could have been killed. It's a wonder I didn't lose my glasses in the incident that I had just experienced. Needless, to say, I never again tried that trolley car stunt.

I am thankful my life was spared and that I could continue my journey through the Myopic Zone. Safety first has been the mode of operation for me (most of the time) since that afternoon experience between the trolley tracks on Chelten Avenue in Philadelphia.

Christmas at 6426 North Norwood Street was always a fun time, as well as a serious time, as our family celebrated the birth of Jesus. We never had an over-abundance of gifts under the Christmas tree, but that did not seem to dampen our Christmas spirit. Of course, there was the imaginary Santa Claus, but the emphasis was not on him or his reindeer. It was on the real Christmas message of "peace on earth and good will toward men." My parents always read the Christmas story before any of us opened our gifts.

We generally decorated the Christmas tree on or before Christmas Eve. As I got older, I was allowed to help carefully hang the colorful ornaments and silver tinsel on the tree. Our Christmas tree had colored bubbling Noma lights that my dad clipped on the branches.

On Christmas Eve, there was never anything under the tree except big empty stockings, one for me and one for my brother. After my parents put me to bed, I had a hard time falling asleep because I was so excited that the next day was Christmas. I looked forward to finding my stocking filled with many little interesting and fun gifts. The stocking had a jingle bell attached to it, and that was important. I would finally doze off into a light sleep, but after a short while, I would wake up. I would jostle the bed to make the bell on the stocking jingle. If no jingle, that meant no stocking was yet hung on the bed post. I would try to go back to sleep, only to wake up after an hour or so. Again, I bounced the bed, and . . . I heard it that time, the sound of the jingle bell! The stocking was filled (by my mom), and had been hung (by my mom) on the bed post ready to be emptied in the morning. Now, finally, I could let myself go into a deep sleep until Christmas morning.

When my parents finally got up, they would come into my room and sit on the bed with me while I opened the gifts in my stocking. When my brother Dick was older, all four of us would sit together as us boys opened our stocking gifts.

Shortly afterwards, my mom went downstairs to the kitchen to fix breakfast. My brother and I were not allowed to go downstairs by ourselves to see the Christmas tree. When breakfast was ready, my dad carried each of us downstairs and covered our eyes, almost knocking off my glasses, as we made our way past the Christmas tree in the living room. "No peeking," he would always say. After a quick breakfast, and the reading of the Christmas story from the Bible, we all went into the living room to the lighted Christmas tree. Finally we got to open our Christmas presents!

I remember asking for a cap gun for several years. The response was, "We don't want you playing with guns." But each year, I kept asking. Then, one Christmas, when I was eight or nine, to my great surprise, I opened a package that contained a Lone Ranger six-shooter, complete with a holster and belt! Wow! I couldn't believe my eyes; I thought my glasses were playing tricks on me! And there were even several rolls of caps in the package with the gun.

Immediately, my parents laid down some ground rules about playing with this treasured present. "Do not aim the gun at anybody!" "Do not shoot caps in the house." "Do not shoot your brother." How could I maintain law and order without aiming my gun at the bad guys? That was a rough assignment. It was bad enough that I, the good cowboy, had to wear glasses to see what was going on. Which cowboys were ever seen wearing glasses! I had no choice, but to swallow my pride, put on my glasses, strap on my holster, and keep law and order in the neighborhood. (Occasionally, I "forgot" the instructions of my parents, and would "accidentally" shoot my brother with my new cap gun.)

My dad always set up our Lionel trains during the Christmas season. The only place with enough room to do this was in the basement. The train tracks were nailed onto a sheet of plywood that was set on top of sawhorses. The layout was a simple oval track and included a green bridge. The track went up one side, across the bridge, and down the other side. There were a lot of houses set around the layout with little light bulbs inside each one. My dad ran the wiring for the houses under the platform. It was neat to watch the train run in the dark with only the house lights illuminated. I liked the smell that was generated by electrical sparks from the engine as it zipped around the tracks. I got to run the train for the first time when I was around eight or nine years old. This was one of the big highlights of the year in our household.

We used this same Lionel train set for several years and later replaced them with an American Flyer train set. The American Flyer trains were smaller (HO scale) and much more realistic than the

Lionel trains (O scale). I don't know whatever happened to the Lionel engine and cars, but I imagine today they would be worth a small fortune.

During a period of time, my dad worked for the Philadelphia Transportation Company as a motorman on a trolley line. Late one night, dad was a bit tired and sleepy. Half way down the block, he suddenly realized he had gone past the trolley stop where a person was standing there in the cold, waiting. Rather than go on down the street, he brought the trolley to a screeching stop. Since there was hardly any traffic on the street at that hour of the night, he literally backed up the trolley half a city block, something that is not easily done. He slowly moved the trolley car all the way back to the corner, picked up the surprised and grateful fare, put the car back into forward, and continued more alertly down the tracks. This added new meaning to the expression that I learned years later, "Hey, wait a minute. Let's back up the trolley!"

Sometimes I felt that I was smarter than my parents, and sometimes I disobeyed them. I learned that disobedience will bring unpleasant consequences, like a good spanking with a leather belt or some other form of punishment. One time, my mom was at the bottom of the stairs, and I was standing at the top. She called up to me with instructions to do something. I did not want to obey her, and stuck my tongue out at her. Not a very good thing to do! She came running up those stairs faster than I ever saw her move. She marched me into the bathroom and proceeded to wash my mouth out with soap, red Life Bouy soap! That was awful, but it taught me a lesson, another principle found in the Bible, "Children, obey your parents in the Lord, for this is right!"

Whenever I needed to be disciplined, which was more times than I like to think about, my parents did whatever they needed to do primarily in love, with only an occasional hint of anger.

My mom conducted a Bible Club in our house at 6426 North Norwood Street, and several of the neighborhood kids came to sing choruses and hear Bible stories. I remember during one of these clubs, a boy who was a bit older than me was very disruptive and noisy. After the club meeting, I walked to the door with him and told him to his face that he was not welcome to come back! I was proud of myself for taking this stand, thinking I had done my mom a favor. However, her reaction was not what I thought it would be when I re-counted this to her later. I was not punished, but she sat me down and gave me a lecture on why she was conducting the Bible Clubs and that I was wrong in my actions. The whole purpose was to share God's love and the Gospel with kids who needed to receive Jesus as their Savior. She wanted this guy and more kids to come and hear the stories from the Bible. I learned another very valuable lesson and principle from my mom that afternoon. It echoed the words that my dad wrote to me a couple of years before, "Daddy does not want you to do the bad things that other boys do. You tell them that Jesus wants boys and girls to be good all the time." And that included the noisy, disruptive neighbor boy. Unfortunately, the disruptive boy never did come back to our house, and I felt terrible!

My dad served his country in the U.S. Army. He was assigned as a chaplain's assistant, a position that was characteristic of his desire to be used of the Lord in some type of ministry. During the close of World War II he was in the infantry, stationed overseas in the Philippines. While there in that country, he felt the Lord leading him into foreign missionary service, with a special interest in the Philippine Islands. My mom shared the desire of my dad to become a missionary however and wherever the Lord would lead.

Little did I realize that in 1951, at ten years-of-age, that my life was about to take on a new and exciting journey through the Myopic Zone, and I would be given the distinction of being called a MK (Missionary's Kid) and a PK (Preacher's Kid). A major move by the Newell family of four was about to take place.

## 3

## MOVE TO KENTUCKY (1951)

---

*And the angel of the Lord spake unto Philip, saying, Arise, and go toward the south unto the way that goeth down from Jerusalem unto Gaza, which is desert.* Acts 8:26

During the time my dad served in the U.S. Army, from March 21, 1945 to May 14, 1946, he spent six months in the Philippines at the close of WW II. He was a First Sergeant at the time of his discharge. While in the Philippines, my dad came to love the people and was challenged to consider foreign missionary service, possibly in the Philippine Islands. I understand that as a child my dad used to play that he was a missionary in Africa, pretending to be in a canoe. In 1947, when I was six years old, my dad and mom publicly expressed their desire to follow God's leading into full-time missionary service.

My parents had prepared themselves for missionary service by doing further biblical studies. On June 11, 1951, my mom graduated from the evening school of the Bible Institute of Pennsylvania, which later was renamed Philadelphia College of Bible, and several years later was renamed again to Philadelphia Biblical University. My dad also studied for two years, taking evening school classes, at the Bible Institute of Pennsylvania. On May 17, 1951, my dad graduated from the Theological Seminary of the Reformed Episcopal Church, a conservative school which was later renamed the Philadelphia Theological Seminary.

My parents had made the necessary preparations for their missionary service even while raising a family and while my dad was working in Philadelphia. He worked at a factory that manufactured labels and stickers of all sizes and colors for various companies and businesses. He also worked a while for the Philadelphia Transportation Company (PTC) as a trolley motorman. He also worked at Hess and Young, a service company that did hot embossing and gold leaf stamping work. George Hess was the proprietor of this business located in downtown Philadelphia.

Now, the next step was for my parents to unite with a mission board to begin their missionary service. At age 32, they applied to the Association of Baptist for World Evangelism (ABWE) with the request to serve in the Philippines. However, the mission board rejected their application and turned them down, stating that they were too old! At this time, I was nine years old, and my brother was five years old. For some reason, God closed that door for foreign missionary service, but He opened another door for missionary work in the United States. My parents had known about the Rural Evangel Mission, a faith ministry, and its work in the mountains of Southeastern Kentucky. They were in contact with Rev. Ernest Hunter, the founder and director of the mission. My parents applied and were accepted for missionary service, not in the Philippines, but in Kentucky.

On June 21, 1951, my dad was ordained to the Gospel ministry by Chelten Avenue Baptist Church. Rev. Earl F. Newell was one step closer to beginning full-time missionary service with my mom in Kentucky. It's interesting to note that some fifteen years later, I would have the privilege of being ordained by the same church in preparation for my own full-time missionary service with my then-to-be wife, Anna Gay.

Many times, I heard the testimony of my parents as they explained how God was directing their steps. God confirmed that He was leading them to serve in Kentucky as home missionaries based on Acts 8:26 where Philip was directed by the Lord to "go toward the south" for a special assignment. My parents were accepted for full-time missionary service with Rural Evangel Mission, and they set their sights on going "toward the south" to Kentucky just as soon as the Lord provided their monthly pledged support from friends and churches.

About this time, a friend of the Rural Evangel Mission was putting the final touches on a vehicle that he was donating to the ministry. This was to be the vehicle that my parents would use in their missionary work in the rough, rural areas of Breathitt County, Kentucky. This rather unusual vehicle was a Dodge Power Wagon formerly used in the military as an Army Command Car. Originally, it had two bench seats with a cargo area behind the second seat. The seats were accessed by four cut-outs, two on either side of the vehicle. It had no roof, only a windshield in front, and a tail gate across the rear opening.

The Dodge Power Wagon underwent a major overhaul. When the work was completed, the second bench seat had been removed and the cut-outs for that seat were covered with steel plates. The top section and roof of an old panel delivery truck had been welded onto the Power Wagon. A different tail gate was fabricated out of wood which closed in the bottom half of the rear opening. The top half was covered with a heavy piece of canvas that could be rolled up or let down to close the opening. The front-wheel drive linkage had been disconnected, and there was no muffler in the exhaust system. The truck was repainted a solid deep blue color. We affectionately named this vehicle the "Blue Bomber" for obvious reasons.

The time came for our departure from Philadelphia in the summer of 1951. My parents disposed of most of our furniture as we prepared to move out of our house at 6426 North Norwood Street. We were extremely limited in space in the back of the Blue Bomber. If it didn't fit in the back of the truck, it could not be taken. My brother and I couldn't take all of our toys, so we had to make some hard decisions on what to leave behind.

My dad carefully packed our stuff in the Blue Bomber, and it was loaded from the floor to the roof with not an inch to spare. The tail gate was securely closed, and the canvas was rolled down and securely tied. There was just enough room on the one remaining bench seat for my dad, my brother, me, and my mom.

I remember the morning we drove out of Philadelphia. We were finally on our way to Kentucky and a whole bunch of new experiences! We all were very excited and just a bit apprehensive as we began this new venture, especially for me, as I continued my journey through the Myopic Zone. At this point, I'm sure that the feelings of our family were very similar to the early pioneers as they journeyed west into the unknown in their covered Conestoga Wagons. Here we were, traveling south into the unknown in the Blue Bomber, our covered Dodge Power Wagon.

My dad referred to several road maps, a luxury the early settlers did not have, and he had our route all laid out. We would go from the city of Philadelphia to the Pennsylvania Turnpike and travel west until we hit U.S. highway 11, a major road running from north to south. We would pass through Hagerstown, Maryland, through Martinsburg, West Virginia, and travel a couple hundred miles down through the valleys of the beautiful Shenandoah Mountains of

Virginia to Abingdon, just north of the Tennessee-Virginia state line. From Abingdon, we would travel sort of northwest toward Kentucky, passing from Pound, Virginia, to Jenkins, Kentucky, over Pound Mountain. From Jenkins we would go the remaining distance to Hazard, Kentucky.

The straps were hooked across the cut-outs; the four of us were in our places. There were no doors to close, no windows to open or close, and no seat belts to fasten. After praying for a safe trip, we were on our way! I imagine we looked something like the Beverly Hillbillies as we made our way through the streets of Philadelphia to the open highway. The weather was clear, and the summer air was warm, a real blessing since the Blue Bomber did not have doors, only the cut-outs with leather straps to keep us from falling out. The ride was noisy in this vehicle without doors and without a muffler, but in a sense it was music to our ears!

Dad found the Blue Bomber to be a cumbersome vehicle to drive, but it was the only transportation we had, and we were thankful to have it. Top speed was about 35-40 miles per hour. It is no wonder trucks and cars were flying past us on the Pennsylvania Turnpike. Drivers were turning in their seats as they past us, probably trying to figure out what type of a truck or car we were driving and who were these people (father, mother, and two kids), and where in the world were they heading!

That's o.k. We kept our chins high and our faces looking forward with eager anticipation of seeing what lay ahead for this missionary family of four headed for the mission field.

Things went relatively well, and as planned, while traveling west on the Pennsylvania Turnpike. Once we exited onto U.S. 11, we could finally say, "We are headed toward the south!" As we drove into the rolling hills and low mountains in central Pennsylvania, northern Maryland, and northern Virginia, it was evident that the Blue Bomber was beginning to struggle under the load. We definitely were not traveling on an interstate highway. (Years later I-81 would be built basically to run parallel to U.S. 11, replacing the hills and curves with a somewhat straight and level four-lane super highway.)

After climbing several rather steep grades, my dad noticed the engine seemed to be overheating, and he pulled off the road to investigate why steam was coming from under the hood. Apparently, there was a crack in the engine block, and it was losing water. This was getting worse as the engine got hotter. This meant that every time the road took a long, steep grade, my dad would have to pull off onto the shoulder and add water to the radiator. Fortunately, we had a thermos jug that could be used for this unexpected task.

We traveled all day and finally stopped at a motel in central Virginia. It was great to be able to stretch out our legs and be away from the roar of the Blue Bomber's engine. After eating a most welcome supper in a nearby restaurant, we made ourselves comfortable for the night.

The next morning, as my dad packed our overnight things into the Blue Bomber, he made a terrible discovery. Overnight, one of the rear tires had gone flat! The good news – we had a spare tire! The bad news – the spare tire was on the bed of the truck buried underneath all of our stuff! So here we are in the motel parking lot, unloading all of our earthly possessions to get to the spare tire. This turned out to be quite a delay in our departure from the motel that second day of travel. Again, we noticed people looking at us and trying to figure out who was this family of four, what was that blue thing they were driving, and where were they going?

Finally, we were able to hit the road again after changing the tire and reloading the Bomber. My dad had to do most of the work, but the three of us tried to help the best we could. We followed the same routine as the day before, adding water quite frequently to the radiator. By this time, my dad had this down to a real science, and the truck almost behaved sort of like a well-oiled machine.

All went fairly well as we pushed ever onward to the south on U.S. highway 11 until we ran into a rain storm. It started as a sprinkle of rain with a very light breeze, but we kept moving steadily ahead. We tried to prepare ourselves for the worst, hoping we could outrun the weather and praying for protection. Before long, however, the rain was coming down in buckets, and the wind was blowing like crazy. The good news – the windshield wipers were working as they should. The bad news – the wind was blowing the rain in the driver's side of the Blue Bomber and out the passenger side, hitting my dad with full force. He was soaked, Richard was soaked, I was soaked, and my mom was soaked! My glasses were dripping wet, and so were my dad's glasses and my mom's glasses. My brother was real fortunate; he didn't wear glasses!

Eventually, we were able to drive out of the storm and into sunshine. But this also meant another stop on the shoulder of the road. After getting dried out and warmed up the best we could, our journey continued into the southern part of Virginia toward Roanoke.

We finally reached Abingdon, Virginia, and turned west off U.S. 11 onto U.S. highway 58, a good highway that ran east to west. My dad's intention was to get across Pound Mountain and into Kentucky before dark.

By this time, there was no mistaking the fact that we were in the mountains. The road down through Virginia was, for the most part, following the valleys of the Shenandoah Mountains and Blue Ridge Mountains. Now, though, we were going straight into and across the mountains, as the road took us up and down and around. The steep grades and curves slowed our progress even more.

We traveled from Abingdon, Virginia, through Coeburn, Wise, and Pound, and made the long, hard climb over Pound Mountain, descending into Jenkins, Kentucky, as dusk fell across the rugged mountains. We found our way to Kentucky state highway 15 at Whitesburg, pointed the Blue Bomber toward Hazard, and continued our westerly journey deep into the mountains of Kentucky.

It was dark as we drove our Blue Bomber into Hazard. Mr. Hunter had arranged for our family to spend a couple of nights in the Grand Hotel located on Main Street. We found our way to the hotel, parked the Bomber in the rear lot, located our room, and collapsed. It had been a very tiring but an exciting trip. But we made it safely, praise the Lord, in spite of the crazy challenges that we experienced along the way.

We experienced some real hardships as our family traveled from Philadelphia, Pennsylvania, to Hazard, Kentucky, but it was a great adventure that I will never, never forget. God was faithful in protecting our family and our things as we made the move to begin missionary service in the mountains of Southeastern Kentucky.

I was born in Philadelphia and spent my first ten years as a "city slicker." Now, I would continue life in the Myopic Zone as a "hillbilly" in the rural mountains of Kentucky. I was going from the dirty, noisy, and fast-paced city living with many modern conveniences to the fresh air of the country with its quieter, slower pace of living with far less of the modern conveniences, and I loved it!

A dozen years later, this newly appointed "hillbilly" would meet a young lady who was a "mountaineer," born and raised in Huntington, West Virginia. According to God's plan, Anna Gay Chapman and I would marry and raise a family while serving as full-time missionaries.    And by the way, I discovered that a "mountaineer" is simple a "dignified hillbilly."   I also learned that labels and names given to certain types of people and locations can be very misleading and can be used in a cruel manner which is very unfortunate and unfair.

I now consider Kentucky to be my stomping grounds and a great heritage that I am not ashamed to embrace.   I am proud to tell people that I was raised in the mountains of Kentucky, and that is where I call home!

## 4

# COCKRELL'S FORK, BREATHITT COUNTY, KENTUCKY
## (1952-1956)

*Trust in the Lord with all thine heart; and lean not unto thine own understanding. In all thy ways acknowledge him, and he shall direct thy paths.* Proverbs 3:5-6

At the age of 10, my parents, Earl and Laverne Newell, and my brother, Richard, moved to Perry County, Kentucky. My parents moved to Kentucky to do missionary work with the Rural Evangel Mission, which was founded by Rev. Ernest Hunter who lived in the Upper Lost Creek area in Perry County. The Hunters had established a children's home as well as a church there on Lost Creek. Our family moved to a house up on the side of a mountain overlooking the children's home. We lived there for about a year. I attended fifth grade at the Rockfork School located about a two and one-half mile walk up Lost Creek from where we lived.

In the spring of 1952, our family moved to Lower Cockrell in Breathitt County. We moved into a house that was rented from Jake Neace who lived on up Cockrell's Fork. We lived very close to where the road crossed the creek and continued on to the post office at Ned. I thought that was a pretty neat name because Ned is my initials backwards (NED, DEN). Right close to our house, Cockrell's Fork flowed into Lost Creek.

I remember that we had to get our water from a well that was in the field across the road from our house. This was a corn field, and we had to carry our water from the middle of the field over to our house. We used to tell people we had running water. That was when my dad, my brother, and I filled the buckets with water and ran back with them to the house.

We had a lot of problems with that well, especially when there was heavy rain and we had tides. The creeks would flood their banks and flow into the field, flood up the road, and run into the well. After a period of time, we began pulling up dead mice with the water.

At that point, we knew some changes had to be made with our water source.

Our house was also located right beside the two-room school there at the mouth of Cockrell's Fork. The school also got water from that well. When we began to have all these problems, the county drilled a new well right beside the schoolhouse. Our family was able to get permission to use that well, and that was a real blessing. We were able to get our water close by. For the first time since we had moved into the house, we had good clean, clear fresh water.

To get from our house to town we had to drive down the dirt road along Lost Creek about two and one-half miles to Whirl Hole where the road turned to gravel. We traveled from that point on the gravel road about five miles to the mouth of Lost Creek where the road ran into Highway 15. We would turn left and go through Haddix to Jackson. On a few occasions, we would travel to Hazard, turning right onto Highway 15 and traveling along Troublesome Creek through Ary and Rowdy, over Duane Mountain, through Bulan and Darfork, and on into Hazard.

While living at Lower Cockrell, my parents worked with missionaries William and Elizabeth Garvin who had already established a church and were conducting Sunday schools in the surrounding communities. The Garvins lived a short distance up Cockrell's Fork. To get to their house, we had to drive our Dodge Power Wagon (the Blue Bomber) right up the creek bed. A couple of times a year, Mr. Garvin and my dad, my brother, and I (and others) would work the creek. We pulled out a lot of rocks and stuff that had washed into the creek during the previous few months and tried to make it as passable as possible. Our landlord, Jake Neace, lived further up Cockrell's Fork, and on a few occasions I would hitch a ride with his son as he would come by the house with his wagon pulled by two mules. Chandler would let me drive the team up the creek, and I thought that was really a great experience.

There was a footbridge that crossed Cockrell's Fork where the road went through the creek. When we had heavy rain and the creek would rise, it usually washed out the bridge. One end was anchored to a tree with a cable, and on many occasions, after the creek receded, my dad, my brother, and I would pull the bridge back in place and set it back on the rocks as it was supposed to be.

Many times, I rode my bicycle from the house, across the creek, and on to the post office at Ned, about a mile up Lost Creek.

One of my best friends was Freddie Hatmaker who was the son of the folks who ran the small store and post office. Quite often, while at the post office, I bought a RC Cola, a package of peanuts (that I dumped into the RC), and a Jumbo Pie at the store. Sometimes, I would help Freddie water their mules in the creek. Occasionally, we swapped transportation, and he would ride my bicycle, and I would ride one of the mules.

It wasn't long before we replaced the Blue Bomber with a new Jeep station wagon. My dad and Mr. Garvin conducted services at the Neace Memorial Church, which was located on past the post office. My mom and Mrs. Garvin taught Sunday school classes in the church. Our family was headed there one time in our station wagon, and part way around the mountain, we met up with a truck coming from the other direction. Since it was closer for the truck to back up to a wider spot, we expected the driver to do that. However, after talking things over with my dad, the man said, "I cannot drive in backup gear." So my dad backed the man's truck to where we could get to a wide enough place to pass. My dad came back to get our station wagon and drove past the truck on to the church.

Our neighbors in the community at lower Cockrell made us feel right at home, and our family really appreciated that very much. I would not trade living those four years in Breathitt County for anything! Just up Cockrell's Fork, within sight of our house, we could see the house of Preacher Jimmy Neace. Just a little distance from our house down Lost Creek, a blacksmith lived whose name was Fletcher Miller. I remember he was a big man, and he rode a rather small horse. He was very friendly and helpful to us. Burnette Neace and his family lived just down the creek and up a hollow. They had milk cows and shared fresh milk with our family.

Living on a dirt road had its challenges, of course. In hot, dry weather the road was extremely dusty, and in the wet, rainy weather it turned to almost pure mud with deep ruts. Every once in awhile around election time, someone would bring in a road grader and work on the road. We had a real nice smooth road for awhile, but before too long it got deep ruts in it again. It sure was handy to have the four-wheel drive Jeep. On more than one occasion, my dad helped pull stuck vehicles out of the mud or ditch and get them back on the road again.

My folks and the Garvins conducted Sunday school classes and church in the two-room school up Ten-Mile Creek. Here again, the only road to the school was right up the creek bed. In the winter time when the water was frozen with ice or when the creek was up, and we could not use the Jeep, my dad would borrow a mule from Burnette Neace. I rode with my dad to the schoolhouse on the mule. I would help get a fire started in the potbelly stove so the room was warm for folks when they came for Sunday school.

Sometime during the four years that we lived in Breathitt County in Lower Cockrell, the county built a road up Cockrell's Fork. Up until that time, there was a footpath that started in the school yard and went behind our house around the side of the mountain up Cockrell's Fork. Basically, they built the road following this path. It was now possible for wagons, sleds, and vehicles to move up and down Cockrell's Fork without going through the creek bed.

It really was nice having the school so close by our house. My brother and I could be at school in five seconds from the time we jumped off our back porch. The schoolhouse was made out of stone and had two rooms with a potbelly stove in each room. The kids in each grade had their subjects taught in the front of the classroom close to the blackboard. Sometimes we had to be disciplined for various reasons. One method of punishment was with an application of a willow switch, and that hurt! Another was to stand in front of the blackboard with your nose pressed against the board. The teacher drew a circle on the board, and you had to almost stand on tiptoes to keep your nose inside the circle. That was a real challenge!

On some of the cold winter days, the teacher would have us bring vegetables, potatoes, and various other things to put in a big container with water that was set on top of the stove. During the morning, this was cooking into a great smelling soup. All of us kids would enjoy the delicious soup for lunch.

When I was in the seventh and eighth grades at Lower Cockrell, the teacher for the upper grades was called Sugarfoot. He was a great teacher, and I learned a lot from him. Every once in a while, he would take a couple of his boy students home for a Friday night and take them squirrel hunting early the next morning. I remember the time Freddie Hatmaker and I went home with Sugarfoot. We spent the night in a side room at his house, and it was so cold, we just about froze to death. We did go squirrel hunting Saturday morning with snow on the ground. We never did shoot anything, but it was a fun experience even with the cold weather.

I have many happy memories of some of the things that we

did at school apart from doing our studies. I loved to play marbles, and some of the other boys loved to play marbles, too. We would play for keeps. Sometimes, I took about ten marbles plus my shooter marble, called a taw, to school. I would not have a good day if I had to go home with just my taw and no other marbles. Other times, I went home with a bag full of marbles that I had won. We played Round-Ring and another marble game called Fatty-Box. There is also a game with marbles where we shot marbles from one hole to another hole, then to another hole, and then to a hole farther away. I can't remember how all that worked, but it was fun, shooting marbles from hole to hole, trying to knock your opponent's marble away in the process. I believe this marble game was called Granny something or other, and we enjoyed that game.

Another game we played was with a peg and a stick. We leaned the peg on a piece of wood on the ground, and with the stick we would hit the end of the peg, flip it up in the air, and whack the peg with the stick. We tried to hit the peg just as far as we could, and whoever hit it the greatest distance, won the game.

Most of us older boys had homemade sleds. I made one out of some boards nailed to two by four runners, complete with handles on the sides. We really didn't need to wait for snow in the winter time. We used these sleds in the early morning after we got to school when the ground was frozen solid. We took our sleds up the side of the hill and slid down across the frozen ground. That was great fun! On those cold winter mornings, we would do this before school started instead of shooting marbles. We could really move fast as long as the ground stayed frozen, but as the ground thawed, it turned into sloppy mud, and that put an end to our sledding.

Just about every boy had either an old rubber tire or a discarded, spokeless bicycle rim. It was fun rolling those things all over the place. We used our bare hands to roll the tires, and we rolled the bicycle rims by holding a stick in the grove of the rim and pushing it along. Who needed store-bought toys!

Each year in the spring, there was a county fair that was held in Jackson. I remember when I was in the eighth grade, our school participated. We marched along the street with a banner proudly indicating Cockrell's Fork School. I carried the Christian flag, and another student (I believe his name was Franklin) carried the American flag during the procession. That year I competed in an art contest and won a blue ribbon for our school.

One of my favorite shooting marbles was actually a steel bearing. Depending on the game we were playing, sometimes I used that as my taw (shooter). One time, I lost my steel marble shooter and had no idea whatever happened to it. Quite a few months later, my dad was preparing a chicken for my mom to cook. While he was cutting up the parts, he found a steel bearing in the gizzard of the chicken. Apparently, the chicken had found my steel marble and somehow managed to swallow it! I sure do not know how the chicken did it, but my steel taw was in its gizzard. It was badly pitted and in pretty rough shape from the internal juices working on it. I lost my favorite steel marble to a chicken. Can you believe that?

Speaking of chickens, on another occasion my dad was preparing a chicken for my mom. Preacher Jimmy Neace happened to be in the yard visiting with us at that time. My dad had killing chickens figured out to a science. Instead of wringing the chicken's neck, we put it between two nails on a block of wood and chopped off its head with a hatchet. With the chicken's feet already tied together, we would hang the chicken on a nail in the apple tree and let it flap its wings while it bled out. It was kind of a gory mess, but it worked quite well. On this particular day, my dad went through the usual routine. He chopped off the chicken's head with the hatchet and hung the chicken up on the nail in the tree to bleed. Of course, the wings were flapping like crazy. Somehow the string holding its feet together got undone, and the chicken flopped onto the ground. It began running around with blood spurting all over the place, making a squawking sound! I almost lost my glasses looking at that sight! My brother went screaming into the house to tell my mom what was going on! My dad and Preacher Jimmy just looked in astonishment at this headless chicken, flapping its wings, and running around the yard making loud squawking sounds like it had just laid an egg. Apparently, when my dad chopped off its head, he severed the chicken's neck just above its voice box, and so here was this unusual sight and sound! It added new meaning to the expression, "Running around like a chicken with its head cut off!" I will never forget that incident and the amazement that we all experienced at that sight.

There were other unusual things that we experienced while living in Lower Cockrell. On one occasion, one of the men in the area had a little too much moonshine to drink. He was on his way home and stopped at our house at about two o'clock in the morning. As he began knocking on the door, and we all peaked out a window, wondering what was going on. My dad went out onto the porch in his pajamas and bathrobe and talked to the man. He wanted my dad to sing some hymns for him. So my dad obliged and sang several hymns to the man. He was satisfied and assured my dad that he would be able to find his way home with no problem. So he went up the road singing to himself as he headed for his house.

On another occasion, there was a shooting up one of the hollows in the area, and the sheriff came out from town to take care of the situation. The sheriff commandeered my dad and our Jeep station wagon and had him drive up the hollow to the house. My dad stayed a safe distance behind the sheriff who went ahead with his gun ready. He was able to take care of the situation and get things under control at the scene. But there was a dead body as a result of the shooting. So the sheriff and my dad loaded the body into the back of our Jeep station wagon, and dad drove the body out to Jackson to the coroner. Fortunately, for my dad and for all of us, that was the only time this type of a thing had to be done.

One afternoon, someone came running by the house and told us to get away from the windows. A man coming up the road was very angry about something and was shooting everything in sight. We then heard a bunch of rifle shots! Our family hurried to a back bedroom and hid behind the chimney until the man went past our house up the Cockrell's Fork path.

One time there was an outbreak of rabies as infected foxes came out of the mountains and attacked and bit cows, cats, and dogs. About this time we noticed our pet cat acting very strange, and it had a glazed look in its eyes. For no apparent reason, it charged across the yard and bit me on the leg. It did the same thing to my dad and brother. It even bit the youngest Francis boy who was in the school-yard. We immediately put the cat up before it could attack anyone else. A neighbor shot the cat for us. Then, we packed its head in a lard bucket with ice so it could be sent to Frankfort for analysis. The report came back that it had rabies, and the four of us that had been bitten had to go each day for two weeks and get injections at Homeplace Hospital in Ary. We survived the ordeal with no ill effects other than being very sore from all of those injections.

While living at the mouth of Cockrell's Fork, and attending the Cockrell's Fork School, I completed the sixth, seventh, and eighth grades. In 1955-1956, I attended my first year of high school at Riverside Christian Training School, located at the mouth of Lost Creek.

I got to school in many different ways. Sometimes I would ride with the mail carrier who came by the house about the time I needed to leave for school. He would head down Lost Creek from the post office at Ned, pick me up at the house, and take me out to the school in his Jeep. He was known as Bunt. If I was going to catch the bus, I had to ride my bicycle to Whirl Hole and leave it at a house by the road. Then, coming home, I would ride the bus back to Whirl Hole, get my bicycle, and peddle on to the house. Gordon Drushel drove the bus from Riverside to the end of the gravel road where it turned around and returned to the school. Gordon's parents founded the Riverside schools. The high school classes were held in a small log building on the school property. On other occasions, my dad would have to take me to school and pick me up.

While living at the mouth of Cockrell's Fork, my parents subscribed to *The Grit Family Newspaper.* I read in the paper how I could possibly earn some money by selling the newspaper myself. So I took on a new venture and tried my hand at selling *The Grit* to folks in our area. At one time, my customers totaled as many as twelve who lived within five miles of my house. I would spend a Saturday afternoon taking newspapers all over the place, riding my bicycle down Lost Creek, up Lost Creek, and up Cockrell's Fork. It took me several hours to deliver the papers and collect the subscription fee. I was pretty proud of myself, being able to have some extra money in my pocket whenever we would go out to Jackson to shop. But it was rough. No matter what the weather conditions, I would have to deliver those newspapers. Sometimes I had to walk instead of riding my bicycle, and that took a lot more time. But I am glad I was able to earn a few dollars by selling *The Grit* newspaper for a period of time.

Our outhouse was located a short distance from the house. At night, we took a chamber pot inside the house which fit under the seat of a chair (with a hole) that we called the commode. We used the commode during the night if we had to. Each morning, my brother and I would take turns emptying the pot. First, we would check very carefully to make sure no one was walking on the path going up or down Cockrell's Fork. Then we would run with the pot out to the outhouse, dump it, and hurry back to the house with it. We rinsed the pot with water from the rain barrel and then hung it on a nail in a tree to dry so it would be ready for use the next night. That was a chore that neither my brother nor I necessarily liked, but it had to be done, and we did it as fast as we could. I must admit, it sure was nice being able to use the commode at night inside the house rather than going outside to the outhouse with a flashlight.

Saturday evening was our bath night. That was usually quite a chore because my dad, my brother, and I would haul a lot of water from the well over to the house in preparation for our baths. In the winter time, we would move the double-size wash tub right in front of the potbelly stove, and set it on chairs to keep it off the cold floor. We would heat the water on the stove in the kitchen and begin filling up the wash tub with our bath water. After bathing my baby sister, Barbara, my mom would get the first bath. Next my little brother, Johnny, got his bath. Then, it would be Richard's turn. Next, it was my turn, and then my dad would get the last bath. We generally would not empty water between baths but rather add hot water to the tub. By the time we were finished with our baths, we had quite a lot of water to empty. That was not too bad, though, since my dad had rigged up a drain pipe that ran under the floor from the kitchen sink outside into the garden area. So on bath night, we had running water, as well. It all ran out the drain onto the ground!

During the summer months, many times my dad, Richard, and I would get our baths in Lost Creek. There was a nice swimming hole right where Cockrell's Fork flowed into Lost Creek, and this is where we would swim. We took a cake of soap with us to the swimming hole and get our baths. We did not have to carry a lot of extra water to the house to get our baths in the wash tub, and that was really nice. But we did have to be on the lookout for snakes!

In 1954, when I was thirteen years old, I was baptized in that same swimming hole in Lost Creek by my dad and Mr. Garvin. Family and friends walked through the corn field and stood along the bank of the creek to witness this significant event in my life.

One of the very interesting experiences I had while in grade school at Cockrell's Fork, was to attend the weekly Bible classes that my dad and mom and the Garvins conducted. If a student could learn 200 Bible verses during the school year, he or she would earn a free week at Camp Nathanael located in Knot County. Of course, the 200 Bible verses did not have to be said all at one time. Each year, I memorized 200 Scripture verses and said them during the Bible class time. The highlight of my summer was to spend a week at Camp Nathanael, which was a ministry of Scripture Memory Mountain Mission at Emmalena, Kentucky.

I always enjoyed opportunities to go to Camp Nathanael in the summertime as a camper. I also attended weekend retreats that were conducted at camp at various times during the year. It was at a special weekend retreat, in 1953 that I knew the Lord was calling me into some type of missionary service, and I dedicated my life to Him for whatever purpose He had for me.

I have many great memories of living at the mouth of Cockrells Fork in Breathitt County. In the summer of 1956, my family moved from Breathitt County to the Heiner Coal Camp in Perry County, just outside Bulan, Kentucky. The Rural Evangel Mission had a new assignment for my folks and that was for my dad to establish a church in Bulan. They were also needed to hold Sunday school classes in Heiner and to visit some of the Perry County public schools in Blue Diamond, Ajax, and Harveyton. At this time, the schools in Southeastern Kentucky were open to Christian workers coming weekly to conduct Bible classes for the students.

Many new adventures lay ahead of our family, and I was ready to take on the challenges, with my trusty eyeglasses, and face my continuing journey through the Myopic Zone.

## 5

## PERRY COUNTY, KENTUCKY (1956-1959)

---

*He that planted the ear, shall he not hear? He that formed the eye,
shall he not see?* Psalm 94:9

In 1951, my parents relocated to Kentucky to do missionary work
with the Rural Evangel Mission, which was founded by Rev. and
Mrs. Ernest Hunter. Pop Hunter and Ma Honey, as they were called,
had established a children's home and a church in the Upper Lost
Creek area. Our family moved to a house up on the side of the
mountain overlooking the children's home and the church building
and Lost Creek in the distance.

The church, the Hunter's house, and the children's home
were located at the bottom of this mountain. There was a path that
led up to the house as well as a crude road. We could drive our
vehicle up to the house only when the ground was dry, which was not
too often in the dead of winter. We had moved some furniture items
and some personal things with us from Philadelphia to Perry County,
Kentucky, in an old Dodge Power Wagon. This vehicle, originally
used as an army command car, had been converted to sort of a panel
delivery truck by a man who donated it to the Rural Evangel Mission.
We affectionately referred to this vehicle as the "Blue Bomber."

It was quite an experience for our family to travel from
Philadelphia to Perry County in the Blue Bomber. This very crude
vehicle did not have four-wheel drive, and we soon discovered that it
was very limited to where it could be driven in bad road and creek
conditions. The back seat had been removed; the cut-out sides were
closed over with steel plating; and the back part was covered with the
salvaged top from a panel delivery truck. The only seat in the front
was accessed through two cutouts (openings) on either side. There
were no seat belts or doors on this vehicle at all. Leather straps could
be hooked across the cutouts to keep everybody somewhat safely
inside. It had no muffler and literally sounded like the thunderous
roar of a big B-52 bomber taking off.

We had the Blue Bomber loaded with some things that we brought for the house in Kentucky, and we had to move those things up the mountain to where we would be living. But we could not drive the Blue Bomber up the mountain. Some friends of the Hunters had a mule and a sled which were used to move all of our household items from the bottom of the mountain up to the house. We also had to purchase some appliances in Hazard, and they were delivered to the foot of the mountain, and hauled up to the house on the sled. It was the first time we had seen a big wooden sled used like a truck, and it was quite fascinating to watch. This was a very practical and efficient way to make that move.

Since we could not drive this power wagon up and down the mountain in rainy and wet conditions, we would have to park the Blue Bomber at the bottom of the mountain and walk up and down the path to get to and from the house.

While living in this house, I attended the fifth grade at the Rock Fork School, a two-room schoolhouse located about two and one-half miles on up Lost Creek. I really did not mind the walk as long as the weather was nice. But on some of the cold winter mornings, it was quite a challenge to get to school without freezing to death. I remember sometimes when getting to school I would be so cold that I could not feel my feet. The potbelly stove was usually glowing a cherry-red and putting out a lot of heat. It sure felt good after a cold walk to school. As always happened, the thick lenses of my glasses would fog up, and I could not see until I wiped off the condensation. That was hard to do with freezing hands and fingers. Another challenge of journeying through the Myopic Zone! If the weather was real bad, either my dad or Pop Hunter would drive a station wagon to the school. The kids from the children's home and I would cram into the vehicle. This helped us keep each other warm on the way to school. It sure was great when we could get a ride to school, and sometimes even home from school, especially when the weather was cold and wet.

It really was an interesting experience, walking up and down the road along Lost Creek. The road went under a very high steel trestle that carried coal cars from the mine entrances near the tops of the mountains on both sides of the hollow. You could hear the whine of the electric-powered motor and the rumble of the cars as they moved across the trestle. The road also went past a place called "Devil's Nose." It actually did resemble a face and nose when you looked across the creek at the rock formation with just the right angle of sunlight and shadows.

Attending fifth grade classes in a two-room country schoolhouse was a new experience for me. I learned a lot of new ways of doing things as our family became accustomed to living in Perry County, Kentucky. I remember carrying my lunch to school in a blue lard pail. This worked great, and my mom was able to get everything I needed for lunch in the lard pail. It worked as good, if not better, than a store-bought lunch kit.

It wasn't too long before I made friends with all of the kids in the children's home. A couple of the boys were my age, and we enjoyed exploring the mountains and doing a number of things together during our free time. One of the great things that I remember was learning how to swing from tree to tree. I always did like to climb trees, and down in the bottom near the creek there was a stand of saplings that were probably fifteen to twenty-five feet high from the ground to the top. We carefully climbed up the tree as high as we possibly could and then tried to see how far we could travel without touching the ground. We did this by swinging the top of the tree back and forth to get momentum going, swinging it in an arch. As the top of the tree leaned further and further from center, we would aim for another tree, and as the top of the tree would bend over, we would grab the next tree and jump onto it. Then we did the same thing again to get from one tree to another tree. I had to be especially careful not to lose my glasses in the process of swinging in the trees and climbing up and down the vines that grew up into the trees. Now I know how Tarzan felt when he was swinging on grape vines through the trees. I really enjoyed those days but have not done too much of that since. It is still a fun memory of getting those trees going, swinging back and forth, jumping into another tree, and then doing the same thing over and over again until we ran out of trees. We would then have to climb down and, if we were not too tired, start the whole process again. The tree-swinging really wore me out, but it certainly was just a fun thing to do! The squirrels probably watched all this in amazement.

We were just really getting used to living there in upper Lost Creek when Mr. Hunter gave my dad a new assignment. He wanted our family to move from Perry County to Lower Cockrell in Breathitt County. There was an empty house there that would be just right for our family, which at that time included my parents, my younger brother Richard, who we called Dick, and me. So in the spring of 1952, our family moved to the house located at the mouth of Cockrell's Fork where it flowed into Lost Creek.

I attended sixth, seventh, and eighth grades at the Cockrell's Fork School. I attended my first year of high school at the Riverside Christian Training School, which was located at the mouth of Lost Creek. From our house the road going down Lost Creek was dirt for about two and one-half miles, and then it turned to gravel until it reached Kentucky highway 15 at the mouth of Lost Creek.

In the previous chapter, I conveyed my memories of Cockrell's Fork in Breathitt County during the four years that my family and I lived there.

In the summer of 1956, my family moved from Breathitt County back to Perry County but this time to the Heiner Coal Camp, located near Bulan, Kentucky. By now our family had increased from four to six. My little brother Johnny and my little sister Barbara Joy were born at the Homeplace Hospital, in Ary, Kentucky. The Rural Evangel Mission had a new assignment for my folks, and that was for my dad to establish a church in Bulan. My parents were also needed to help Miss Hester Treher, a Rural Evangel missionary, to conduct Sunday school classes and Bible classes in schoolhouses in the communities of Blue Diamond, Ajax, and Heiner.

My parents rented a house from E. Raymond Haddix, who at that time was working with the Scripture Memory Mountain Mission (SMMM) and Camp Nathanael, located in Knott County at Emmalena, Kentucky. Our house was once a coal company house, one of four located up a small hollow above what used to be the commissary building. The commissary building was now the home of the Haddix family. More company houses had been built up on a ridge to the left side of the hollow and a few on the right side.

Our house was built on stilts and needed some repairs and remodeling. With the help of some others, my dad added two bedrooms and a bathroom to the side of the house. It was nice to have a regular inside bathroom for the first time since our move to Kentucky in 1951. The outhouse was situated behind the house a very short distance up the hollow, and we used it until the bathroom project was complete.

We also had a coal furnace and vent pipes installed under the house. This required a good amount of digging and clearing away dirt to make this all fit. We even had room to connect a stoker to the furnace. The entire underside of the house was closed in with boards.

I remember some of the interesting experiences we had with wild critters in Heiner. On several occasions, we had bats flying around inside the house. Where did they come from? After some investigation, we discovered a bunch of them nestled between the outside weather boards and the inside wall of the house. At dusk, it got to be a game with my dad and brother and me, taking turns trying to shoot the bats with a BB gun as they squeezed out from cracks in the boards before flying away. Needless to say, this quickly turned into a major frustration instead of a game. I could not see through the gun sight very well because of the rather thick lenses in my glasses. This was another reminder that I was journeying through the Myopic Zone. Eventually, we had to tear off some of the siding, exterminate the bats, and cover that section of the outside wall with new, tight-fitting siding.

One evening as our family was quietly sitting in the living room reading and doing homework, we began hearing a strange sound in the ceiling. It was a slight scrapping sound and moved from one side of the ceiling to the other. Surely bats were not making that sound! We had a trap door in one of the bedrooms which my dad carefully pushed into the space between the ceiling and the roof. I had a flashlight as we both stood on the ladder. Suddenly, the light picked up two beady eyes looking right back at us.

I almost lost my glasses as I jumped down to the floor. My dad grabbed the flashlight and aimed it at the eyes that were attached to the head of a gigantic black snake. We quickly put the cover back into place and discussed our plan of action.

There was another trap door in the utility room ceiling just above the back door. My dad opened the back door as wide as he could and armed himself with a broom. I went back to the first trap door armed with the flashlight and the BB gun. We then uncovered both openings. I saw the snake and shot at it with the BB gun. It slithered uncertainly toward the other opening by the back door where my dad was hiding with the broom clutched in his hands. The snake looked down from the opening. As I continued to wildly shoot, the snake's head came further out of the opening. It momentarily hung by its tail, looking all around in a confused state. Suddenly, it lost its grip and flopped onto the floor. In a flash, my dad hit the snake with the broom and swept it out the back door. Like a streak of lightning it was gone before we could say, "Land snakes alive!" It never looked back as my dad slammed the door shut!

After both trap doors were securely closed, everyone congratulated each other as my mom and little sister Barbara climbed down off the kitchen table and as my brothers Johnny and Dick screamed and cheered! We put the BB gun, flashlight, and broom back into the closet ready for whenever the next adventure presented itself.

On a more serious note, property was given by a family in Bulan where the church that my dad was organizing would be built. The new church was named the Bulan Community Church. When not in school, my brother Dick and I helped my dad as much as we could during the construction of the building. Friends in the Bulan area also helped with the building project.

A few years before our family moved to Heiner, the community had ceased to be an operational coal camp. Most of the original houses had been bought by private owners, and some were available for rent, like ours. Many of the houses had been remodeled and enlarged.

Springs from the worked out mines up the mountain provided good drinking water for Heiner. A pipe line was run down the mountain that gravity-fed water to the community.

The coal mines up near the top of the mountains had been worked out (from the inside). However, there was still coal that could be removed. This was done by auger mining, a method new to us. We watched with interest as bulldozers exposed the coal seams by digging out roads around the outside of the mountain. This made it possible for heavy equipment with huge augers to move along the seam of coal and drill from the outside to pull out the remaining coal. The coal was loaded into trucks and hauled down the mountain to the tipple where it was processed and dumped into railroad hoppers.

Unfortunately, this was a messy operation and there was a lot of soil and water erosion that resulted in permanent scarring of the mountain beauty. During heavy rains, dirty water from the auger mining operations washed down the hollows and into the creeks and rivers. Eventually, measures were enforced to prevent some of this destruction from getting worse.

The tipple at Heiner continued to be very active for many years after we moved into Heiner. This was served by a spur rail line of the Louisville and Nashville (L&N) Railroad. The line ran from Heiner (known as Pioneer) down the hollow to Bulan (Duane), and there the tracks formed a wye. From there a spur line ran up another hollow to Tribbey and Hardburly.

From these communities, the L&N tracks led through Ajax, past the mouth of Lotts Creek, through Darfork, into Walkertown (where it crossed the North Fork of the Kentucky River), and into the northern section of the Hazard Railroad Yard.

The line from Heiner to Ajax was known as the L&N Railroad's Danger Fork Branch. The line from Hardburly to Bulan was known as the L&N's Jake's Branch. I was fascinated by the railroad and tipple operations that we saw every time we traveled from Heiner out to Hazard. This sparked an interest in railroads, particularly the L&N, which continues even to this day!

After making our move from Cockrell's Fork in Breathitt County to Heiner in Perry County, we had to make some decisions about my second year of high school. I had completed my first year at the Riverside Christian Training School at the mouth of Lost Creek in Breathitt County, Kentucky. Since we now lived in Perry County, my parents enrolled me as a sophomore in the M.C. Napier High School located at Darfork, Kentucky. I remember that this was quite an adjustment for me after going to such a small, private school for my freshman year. M.C. Napier was a much bigger four-year high school, and there were a very large number of students who were enrolled. To get to school, I had to catch the school bus where the main gravel road coming from Upper Lost Creek and down from Harvey Ridge branched off to Heiner. The school bus ran out to Bulan to Kentucky highway 15 and on to Darfork.

As I began my sophomore year at M.C. Napier, I made new friends. I was very pleased to renew some acquaintances that I had made at the children's home in Upper Lost Creek back in 1951. A couple of the kids were around my age, and I was happy to see them again.

I remember one morning as I was waiting for the school bus, it began to rain. I got back up under some overhanging rocks beside the road to get out of the wet weather and keep my glasses dry. A very bad idea! A few days later, I began to break out with a rash on my face and hands. This turned out to be a severe case of poison ivy, and I had blisters that were oozing all over my face. It was very itchy and very painful. We had to use massive doses of calamine lotion to help this major problem on my face. For a time, I could not wear my glasses and had to miss a couple of days of school. I later looked more closely at the top of the overhanging rocks and discovered big patches of poison ivy growing in the bushes and shrubs. So I learned my lesson to stay away from overhanging rocks no matter what. And to keep away from poison ivy!

On one particular morning, as the school bus pulled into the M.C. Napier High School parking lot, I saw a bunch of students and some teachers standing by the flag pole looking upward. Were they looking at birds, or maybe bats? I soon learned that someone lost control of the rope with the clip on the end of it that attaches to the top of the flag. The rope had slid up through the pulley and back down until the clip jammed in the pulley. This prevented the entire section of rope from ending up on the ground. The end of the rope with the clip attached had to be pulled back through the pulley to the bottom of the flag pole.

Several boys had already tried unsuccessfully to shinny up the flag pole to retrieve the end of the rope. I figured since I was such a good tree climber, I could very easily take care of this situation. The top of the flag pole was only about twenty or twenty-five feet up.

After making certain that my glasses were securely in place, I began shinnying up the flag pole. I got to within two feet of the pulley, but somehow could not go any further even with all the cheering for me that was going on below. I hung on for dear life and carefully eased back down the pole to the ground. It took me a while to catch my breath and let my knees stop shaking from the effort! This time I'm afraid I bit off more than I could chew!

Eventually, one of the other boys made it all the way to the top, grabbed the clip at the pulley, and pulled it and the end of the rope back to ground level. Without delay, the American flag was correctly attached and proudly raised. After a belated pledging of allegiance to the flag, we all went to our respective homerooms, and classes resumed as normal.

Christmas 1956 was a very special Christmas for me. My mom and dad gave me a Scofield Reference Bible! This King James version of the Bible had cross references, a concordance, subject index, and other helps. It was the New and Improved Edition from the original Scofield Reference Bible published in 1909.

I used this treasured Bible throughout my remaining high school years, and it was invaluable during my four years of studies at Philadelphia College of Bible. I continued to use this as my main

Bible for over forty years until the pages began to tear and the covers started to disintegrate. Over those years, I have highlighted many Scripture verses and added numerous notes and comments of my own. As of this writing in 2010, I still refer to this special Bible from time-to-time. The inscription in the flyleaf of the Bible reads: "To David from Mother and Dad, Christmas 1956" with the Scripture verses: "1 Chronicles 28:9" and "Psalm 119:9 and 11." These have been and are very special verses, helpful guides in my Christian life.

"And thou, Solomon my son, know thou the God of thy father, and serve him with a perfect heart and with a willing mind: for the Lord searcheth all hearts, and understandeth all the imaginations of the thoughts: if thou seek him, he will be found of thee; but if thou forsake him, he will cast thee off for ever" (1 Chronicles 28:9).

"Wherewithal shall a young man cleanse his way? by taking heed thereto according to thy word (Psalm 119:9). "Thy word have I hid in mine heart, that I might not sin against thee" (Psalm 119:11).

The devastating "Flood of 1957" will always remain in my memory even though our family and house was not greatly affected since we lived in Heiner, well removed from the North Fork of the Kentucky River. I was a sophomore at M.C. Napier High School, and classes were disrupted due to the flood waters in Darfork. When it was possible after the flood waters receded, my dad drove us boys out to Hazard where we saw a tremendous amount of destruction. As we drove along the stretch of highway above the river between Darfork and the Mother Goose Market, we saw that a beer joint had been washed away. The buildings on either side of the beer joint remained in place. It was as if that particular structure did not need to be there and was purposely swept clean away by the flood. Our family was extremely grateful to God that our home was not in the direct path of the flood waters.

I finished my second year of high school at M.C. Napier in 1957. During the summer months, some folks began talking with my parents about the possibility of me transferring from M.C. Napier to the Hazard city high school for my junior year of high school. So they did arrange for me to attend Hazard High when school started at the end of the summer of 1957. Now I faced another change in my high school attendance career! My first year was spent at the Riverside Christian Training School in Breathitt County, Kentucky, at the mouth of Lost Creek. My second year of high school was at M.C. Napier at Darfork, Kentucky, in Perry County. Then my third year high school studies, and my fourth year, were completed in Hazard, Kentucky, at the Hazard High School.

For various reasons, it was not until I began my junior year that I was able to get involved in a few extra-curricular activities. None of these were contact sports since I wore eyeglasses!

Also, it was not until my junior year in high school that I felt it was time for me to act like a real man and learn how to shave. The "peach fuzz" sprouting on my face was becoming more evident. As usual, I faced the major obstacle of my glasses in my journey through the Myopic Zone. Do I shave with them on or off? Neither choice was good. If I kept them on, I got shaving cream on the ear pieces and the lenses as I tried put the razor where it was needed. If I kept my glasses off, I would nick myself because I could not see well enough to know what the razor was doing. The fact that we had one bathroom did not help for it seemed like everybody in the family needed to use it right at the times when I was frantically trying to shave. After weeks and months of practice, and encouragement from my dad, I was able to get a halfway decent shave. At first, this was a weekly chore, but a couple of years later it turned into a daily event.

Ever since I could hold a pencil, I found myself interested in sketching, drawing, and doodling. When I was in grade school, I was given a set of paint-by-number drawings. There were two canvas panels with the outline with a number indicating where each color should be painted. I labored through the first painting, following the numbers and colors very faithfully. Then, when it came to the second painting, I decided to venture on my own and paint a scene totally different from what was printed on the little canvas panel. I ended up with an interesting scene using the paints that came with the paint-by-number set. I was an artist! This was the first of many drawings, sketches, and oil paintings that I would make in the years to come. I soon realized that this was a special talent, gift, and ability that God had given me, and I dedicated myself to use it for His honor and glory in the days, weeks, months, and years ahead.

My art ability was not unnoticed at Hazard High, and I found myself involved in preparing a number of drawings and posters for various activities at the school. My English teacher, Mrs. Ross, recruited me to draw a big poster of an Elizabethan Theater. She proudly hung this in the front of her classroom where it remained for many years. My French teacher, Mrs. Kirby, also enlisted my drawing talent for making a series of cards that illustrated words in

English with their French translations. She put these all around the top of the chalk board in her classroom. I was also asked to make posters for special events throughout the two years I spent at Hazard High. These were placed in the hallways of the school.

I really did enjoy the two years I spent at Hazard High. I learned a lot and experienced many new experiences. One problem I encountered was the fact that I could not ride the school bus from Heiner out to Hazard. So we spoke with Mr. Emory Haddix who lived in Heiner and worked at the Sterling Hardware Store in downtown Hazard. He agreed I could ride with him out to Hazard and then walk up High Street to get up to the high school. If it was raining, he would kindly take me right to the school door. After school, I walked back down off the hill to Main Street where the Sterling Hardware Store was situated. I would find a comfortable chair in the furniture section in the back of the store and do my homework, while trying not to fall asleep. By the time Mr. Haddix finished work at the end of the day, I usually had completed all my homework, and I was certainly ready to head home.

The principal of Hazard High carried a whistle with him as he patrolled up and down the hallways. His name was Mr. Wesley, and he could sure blast that whistle, when necessary.

During my junior year at Hazard High, I had a major accident on my bicycle. There was a steep bank across the little stream from where our house was located in Heiner. There was a flat place about ten or fifteen feet on top of the bank. My brother Dick and I decided to dig out a path up the side of this hill to the flat place on top. It was just barely wide enough to ride a bicycle down the path and across the bridge that we built at the bottom that crossed the little stream. We had to be very careful that the pedals did not hit the side of the hill which could easily throw us off balance. One Sunday afternoon, I was on top of this bank with my bicycle and had the very brilliant idea of making a turn onto this path and going down and across this little bridge into our yard. The problem was I could not make the turn at the top without getting off my bike. I got all jammed up, missed the path, and lost my balance! The bicycle and I went flying over the side of this embankment and landed in the yard below. My bicycle crashed on top of me and knocked the wind out of me. I could hardly catch my breath for several minutes as I lay on my back with the bicycle on top of me. One of my first thoughts, "Where are my glasses; are they broken?"

That evening I was in pretty bad pain, so my parents took me to the Homeplace Hospital in Ary, Kentucky. The doctors and nurses examined me and could not find any apparent injury that could be treated at that time. They told my parents to watch me carefully, and if I continued to have pain, especially across the top of my shoulders, and if I craved water, to bring me back to the Homeplace Hospital immediately.

By Tuesday morning, I was experiencing severe pain across my shoulders and around the area of my stomach, and I could not get enough water to drink. So back we went to Homeplace. My folks described what I experienced, and I again described my bike accident. The doctors conferred and agreed that I had a ruptured spleen and was bleeding internally. That sounded scary! It was even scarier when they said they would have to do an operation and remove the spleen immediately. Since I had been bleeding internally, the doctors had to pump the blood out from my stomach area. In order to do this, they inserted a tube into my nose which was pushed down my throat. That was awful! They kept saying, "Don't gag, just pant like a dog." I felt like a dog! Actually I felt much worse than a dog at that point. After they had successfully gotten the tube down my throat, they proceeded to put me to sleep in order to perform the operation. Dr. Cameron, who had served as a missionary doctor in China, was one of the doctors who performed the surgery. Dr. Martin assisted with the operation. They were very kind, and they knew exactly what they were doing. The nurses were kind also. I especially remember Miss Goodell and a couple of the other nurses who were part of this momentous occasion.

When I woke up from the operation, I was extremely sore and in a lot of pain from the fourteen-inch incision that was made in the front of my chest and stomach. I had to stay in the hospital for about a week following the surgery. I thank God that the surgery was successful and that my life was spared.

While at Homeplace Hospital recovering, Mr. Wesley, the principal from Hazard High, came to visit me. I really appreciated that very much. As we talked, he made a comment, "You know that without a spleen, you cannot live in the tropics." Actually, this was not an accurate statement, since years later I lived for eighteen years in the tropics, nine of those years on Bonaire in the Netherlands Antilles, and the other nine years on Guam in the Western Pacific.

I could not attend school for three weeks after returning

home from Homeplace Hospital. During that time, I was able to keep up with most of my school work. However, I had to be extremely careful of how I moved, and I was restricted from lifting anything heavy for many weeks after that. When I returned to classes at Hazard High, some of my fellow students carried my books for me because of their weight. I learned after returning to school that the teacher who taught the health classes had indicated to somebody that a person could not live without a spleen. One of my classmates took me to meet the teacher and explained to her that I was living proof that a person could in fact live without a spleen. The spleen is an organ in the body that acts as a reservoir for blood, and it filters out impurities in the blood, as well. The liver does double duty and picks up some of the functions of the spleen when the spleen no longer exists in a person's body. I was told by the doctors that I would have to be very careful that if I ever experienced a severe cut, I should get the wound covered and the bleeding stopped immediately. Otherwise, without a spleen, I could die because of loss of blood.

Another major event took place during my junior year in high school. I got my driver's license! My dad helped me in the learning process, and I passed the driving test on the first try. I had to do the parallel parking on the bypass around Hazard. At this time, our family had a 1957 two-tone green station wagon. There was nothing real fancy about the station wagon, but it was nicer than the vehicles we had up to this point. In 1951, when our family moved to Southeastern Kentucky, we drove the Blue Bomber (the old Dodge power wagon). In 1953, a new Willys Jeep station wagon was provided for our family which we used for four years. In 1957, the Jeep station wagon was traded for the Chevy station wagon. We certainly needed the Jeep when living in Lower Cockrell in Breathitt County. But when we moved to Heiner in Perry County, my folks did not have to travel on dirt roads and across, up, and down creeks. Instead, almost all of the driving was done on gravel and paved roads.

Of course, my driver's license had imprinted on it "restricted to glasses" due to my nearsighted vision and the need for very strong corrective lenses. This was another reminder that I was journeying through the Myopic Zone.

I completed my senior year of high school at Hazard High in Hazard, Kentucky. Thankfully, I did not have to attend a fourth high school during my senior year. Studying in three different high schools was quite enough! I graduated on May 29, 1959. What a happy day! I remember our class sang "Look for the Silver Lining" during the commencement program. It was quite an honor to be recognized for my art contributions at Hazard High. I also received a special Quill and Scroll key and chain which I thought was really cool. I was voted the "Most Talented" boy in our Senior Poll for the "Class of 1959," and Bobbie Webb the "Most Talented" girl. That also was quite an honor for me!

My senior year was the best! However, it did have its challenges as I needed to have passing grades for all of the required courses in order to graduate. Somehow in the transfer from Riverside to M.C. Napier to Hazard, I had not taken a health class. To take this class, I had to give up band and my trumpet lessons with Mr. Harlan Stone. The regular health class could not be worked into my class schedule. It was finally determined that instead of a regular study hall, my schedule was rearranged for me to go to the study hall of the health teacher. Under her supervision, I outlined every chapter in the health textbook and took the regular exams after completing each chapter. This was rather a unique approach to the dilemma, but I passed the course. So you could say that I basically taught myself the health class in order to meet all the requirements for graduation.

A special assignment given to me was to work on the school 1959 yearbook (or annual) as Art Editor, and I really enjoyed it. That edition of *The Bulldog* was one of the best, not necessarily because of me, but because every editor and staff member of the annual team did a great job with their responsibilities. It was a pleasure to work with each one!

For sketches and drawings, I liked to work with India ink on paper. Several sketches that I drew were used in the annual, including a bulldog, a front view of the Hazard High School, the senior class ring, the dedication page with a sketch of an Elizabethan Theater, and a page with a football and a football jacket that recognized Hazard High as the Eastern Kentucky Mountain Conference Champs.

During my senior year in high school, Southeastern Kentucky was thrown into turmoil as a result of a major strike by union coal miners. There were numerous shootings and dynamite blasts as the strike intensified and non-union miners tried to cross picket lines that had been set up around the mines. I remember that the Hazard High School gymnasium was used to house National Guard soldiers who were deployed by the governor to help restore and maintain law and order in and around Perry County.

One of the highlights each summer was spending time at Camp Nathanael in Knott County at Emmalena, Kentucky. First, I was a regular camper, then a junior counselor, and finally a summer worker and counselor. I consider the experiences I had during my summers at Camp Nathanael to have played a major part in my social and spiritual development. I especially liked the Youth Leadership training camps that were conducted at the end of the weeks of regular camp. Those few who were a part of this special training were recommended by the Scripture Memory Mountain Mission. It was a privilege to be selected for this ten-day training program. Our group would visit local churches and conduct special services with singing, testimonies, and preaching. This gave us hands-on opportunities to put into practice the things that we learned and helped me get over my apprehension of public speaking.

I remember as a grade school camper, at the end of the camp week on Saturday morning I wanted to buy something (probably candy) at the camp store before going home. To my dismay, I lacked a few cents on my store card for the item I had selected. Mr. Bob Beckwith saw my dilemma and said, "Bein' it's you, what you have there is enough," and he handed me the item. That really made me feel special, and it was typical of the kindness that every missionary worker at Camp Nathanael showed to campers.

The Lord used the many summers, and the other times that I spent at Camp Nathanael as a camper and counselor, to grow into a deeper relationship with my Lord and Savior, Jesus Christ, as the Word of God was faithfully taught, and as I was challenged to obey His instruction. I learned more about world-wide missions through the various missionary speakers who were continually being featured at camp.

I dedicated my life to the Lord at camp, willing to go into full-time missionary service, if that was God's will for me. Little did I realize that several years later in 1966, after completing Bible College, studying radio electronics for another two years, marrying Anna Gay Chapman, and being ordained into the Gospel ministry that we would be preparing to go to the mission field with Trans World Radio. We conducted our first deputation meeting at Camp Nathanael, sharing how God was leading us to the mission field. A few years later, one of the cabins at Camp Nathanael was named "Bonaire" which was the first foreign country where we served as missionaries. (Bonaire is one of the ABC islands in the Netherlands Antilles located in the southern Caribbean about forty miles north of Venezuela. This is where Trans World Radio had established super-power transmitters for broadcasting Christian programs in many foreign languages into many parts of the world.) Perhaps, Anna Gay and I should have been married at Camp Nathanael!

Nothing reminded me more than Halloween that I was traveling through the Myopic Zone. I really am thankful that my parents allowed us kids to enjoy Halloween as a fun time and not a bloody, scary one. Since I wore glasses, it was always a challenge to come up with a mask that would work for me. If I put the mask on over my glasses, they would steam up very fast and I could not see. I tried putting my glasses on over the mask, but they kept falling off. The only other option was to not wear my glasses at all. Always the embarrassing problem was that I could not see what was going on or where I was going, so I had to depend on somebody to help me. Quite a dilemma! But somehow I still ended up with as much candy as my younger brothers and sister.

I remember some of the ingenious Halloween costumes that kids wore in the Southeastern Kentucky Mountains. They were homemade, and the masks were homemade, as well. They were quite unique and served their purpose much better than store-bought costumes and masks. They were really funny and not necessarily scary.

Christmas time was another challenge with my journey through the Myopic Zone, especially during the school and church plays. Whoever saw a wise man wearing glasses, or a shepherd, or Joseph? Horrors! I guess I let my pride get the best of me sometimes as I dutifully put on the bathrobe, wrapped my head in a towel, and put on my glasses. A couple of times I tried to play my part without wearing my glasses. Bad idea! I could not see because of being so nearsighted, and it was complicated trying to decide where to park my glasses. By then, I was so concerned about these particular matters that I would forget my part!

How easy it is to forget the main thing about Christmas, like me worrying about the technicalities of wearing or not wearing glasses. Christmas is the celebration of the birth of Jesus Christ, God's Son, who came into this world to provide salvation through His shed blood on the cross of Calvary. "For God so loved the world, that he gave his only begotten Son, that whosoever believeth in him should not perish, but have everlasting life" (John 3:16).

The Christmas seasons were very special in all of the communities where my parents ministered and lived. There were Christmas programs and plays in each schoolhouse or church. My dad led in singing Christmas carols and taught and preached from the Bible. My mom played the pump organ that we carried to the schoolhouses in the communities.

Each Christmas, many gifts for adults and children of all ages were provided for distribution by friends and churches that contributed to my parents and their ministry. Boxes of unwrapped gifts were sent to our house and opened in preparation for Christmas. Each person who attended the services in each community received a gift. Each person had to be identified with a specific gift. Then the fun began! Our family wrapped each gift and placed a name tag on it. I loved to wrap presents, and still do. We had boxes of gifts marked for each community where a special Christmas program and party would be held. It was such a blessing to see the joy on the faces of adults, teenagers, and children as they received their gifts which was an expression of God's love from the friends and churches that made this possible.

It was always a miracle each Christmas to see how the Lord provided just the right items needed for the special folks that faithfully attended Sunday school and church services in the schoolhouses and in the Bulan Community Church.

My parents served as what is called "faith missionaries" in Breathitt County and Perry County, Kentucky. As a "faith mission organization," the Rural Evangel Mission did not pay any financial support to my parents or its other missionaries. The support for our family came from individuals and churches who believed in our missionary work and wanted to be a part of it through their monthly prayer and financial support.

I learned first-hand that this principle of "living by faith" works. As a family, time and time again, we saw God supply our financial, physical, and spiritual needs in many unusual ways.

For example, on more than one occasion, we would run out of a food item and did not have the money right then to replace it. At just the right time, a friend would stop by the house with the exact item that my mom or dad needed. My mom and dad were very frugal, and I am thankful that they also engrained this principle in me.

From these experiences, I learned many practical and lasting

69

lessons in "living by faith." This principle stayed with me from those days in Kentucky as I stepped out "in faith" to attend Bible College and technical school, in preparation for beginning a career in missionary service. God has been faithful to the promises in His Word that He will supply all our needs.

My folks instilled in me the importance of maintaining a good work ethic. My dad used to say, "If a job is worth doing, it is worth doing right." And I have passed this principle on to my children, as well. Some have called me a "perfectionist," and maybe that was one of the results of a godly heritage. I may not be as much of a perfectionist now, but I still want to do my best in whatever job or project I undertake. It is not as easy now, especially with my recent experiences in my journey through the Myopic Zone, dealing with the retina detaching in my right eye.

Years later, as a second generation missionary, I have conveyed these same principles to my wife and to our children as we have served in faith missions overseas and in the states since May 31, 1966, with Trans World Radio (TWR), Source of Light Ministries International (SLM), and Neighborhood Gospel Missions (NGM).

These memories are just a few of the experiences I had in those years from 1956 through 1959 while living at home in Heiner, Perry County, Kentucky. A big milestone of some sort was reached in high school when I had to switch from regular eyeglasses to glasses with bifocal lenses because my vision was deteriorating. The bifocals sure helped me see better for reading and close up work while maintaining my distance vision. Every year my eye examinations showed that I needed stronger lenses to correct my myopic condition.

After graduating from Hazard High, I moved to Philadelphia, Pennsylvania, in the fall of 1959 to continue my education at Philadelphia College of Bible. I moved into the dorm, and this began a whole new chapter in my journey through the Myopic Zone.

## 6

## BACK TO PHILADELPHIA  (1959-1963)

---

*Thou has beset me behind and before, and laid thine hand upon me.*
Psalm 139:5


During my senior year at Hazard High School, I obtained a lot of information from several Bible Colleges and Bible Institutes to determine where I could possibly study in preparation for my future missionary service, wherever that might be.

Some of the schools I checked out were Tennessee Temple in Chattanooga, Tennessee; Bob Jones University in Greenville, South Carolina; Moody Bible Institute in Chicago, Illinois; Bryan College in Dayton, Tennessee; Philadelphia College of Bible in Philadelphia, Pennsylvania; Southland Bible Institute in Pikeville, Kentucky; and Appalachian Bible Institute in Bradley, West Virginia.

Actually, I had considered going to art school where I could develop my artistic abilities. I did not find any Bible College that offered this course of study so I did not seriously pursue this line of thought. Even without any formal art training, I soon discovered that God would give me many opportunities to use my art talent in Bible College and on the mission field.

I was especially drawn to Philadelphia College of Bible (PCB) since my dad attended evening classes at the Bible Institute of Pennsylvania, and my mom was an alumni of the same Bible Institute which several years later grew into PCB. I was also interested in getting a B.S. degree in Bible as well as studying a major in missions. I was accepted at PCB and enrolled in the missions program with my goal of graduating in four years with a B.S. in Bible.

In my move to Philadelphia, I had to step out of my comfort zone by faith and begin to be more independent of my family and home surroundings that I had grown to appreciate during my last couple of years of high school. The time had come for me to pack my things, clean my eyeglasses, and face a new phase of my journey through the Myopic Zone. I knew for a fact that God had led me to

Philadelphia College of Bible. And I knew that He would provide for my financial needs for the tuition, room and board, and book expenses.

I soon learned about syllabus notes and term papers; I learned how to balance studies between part-time work, sleep, and social events; and I learned the need to adjust to city living deep in the heart of Philadelphia.

Real quick, I learned how to type my term papers and reports on an old Underwood portable typewriter (which I still have in my possession). I used what some called the "Hunt and Peck Method." I hunted for the right key and banged it down with my right index finger. Others referred to my way of typing as the "Columbus Method," which simply means I would eventually "discover" the correct key on the keyboard with my right index finger, and hit it. I can honestly say my one finger put me through college. Unfortunately, I still made many mistakes which had to be corrected by either erasing (which was quite messy) or by applying correcting tape over the error and retyping (which was a pain because it took too much time). Some of my classmates paid girl students to type their papers. I just couldn't afford to do that, so I had to toil ever onward, looking for the right key through my thick bifocal lenses.

My short-term goal was to complete my Bible training and graduate in four years, and then see how and where the Lord would call me into full-time missionary service. I was confident that I was surrounded by God's guiding hands and that He would open and close doors in my journey through the Myopic Zone. The four-year adventure at PCB had its difficulties that were outweighed by great blessings as I studied and learned many valuable lessons through the classroom experiences as well as through interacting with my classmates, and the godly men and women who served on the faculty and staff. The reality that college studies were different from high school classes hit home real quick, but I knew that the Lord had definitely led me to PCB. I also had to make the adjustment from the openness of country living in Kentucky to the confinements of city life in downtown Philadelphia.

The address of Philadelphia College of Bible was 1800 Arch Street, located on the corner of 18th Street and Arch Street just a few blocks from the City Hall building with the statue of Billy Penn on the very top. Being in center city was a blessing since public transportation was within walking distance of the college. The Broad

Street Subway and the Frankford Elevated Train were the main means of travel for most of us students who did not own vehicles. The entrance to Suburban Station of the Pennsylvania Railroad was right across 18$^{th}$ Street from PCB. The Greyhound Bus Terminal was just about two blocks away, and the commuter trains of the Reading Railroad were accessed through the Reading Terminal just a few blocks to the east of the college.

One could go into the entrance to Suburban Station and walk through underground concourses to City Hall at Broad and Market Streets and catch the Broad Street Subway. Some of the underground concourses were usually crowded with people walking here and there, and others were sort of spooky because of the dim lighting and the lack of people. Who knows how many innocent people have been mugged in these underground passageways. I never had any problem, but I was always greatly relieved to get back to the street level sidewalks.

The center city location of PCB was also helpful for our Christian service assignments in local churches, in rescue missions, and for street meetings on key corners of the city as well as in the city parks.

My first year Christian service assignment was teaching a weekly evening Bible class of rambunctious boys at the Sunday Breakfast Association, a rescue mission in Center City Philadelphia. Other Christian service assignments included leading street meetings, conducting a weekly Bible Club, and driving a college VW bus to transport Christian service teams to various locations in and around the city for special meetings.

I remember one time I was driving students to a meeting location, traveling on the Schuylkill Expressway. The van was sputtering along as fast as it could under the heavy load. Someone had the bright idea of seeing if we could increase our speed, so everyone began lurching forward in unison. The VW bus was literally surging faster down the highway. This added to the interest of us students on the trip, but it was not the safest way to travel, especially in heavy traffic, so this experiment was stopped rather quickly.

The physical construction and layout of Philadelphia College of Bible (PCB) was rather unique in its location in downtown Philadelphia. Everything related to the college was neatly packed into a nine-story building. We did not have a typical wooded campus; instead, we had steel fire escapes suspended over concrete sidewalks. The closest thing we had to a campus was Logan Circle, part of the Fairmount Park system that was located about three blocks to the north on Arch Street. This beautiful spot had an ornate fountain surrounded by many trees and many varieties of flowers.

The college building itself was formerly used by the YMCA, and now it had been remodeled for use by PCB. The basement was used for the kitchen, cafeteria, dining room, and maintenance. The auditorium, bookstore, administrative offices, and snack shop were located on the first floor which had main entrances from Arch Street in the front of the building and 18th Street on the side. Part of the second floor was used for a balcony around the auditorium, and the rest of the floor space housed faculty offices and classrooms. The third floor was used for classrooms, the library, and faculty offices.

The girls' dorm rooms were located on the fourth and fifth floors. The boys' dorm was located on the sixth and seventh floors. The eighth floor contained a gymnasium, a student lounge, a game room with ping pong tables, and a few rooms in a small wing that was used for a boys' dorm. The ninth floor housed the radio room (ham shack) and provided access to the roof.

The roof held a big water tank that we were convinced did not hold a drop of water but instead was full of beef gravy! Every meal in the cafeteria, no matter what the meat dish, was served with beef gravy. Beef gravy with chicken. Beef gravy with pork chops. Beef gravy with scrambled eggs. Beef gravy with spaghetti. Beef gravy with sausage. And, yes, we did have beef gravy with beef gravy, as well as with hamburgers and roast beef.

Several light wells had been constructed as part of the building's design. Two stairwells provided access to the various floors, and two side-by-side elevators were built into the center part of the building which opened onto each of the eight floors from the basement to the top floor. The access to the ninth floor was by a stairway.

This layout of PCB definitely had its advantages. Everything was under one roof, and all floors could be reached by either the stairways or the elevators. We did not have to walk outside through the elements in inclement weather to get to the classrooms, dorms, and dining hall like typical colleges. The disadvantage was the feeling of being confined, something I had to adjust to since moving from the wide-open spaces of my home in Kentucky.

Many students lived close enough to PCB so they could go

home on Friday afternoon after classes and return to PCB either Sunday evening or early Monday morning. A few of us lived too far away and had to remain in the building throughout the entire weekend.

I remember one Saturday evening when there was not a whole lot happening in the building. The dorms were quiet; there were a few students in the lounge on the ninth floor, and there were a few in the snack shop on the first floor. One elevator was operating, and I was substituting for the elevator operator. Another student who worked in maintenance and I figured we would add some excitement to this rather dull and boring evening.

I stopped the elevator between floors so my buddy could get on top of the cage. We opened the trap door on the ceiling of the elevator just a crack. Eventually, a signal came to the elevator for a pickup on the sixth floor, a girls' floor! Great! I operated the hand control and moved the elevator car up to the sixth floor where three girls were waiting. I opened the elevator gate and opened the hallway door to let them into the elevator, giving them a nice friendly greeting and a big smile. As I started slowly back down toward the first floor, my buddy began poking a rubber black snake down through the ceiling trap door. Suddenly, there were piercing screams from the girls as they saw the snake coming into the elevator car from the roof. Fortunately, none of them hyperventilated. I was so excited, I almost lost my glasses. We learned that the students in the snack shop heard the screams from somewhere up the elevator shaft and wondered what on earth was going on. What a great practical joke! At least I thought so, and so did the girls after they calmed down, realizing it was just a fake rubber snake. It sure livened up the evening, too.

At times, both elevators had to be in service. On another occasion, I was substituting for one of the student operators. Normally, both elevators would be parked on the first floor with doors open ready to take people to one of the upper floors. If we received a signal from an upper floor, one elevator or the other would go for the pick up. It was rather interesting to have a race to see which elevator could reach the floor first. There was a special knack to closing the cage and door, cranking the control to fast up, stopping at the floor, and opening the cage door and the floor door.

The floor of the elevator had to be relatively even with the hallway floor in order to open the door into the hall. If it was too far off, the door could not be opened even though the cage door of the elevator could be opened. However, some of us knew it was possible to defeat a safety catch so that the hallway door could be opened no matter how far above or below the elevator floor was positioned from the hallway floor. Only occasionally did I defeat this safety feature for various reasons. Enough said on that subject!

For my freshman year, I was assigned to a very small dorm room on the seventh floor along with another first year student. It was quite an adjustment for both of us, to say the least. The one thing we had in common was both of us were MK's (Missionary Kids). Bob's parents were missionaries in the wild jungle country of Africa, and that is where he was raised. My parents were missionaries in the wild mountain country of Kentucky, and that is where I was raised. That is where the similarity ended. He liked to stay up late and do everything but study, but I wanted to get my studying done and get to bed with the lights out at a reasonable time. I considered myself self-motivated and self-disciplined, but Bob was just the opposite. Somehow, by the grace of God, I made it through the first year (and so did he).

There was a small wing with about ten single dorm rooms on the eighth floor. I put in my bid for one of these rooms before finishing my first year, and one was assigned to me. What a blessing! I managed to keep the same room for my second, third, and fourth years at PCB.

As I settled into my college life, it did not take long for some of my classmates and faculty members to recognize my God-given art ability. I was soon drawing posters and announcements for various functions at PCB. I was happy to be involved in drawing and sketching and receive compliments for my art work.

On one occasion this was not quite the situation, though. I was asked to draw up a poster announcing the annual Valentine Social. I used the theme from the Li'l Abner comic strip and drew likenesses of the main characters, who were Abner and his friend Daisy Mae. The Social Committee placed the poster in the first floor hallway. Not long afterwards, I was called into the office of the Dean of Women. She had the poster in her office and explained to me that I had done too much justice in drawing the likeness of Daisy Mae and that the depiction of her needed to be modified to make her more flat-chested. So I redrew the character to the accepted standard and placed it on top of the original sketch. Everyone was happy, and the poster was returned to the hallway to announce the upcoming social event. This incident made me aware that I needed to be careful in what I drew and how I drew it. I certainly did not want to offend anyone, and I wanted to make certain my drawings were not a dishonor to the Lord.

I had a lot of lessons to learn in college, and a lot of these were outside the formal classes of study required for graduation. I learned how to navigate in and around the city of Philadelphia. I learned how to interact with people and co-workers in the work force since I had to work at various part-time jobs to help pay for my college expenses.

My parents were not able to help very much because they had a limited income with their missionary support. Some friends of the family and churches in Kentucky would occasionally send some money to help me. It was amazing to see how God supplied for my financial needs at just the right time. For example, at the end of one month I owed $20.00 on my college bill. I had no extra cash, and the deadline was within a couple of days away. I asked the Lord to supply the funds I needed. Someone sent a check which I received in my mailbox the day the final amount was due. I thanked God that He had laid me on someone's heart, and they responded by sending me $20.00 (just the amount needed to cover the balance of the monthly payment).

This happened over and over again throughout my four years at Philadelphia College of Bible, and it was proof to me that I was right where God wanted me to be and that His hand was on me and that He would provide just what I needed at just the right time. This applied to all aspects of my life both physically and spiritually, but I had to do my part by working part-time.

I had transferred my church membership from the Neace Memorial Chapel in Breathitt County to the Bulan Community Church in Perry County after our family moved in 1956. I transferred my membership again in 1959 when I moved to Philadelphia to attend college at PCB. Since my parents were members of Chelten Avenue Baptist Church in Philadelphia, I moved my membership there, as well. The church was located in the Germantown section of Philadelphia close to where I used to live at 6426 North Norwood Street, but a pretty good distance from PCB.

It took me about an hour to travel to the church. I had to walk several blocks to the Broad Street Subway and take it north before transferring to a bus that took me to within a couple of blocks of the church. Eventually, one of the members of Chelten Avenue Baptist Church, Ed Babe, drove his station wagon to PCB to pick me up along with some other students and take us to the church for Sunday services. This was a good bit faster than traveling by public transportation. Ed would do the same thing on Sunday evenings if I or others were able to get to Chelten.

My first part-time job was working for a small printing company in Center City Philadelphia. I was hired to keep the shop orderly and clean, to help set up various jobs for printing, and to deliver printed materials to customers. Most of the customers were located within a few blocks of the business so I did a lot of walking on the crowded city sidewalks and across the busy streets, trying to dodge pedestrians while trying to avoid running into trolley cars, city busses, and cars and trucks. This was especially tricky while pushing and pulling a hand cart loaded with boxes. There was always noise – the sound of horns blasting, traffic cop whistles, clattering trolley wheels, vehicle engines, and sirens from police cars and fire trucks. Of course, there was always the smell of pollution from vehicle exhaust and garbage trucks loaded with all kinds of good stuff. There was always something of interest going on.

The printing business was run by a husband and wife team. The wife had a very foul mouth, and she cursed and shouted at me for no apparent reason that I could tell. Her husband was much more reasonable to deal with, and his language was nothing like his wife's. On more than one occasion I was ready to quit, but I managed to put up with the nonsense during my freshman year and was thankful that I had a job to help with my college expenses. I wanted to be a good testimony to the business owners in spite of the rough working environment, and I had several opportunities to witness to the owners as well as to the other employees.

The part-time job I had during my sophomore year was not as hectic as the job at the printing business. I, along with two other PCB students, worked for E. Brooke Mattlack, a trucking outfit known as "the pipeline on wheels." This company shipped oil products nationwide in big semi-tractor tanker trailers. We worked in the billing department, separating and sorting bills of lading and invoices. We filed the paper work and mailed out the invoices to businesses that had used the trucking company to purchase and transport the petroleum products. The neat thing about this job was that it was not within walking distance of the college like my previous job. Instead, we had to travel by train using the Pennsylvania Railroad's commuter line that originated in the Suburban Station that had an entrance right across the street from PCB.

It was not a long ride, and rarely did we have to pay a fare. The rail line went from Suburban Station, where the tracks were underground, and traveled west for several blocks going from below ground to a bridge crossing the Schuylkill River to the Pennsylvania Railroad's 30th Street Station. From this station, connections could be made to other commuter lines as well as to the railroad's Main Line that served passenger trains going south to Washington, DC, and also to northern and western cities and states.

Most of the time, the conductors would not collect fares or tickets until the commuter trains left 30th Street Station. But this is where we would get off the train and walk to the E. Brooke Matlack offices just a couple of blocks away.

I was happy to be able to travel by train, even though it was just for a few minutes going just a few city blocks. I missed the L&N Railroad in Kentucky and the long lines of coal hoppers being shifted from the Heiner tipple to the Hazard railroad yards. I did ride the Philadelphia subways from time-to-time, and I always enjoyed those experiences.

My part-time job during my junior and senior years at PCB also required me to travel by train, but this time I had to go a greater distance. I was offered a job at Brackbill's Farm Market in Ardmore, Pennsylvania, about a thirty minute commute on the Pennsylvania Railroad's line that ran between downtown Philadelphia and Paoli. I couldn't believe my good fortune! I caught the train at Suburban Station which stopped at 30th Street Station and then continued on to the station at Ardmore. I didn't mind having to buy tickets; it was worth the expense since I got to travel on the train!

Actually, I was able to get a special reduced meal ticket at PCB that covered only breakfasts and suppers. I left for Ardmore immediately after my last morning class and ate a quick, free lunch at Brackbill's before starting work. This arrangement helped offset the cost of my train travel.

I really enjoyed working at Brackbill's Farm Market and learned many new things in the process. Mr. Brackbill had several farms and grew a lot of the produce we sold in the market. Ardmore was the location of one of his farm markets and was managed by Henry Fietz. This location was sort of ritzy, and a lot of the customers were rather well to do people. It was an interesting experience dealing with them as we sold several fancy type food items.

For example, we sold lunch meats that had to be sliced. A popular item was dried beef that came in big chunks. We used an electric slicer to cut through the chunks at the thickness desired by the customer. We sold whole fresh chickens that the customers wanted us to cut up for them. That was some challenge, believe me, and I had to learn how to do this. In Kentucky, my dad always cut up the chickens for my mom, and I had no expertise in this matter. Woe is me! My first few cut up chickens were more like mutilated chickens. It's a good thing the chicken was dead and unable to respond to my lack of culinary skills. Eventually, I got the hang of it and could cut up a chicken almost as good as a professional butcher.

Brackbill's also sold fresh turkey parts, thankfully not the whole fresh bird. We sold turkey thighs, drum sticks, and sliced white breast meat. One time a lady asked me, "May I please have two turkey hips?" I didn't understand what she wanted so I asked her to please repeat what she wanted. "Two turkey hips!" I almost asked her again, but then it hit me, "She wants turkey thighs!" I guess hips and thighs are synonymous. Anyway, I understood the order and neatly wrapped up her two turkey "hips," and she went away happy.

We sold special salads that a German lady, Mrs. Hegadesh, made right there in the store kitchen. She made chicken salad, pepper hash, and several other delicious dishes. The store also sold fresh asparagus grown in New Jersey. Sometimes Mrs. Hegadesh would fix this for me for lunch, and it was delicious.

Mr. Brackbill grew the most beautiful chrysanthemums, and that was a popular item in the fall. One of the most popular items in summer was freshly picked corn from the Brackbill farms. Mrs. Hegadesh would fix fresh corn on the cob for us employees, and was that good!

Another item that was a best seller in the fall was the freshly squeezed apple cider. This was the best apple cider I have ever tasted. I guess that is because everything went into the squeezing – apple cores, worms, seeds, and who knows what else. And there were no preservatives. Yum! Yum!

I had the opportunity of taking some of the food items that

were left over at the end of the day back to my dorm room. The window in my room opened into an outside light well, and I was able to build a little shelf arrangement on the outside window ledge where I could keep things in the cold outdoors. I had no small dorm-size refrigerator, since they were not available in those days, when I was in college.

I was not the only Kentucky hillbilly that attended Philadelphia College of Bible. Donna Baker was also a freshman. She lived in Mayking, Kentucky, a small town deep in the coal mining regions of the mountains. Beatrice Pendleton was a year ahead of Donna and me. Bea was also from a small town near Mayking, Kentucky. The girls had been introduced to PCB by Bill Shade who was a Christian worker in Southeastern Kentucky and who was a graduate of the college. Bea wrote the following comments in my 1961 year book:

"Dave, from one hillbilly to another may I say best wishes in everything you do in the future. Have fun at camp this summer. May the Lord bless you richly, In Christ, Bea.

"P.S. Thanks for your trouble in carrying our bags on the way to Kentucky."

My social life took on a new dimension during the summer of 1961 while working at Camp Nathanael. Another college student, Leslie Stone, was working at camp that summer, as well. Leslie's dad, Harlan Stone, was the Hazard High School band director. He taught me trumpet lessons during my junior year at Hazard High. I had known Leslie from high school, and also we attended camp together as campers and junior counselors. She completed her senior year at Hazard High while I finished my first year at PCB. As we both worked again at Camp Nathanael during the summer of 1961, our friendship deepened, and we exchanged our high school senior class rings. However, maintaining a long-distance friendship had its many drawbacks. God had other plans for our lives, and after a year or so, we broke off our relationship.

Leslie had moved to Tennessee in 1960 to begin her first year of training at Bryan College. While studying there, she met a guy who also was attending that college, and they developed a very close friendship in late 1962. Leslie and I returned each other's high school senior class rings, a prudent but tough decision under the circumstances.

I had occasionally dated Donna Baker, from Mayking, Kentucky, during our first two years at PCB, and we became very good friends. At the time, we both felt it would be best that we not get too serious about going steady, but date others at PCB and get to know them through the various social events that were a part of our college life. Donna wrote this in my 1961 year book as our sophomore year was coming to an end:

> "Dave, this has been a good year in Him. Our friendship has and I hope will continue to be a blessing. May the Lord bless you in Kentucky this summer. Donna."

Dorm life had its challenges and mainly revolved around studying and sleeping. Sometimes other things would become a part of both of these activities. It was very easy to get caught up in bull sessions that covered every topic from A to Z, some of it related to class subjects, Bible doctrines, politics, and just plain fun. Some things under the fun category included games such as chess, checkers, and Rook. It seemed like the card game Rook was developing into the main pastime for a good many of men dorm students. Some guys would spend hours playing Rook that drastically cut into their study and sleep schedules. Thankfully, I was able to exercise self-discipline and limited my bull session and Rook activities to reasonable amounts of time. Unfortunately, none of us had parents who could put a check on unreasonable activities and remind us to turn out the lights and get some sleep. Eventually, the Dean of Men had to put some restrictions on activities that tended to move into the unreasonable realm.

At the end of a very busy day, I was thankful to remove my thick-lensed bifocal glasses, put them carefully on my dresser, and turn out the lights in my room. On a few occasions, I had to visit my next door neighbor and remind him, and the others in his room, that it was quiet time and they needed to hold down the noise so us guys that needed to sleep could do just that.

During my senior year, I was on the Dormitory Council and was responsible for maintaining law and order (something I learned to do with my famous Lone Ranger cap gun years before) in the one and only dorm wing on the eighth floor. I coordinated our devotional times and had to continually remind guys that the quiet time didn't necessarily mean lights out, but it did mean to be quiet as they wrapped up a bull session or finished out a game of Rook. At various times, I did have to write up guys that ignored the rules. They had to answer to the Dean of Men and receive whatever disciplinary action was required. I also had opportunities to counsel some guys individually who had questions about all aspects of their social and spiritual lives. We had some very profitable and thought-provoking bull sessions throughout the year, as well.

With many students living in the dorms on the upper floors of the building, safety was a big consideration. Evacuation plans were in place and were constantly being monitored. Part of this included periodic fire drills which meant clearing the entire building of all students, faculty, and staff. It was a very interesting sight to see hundreds of people spilling into the streets outside the building whenever we had fire drills. It was particularly interesting when these fire drills were conducted at night which primarily affected dorm students. Everyone had to leave the building mostly by going down the outside fire escapes. Many girls, and some guys, were quite apprehensive about this, but those that weren't scared encouraged and helped those who found it unnerving to descent to street level on outside steel fire escapes from the upper floors where the dorms were located. These events were especially interesting in cold winter nights when overcoats had to be quickly put on over pajamas and bathrobes. Oh the joys of living in the dorms in a nine story building!

During my sophomore year at PCB, I was selected to be a part of the All School Social Committee. The description under the photograph of our committee in the 1961 yearbook read:

"This hard working committee adds spark to school spirit and social life. Many are the long evenings spent in planning, decorating, and staging for the successful Thanksgiving, Christmas, Valentine, and Spring Socials."

The only time throughout the school year that I could get back home was during the Christmas break. I missed the family and the mountains, and I was sure ready for a change of pace for a few weeks. The down side was the fact that the semester didn't actually end until we had our finals which were scheduled right after returning to the college. It took away some of the care-free spirit of the holidays, but that was something I had to live with, and it didn't detract too much from the joy of being home.

The streets of downtown Philadelphia were brightly decorated with colorful Christmas lights. The large department stores as well as smaller businesses were full of colored lights and Christmas music could be heard on almost ever corner. One department store in particular, John Wanamaker's, attracted my attention.

When I could fit it into my schedule, I liked to go into the great open area on the first floor and look at the huge lighted Christmas tree in the upper balcony. In the same section, a gigantic pipe organ was installed. A large fountain with many water jets was also located in the balcony section. As the music was played on the organ, the jets of the fountain shot streams of water in all sorts of interesting patterns in time with the music. The lights in the fountains and the lights on the Christmas tree flashed in many light combinations. This was a beautiful sight to see and a wonderful sound to hear. It sure put me in the Christmas spirit! And I couldn't wait to get home for the holidays!

Traveling to and from Hazard, Kentucky was quite an experience in itself. I boarded a Greyhound bus at the bus terminal that was located just a few blocks from PCB. Bea Pendleton, Donna Baker, and I coordinated our schedules so we could travel together. The Greyhound Bus Lines took us from Philadelphia to Wilmington, Delaware; to Baltimore, Maryland; to Washington, DC; to Roanoke, Virginia; and to Abingdon, Virginia. We had to change from Greyhound to the Bristol-Norton Bus Lines, a smaller bus line that ran from Abingdon through Coeburn, Norton, Wise, and Pound. This bus line traveled over Pound Mountain and down into Jenkins, Kentucky, the end of the line.

The parents of Bea and Donna met the bus in Jenkins, and I continued my travels alone. At Jenkins, I had to transfer to an even smaller bus line, the Jenkins-Hazard Bus Line that ran between Jenkins and Hazard. What a relief to finally see the Main Street of Hazard after a grueling twenty-four hour journey stuffed into buses with all sorts of passengers, some who insisted on smoking. My family would be waiting for me at the Hazard Bus Station, and what a welcome sight they were for my nearsighted, bloodshot, runny eyes trying to focus through my thick bifocal lenses!

On one of the infamous return trips to Philadelphia, I arranged to meet Donna Baker in Jenkins, Kentucky, and we would travel together on the Bristol-Norton line to Abingdon, Virginia, where we would change to the Greyhound line and proceed to points north.

Donna's parents had already dropped her off at the Jenkins Bus Station when I met up with her. We purchased our tickets and settled down in the crowded station to wait for our bus to arrive. This was a busy place, and several buses were scheduled to make brief stops in Abingdon as they journeyed south, east, west, and north.

Every time a bus came into the station, the ticket agent rattled off destination after destination in some unintelligible language unknown to me (and most likely unknown to all others in the waiting room). I kept watching the time, but our bus was not scheduled for several more minutes. Our departure time came, but no bus. A few minutes later, still no bus. I decided to check with the agent to see why the delay. She replied to my question, "Oh, the bus for Roanoke left ten minutes ago." I thought, "That cannot be! How did I miss the announcement? Why did it come early and leave early?"

When I told Donna, she broke into tears. It made me feel bad, and I had to take responsibility for this unreal situation. I needed to do something and prayed a quick prayer, asking for God's help. I quickly returned to the agent and asked if the bus could be stopped and if we could catch it. She radioed the bus driver who reluctantly agreed to stop the Greyhound at a restaurant parking lot about 20 miles out of Abingdon. I found a taxi driver who agreed to take us to the place where the bus would be waiting.

We quickly dumped our suitcases in the car, and the chase began as we roared out of the station, gravel flying. I hardly had time to explain all this to Donna, and she was a nervous wreck. And so was I, but tried not to show it too much.

It seemed like it took us a good half hour to reach the restaurant, but there it was just up U.S. highway 11. And there in the parking lot was our Greyhound bus! What a beautiful sight! Our ride skidded to a stop, and we quickly transferred our bags to the bus. Needless to say, the bus driver and many of the passengers were not happy with the delay this incident had caused. Donna and I collapsed in our seats and thanked the Lord for helping us through this unexpected ordeal which certainly could be described as one of life's finer moments. The day we missed our bus will never be forgotten!

Fortunately, my travels by bus ended after I finished my second year of college. Somehow, we found that the Chesapeake and Ohio Railroad had passenger train service through Kentucky to the Northeast. I could catch the C&O at Winchester, Kentucky, and travel by rail right into Suburban Station in Philadelphia. Not only did this knock several hours off the 24-hour bus trip, but I could actually ride in the comfort of a train! In fact, I could get on one passenger coach and stay on it for the entire trip. My coach would be switched from one train to another at Charlottesville, Virginia, and

Washington, DC, and all I needed to do was sit back and watch all the railroad activities in the station yards. This was the epitome of travel!

The only drawback was that I could not travel with my fellow Kentuckians since Bea and Donna continued their travels by bus. Winchester, Kentucky, was the opposite direction from Jenkins and Hazard. But in fact, it took less time for my dad to drive me to Winchester than to Jenkins. This cost of train travel was just a little more than the bus, but it sure was worth it. So, I rode the train during my junior and senior years at PCB.

The C&O ran from Winchester to Ashland, across the Ohio River into Huntington, West Virginia (a very special city where I would learn later lived a very special person). From Huntington, the C&O ran through the mountainous coal mining regions of West Virginia; through Virginia to Washington, DC; with a connection to the Pennsylvania Railroad and on to Baltimore, Maryland; Wilmington, Delaware; and Philadelphia.

Some of the courses that I took at PCB were real challenges. The most difficult for me were Physical Science, Spanish I and II, and Doctrinal Distinctions. The Doctrinal Distinctions classes were taught by Dr. Clarence Mason (referred to as Dean Mason). One of the requirements for passing this course was to prepare a term paper outlining the history and doctrinal position of the particular denomination of the church where the student had membership. In my case, I had transferred my membership to Chelten Avenue Baptist Church which was a part of the Conservative Baptist denomination. I spent many exhausting hours doing research, writing the first draft, and typing (with one finger) the term paper. I surely gave my thick bifocal lenses a real workout! It actually was more like a thesis by the time I completed this 100-page project. Thank the Lord; I received a very good grade for my work.

Dean Mason was a great professor and communicator. He often came up with some choice expressions in the classroom. One of the classics I remember had to do with personal attitudes. He exclaimed, "Don't be like some people who have constipation of the brain and diarrhea of the mouth!" If you think about the implications of that statement, you get the point.

There were several extra curricular activities available for students. During my freshman year, I got involved in a committee that began laying the groundwork for a college newspaper. We determined that the name of the paper would be *The Scroll*. I did not continue with this the following year because I learned more about the Radio Club and felt inclined to join that club as I began my sophomore year.

The Radio Club was actually an amateur radio station that was organized a few years prior by the then president of PCB, Dr. William Myrop. This designated ham station of the Amateur Radio Missionary Service (ARMS) with call sign K3CBM was located in what was known as the "ham shack" on the ninth floor of the college. I had befriended fellow-classmate, Dick Seymour, who was already a licensed amateur radio operator. I attended a few Radio Club meetings, and I was hooked. Ham radio had a very significant role to play in foreign missions and could be used as a tremendous communications tool.

I began to learn the relevant electronics theory as well as how to send and receive Morse code. The theory was the basic knowledge required to maintain and operate a ham radio station. In order to pass the Federal Communications Commission (FCC) test for a ham license, one had to be able to send and receive code at a minimum speed of 13 words per minute.

After months of practice and study, I passed the FCC test and was issued my Amateur Radio Operator License with call sign WA4DUP. I immediately became a member of ARMS, and now I could legally operate the K3CBM station! I could transmit in either Morse code or voice. When using the voice mode, it was common to use phonetics to help with the station identification and communications since there was always some sort of interference on the operating frequency. For example, I would say, "This is WA4DUP, William Able Four Delta United Pacific calling K3CBM, Kilowatt Three Charlie Baker Mike." I learned new lingo, such as: "The handle here is Dave (my name is Dave). My QTH is Philadelphia, Pennsylvania. Your RST is 559. There is heavy QRM on the frequency. Please QSL." (QTH means location; RST means signal strength; QRM means noise; QSL means confirm our contact.)

We made some long distance contacts from K3CBM with ham radio operators in all parts of the states and around the world. Some were regular guys and gals and others were missionaries on the field. The contacts with missionaries were especially exciting, and sometime we could relay important information by telephone or by another ham radio contact. I saw first hand and by experience, the tremendous advantages that shortwave radio had in direct relationship to missionary communications as well as missionary radio broadcasting that could span hundreds and thousands of miles.

I knew the Lord was directing me to be specific in my preparation for missionary service, using radio waves, as I completed my formal training in missions at PCB. I spent as much time as possible in the K3CBM ham shack.

We had various radio and electronic parts that had been donated to K3CBM by Christian hams in the area who were members of ARMS. I found a schematic for a simple 50 watt transmitter that could be used for sending Morse code with a telegraph key, and I decided to try to build it from scratch. Dick Seymour and I discovered several electronic stores down Arch Street on the other side of Broad Street close to the Reading (Railroad) Terminal. I liked to browse through these stores when time permitted and found some used parts that I needed for my homebrew (home built) transmitter.

After months of work on this project, on the side, I had my homebrew transmitter put together. A friend of the Radio Club tested my creation, corrected some wiring glitches, and put the rig on the air. I set this up in my dorm room along with a very simple super-regenerative shortwave radio receiver. I was granted permission to string a wire antenna across the light well just above my dorm room on the eighth floor. It was easy to feed a coaxial cable lead in from the dipole antenna down to my window and into my room. WA4DUP was operational and on the air! I remember one of my first contacts late one night with a ham in California using code. That was some distance from Philadelphia! Real DX! I got so excited; I almost knocked my glasses off!

In one of my mission classes, I followed my new-found interest in radio and did a research paper on HCJB (Heralding Christ Jesus' Blessings) a missionary broadcasting station with shortwave transmitters in Quito, Ecuador.

In 1962, I took a particular interest in the FMF (Foreign Missions Fellowship) project of raising funds for Trans World Radio (TWR) to purchase high-power vacuum tubes for its super power shortwave transmitters that were being installed on Bonaire, Netherlands Antilles. TWR was a faith mission whose goal was to direct Christian broadcasts by shortwave to several countries around the world. I knew by this time, God was directing me to a ministry that was involved in broadcasting by shortwave radio.

I had already gotten information from JAARS (Jungle Aviation and Radio Services), the technical arm of Wycliffe Bible Translators, and from MAF (Missionary Aviation Fellowship). Both of these mission organizations were founded to provide communications with and between missionaries in the field. But now I would be focusing on missions that emphasized beaming Christian programs around the world.

In the meantime, I continued drawing posters and using my artistic talent bent on various PCB projects. It was a special blessing to have comments such as these from my classmates:

"Dave, artist, photographer, term paper doer, and friend, May you have many great and happy years ahead in the Lord's service. Proverbs 16:9 Dick"

"Dave. I would just like to tell you how much I've enjoyed your many posters. Keep trusting in the Lord and keep smiling. Bill"

I was especially interested in trying my hand at chalk drawings. One of the faculty members, Charles Foster, was a chalk artist, and he used this as he represented PCB in church meetings. He introduced me to lectures chalk, large blocks of colored chalk used to do large illustrations. He gave me a few basic colors and a roll of newsprint paper so I could practice. In fact, he asked me to pinch hit for him on a few occasions when he could not work an invitation for a meeting into his schedule.

At first, I was a bit nervous, but with practice and with my limited materials, I was able to improve my presentations. This was a whole new experience for me, and I liked to accept challenges in my journey through the Myopic Zone.

Each year PCB had a week of special emphasis on missions. In 1962, the theme was "Motives that Move Men." During one of the services, Mr. Foster set up three easels on the platform. The middle panel had a picture of Christ on the cross which he had drawn before the meeting. The panels on either side were blank. As the missionary challenge was being given, Mr. Foster drew a picture on the right panel of a winter scene. At the same time, I drew a picture on the left side of a tropical scene. We both finished our chalk drawings at the same time as the person speaking made his closing remarks. This was the first time I had drawn like this before a crowd of people. The Lord helped with this unique presentation that reminded all of us that Jesus died on the cross providing salvation for all peoples of the world from the cold north to the hot south. I had several favorable comments from students and faculty with the encouragement to keep drawing!

At one point during my senior year at PCB, Mr. Foster set up a meeting for me at Chelten Avenue Baptist Church where I now had my membership. He explained that he would have his easel and chalk board with paper, colored lights, and lecturers chalk set up in the church auditorium, ready for me to make my presentation. All I needed to do was get to the church, preach the message, and illustrate it with a chalk drawing.

Everything went according to plan. I preached a message and then illustrated it with the colored chalk, with some special effects using fluorescent chalk and the colored lights and the special black light. Then, I concluded with some additional remarks, closed in prayer, and took my seat.

To my utter surprise, the pastor called me back up to the platform and proceeded to present me with the equipment I had just used. He said this was a gift from the church, and they wanted me to have the whole outfit so that I could continue to present the Gospel using the visual media of chalk drawings. I was flabbergasted! I never dreamed that I would ever have such a great tool. The Lord had given me the ability to draw, and now he had given me the means to use this ability for His honor and glory. What a tremendous blessing!

I later learned that the easel I used for my drawing did not belong to Mr. Foster. The Men's Fellowship at the church had constructed the aluminum easel, lighting panel, and lighting controls patterned after the equipment Mr. Foster used for his chalk drawings. He had worked with the men in putting this all together. The easel could be taken apart so it could be easily carried along with everything else.

At a later time, my dad and I constructed a wooden box with handles that made transporting the chalk drawing equipment much more convenient.

I still have this equipment and the wooden box which I have had the privilege of using in many different parts of the world in church services, missionary conferences, and special meetings and campaigns.

Each summer, I traveled home to Kentucky prepared to spend several weeks at Camp Nathanael as a worker and counselor. I always looked forward to serving the Lord in this way and to receiving a great number of blessings. Many of the students got good paying summer jobs, but I went to camp, and the Lord continued to supply my needs for tuition, room and board, and books.

I graduated from PCB on June 1, 1963, with a Bachelor of Science Degree in Bible and an emphasis on missions. I value my training at Philadelphia College of Bible, and now this chapter of my journey through the Myopic Zone with my super-thick bifocal lenses had come to a close.

## 7

## AN UNEXPECTED REUNION IN KENTUCKY (1963)

---

*I will lift up mine eyes unto the hills, from whence cometh my help.*
*My help cometh from the Lord, which made heaven and earth.*
Psalm 121:1-2

For the first time in almost a dozen years, I would not be spending part of my summer working at Camp Nathanael in Emmalena, Kentucky. Instead, I planned to spend the summer of 1963 in the areas around Philadelphia, Pennsylvania, working for a construction contractor.

This strategy was formulated prior to graduation since I needed to earn some extra money to cover my post-college training courses at Philadelphia Wireless Technical Institute (PWTI). Also prior to my graduation from PCB I knew I needed training in radio electronics in preparation for serving the Lord in a Christian radio broadcasting ministry. I checked into enrolling in the radio course at Moody Bible Institute (MBI) in Chicago, Illinois, and learned that I would be required to repeat almost all of my missions and Bible subjects since MBI and PCB were on different study schedules. I discovered that I could get my electronics training right there in Philadelphia, so I enrolled in Philadelphia Wireless Technical Institute on Pine Street located in the downtown part of the city within a few blocks of PCB.

The plan was for me to room with my grandmother whose house was located in the Mayfair section of Northeast Philadelphia. I am thankful that she agreed to this.

I also was able to get a part-time job at the Franklin Institute which would start at the same time my classes started at Philadelphia Wireless. The Franklin Institute was a famous museum in Philadelphia that had all kinds of scientific static displays, including a real Baldwin steam locomotive. In addition to the museum, the Franklin Institute had several labs where scientific experiments and projects were being developed. My job was working with a project involving the newly launched Syncom Satellite. This was the first communications satellite to be put 38,000 miles into space in a synchronous orbit. We processed data from signals transmitted from earth stations up to the satellite where they were relayed (retransmitted) to receiving earth stations on land and on board ships.

The test messages read: "The quick brown fox jumped over a lazy dog's back. 1, 2, 3, 4, 5, 6, 7, 8, 9, 0." This message contained every letter of the alphabet plus every digit in our numbering system. We used IBM punch cards and paper tapes along with the Franklin Institute's monstrous computer system built by Univac that was housed in a large air conditioned room. We literally could walk inside this computer. Thousands of vacuum tubes were configured into this computer system. Today, 35 years later, the functions performed by this gigantic computer can be performed more efficiently and much faster using a thumb-size computer chip. We surely have come a long way in technology!

One of my first orders of business after graduating from PCB was to find a vehicle to purchase with my limited available funds. I found a 1953 Chevy four-door sedan for $64.00 at Reedman's Used Cars, a huge car dealer in Northeast Philadelphia. I realized it had its issues, but it ran (at the time I looked at it), and I could pay for it. And pay for it I did! I probably should have been more concerned about the message stamped in big red letters on my bill of sale: "SOLD AS IS."

First gear, and the third and fourth gears, operated nice and smooth, but second gear apparently had some teeth missing, and it sounded like a machine gun when driving in that gear. I would start in first and go as fast as I dared before shifting only briefly into second, and then immediately into third and on to fourth. The tires were good, and the body of this black car was in fair condition. The seats needed seat covers which I bought as soon as I could. I named this car "Black Moriah." I needed this car for my summer job and then for driving to and from Center City Philadelphia when classes began in the fall of 1963.

On more than one occasion, Black Moriah decided to stall in busy intersections and refused to start. I eventually had to install a different ignition switch, and that seemed to correct the starting problem. Unfortunately, Black Moriah embarrassed me more times than I like to remember. I also learned that my black vehicle was a great oil guzzler. It was almost to the point where I would pull into a service station and say, "Please fill up the oil and check the gas!" In spite of its shortcomings, I loved having my Black Moriah, my very own vehicle.

Things went relatively well with my summer job. It required me traveling to various construction sites in and around Philadelphia and as far away as Conshohocken and Valley Forge. On one job, I had to drive a dump truck, hauling dirt from the construction site to a land fill. I was given a crash course in driving the truck and dumping the load. The truck had a governor on the engine that restricted the speed. It made me a bit nervous driving on the highway because other vehicles soon backed up behind me and my load of dirt. In spite of my thick lenses, I thought that I handled the truck driving quite well.

I remember a close call with the truck that could have been a disaster. I had backed the truck to the edge of the land fill and proceeded to raise the bed. Then, it suddenly dawned on me that I had not released the tailgate. I quickly took appropriate action and got the load safely dumped before the truck, me, and the dirt tipped over backwards and crashed upside down into the ravine. I cleaned my steamed-up glasses and thanked the Lord for His protection.

At that time, I sure would have preferred to be working at Camp Nathanael in familiar surroundings. I remembered the great blessings that I had received while helping at camp. Over the past few summers, I had met several guys and gals who were students like me preparing for the Lord's service.

I met one gal in the summer of 1960 who was a student at Appalachian Bible Institute (ABI). She was Anna Gay Chapman, had completed her second year at ABI, and was also spending that summer at Camp Nathanael. We were both working in the kitchen, and we introduced ourselves while up to our elbows in sudsy water washing dishes. I had met students from Bob Jones University, Bryan College, and a couple of other Bible Institutes and Colleges. I enjoyed hearing their testimonies and learning of their plans for the future. At the end of summer camp 1960, we all returned to our respective schools to continue our education and training.

Now, in mid-summer of 1963, I suddenly found myself without a job. The big projects anticipated by the contractor had slackened up, and since I was the last hired, I was the first fired (to be laid off). No work for the company meant no job for me! Oh me! What do I do now?

What else could I do but head for "my old Kentucky home," and that is exactly what I did. I had already planned to spend the last few weeks of summer at home and then return to Philadelphia in time to begin my training in radio electronics at Philadelphia Wireless Technical Institute. I said goodbye to my grandmother, loaded a few things into Black Moriah, and headed south following the same route that my family took in the Blue Bomber in 1951.

My parents, Dick, Johnny, and Barbara (and our boxer dog Pudgy) were glad to see me and I was glad to see them after a long uneventful trip in my 1953 Chevy with its machine gun-sounding second gear. Of course, I had to add almost as much oil as I did gasoline on my drive home. I had just enough money to get home and ended up with a quarter in my pocket!

I wasn't home more than a couple of days before Mr. E. Raymond Haddix, the one from whom we rented our house in Heiner, invited me to come by his house for a visit with his family. At that time, Raymond was the Director of Scripture Memory Mountain Mission (SMMM), the home of Camp Nathanael. The Haddix house was also located in Heiner and was within sight of our house.

To my surprise, a special friend of the Haddix family was visiting with them, and I met Anna Gay Chapman for the second time. She was the gal I met in the summer of 1960 when we were both working at Camp Nathanael. Anna Gay had been visiting relatives in Florida after completing two years of nurses training at King's Daughters Hospital, in Ashland, Kentucky. She was on her way home to Huntington, West Virginia, and stopped to visit Raymond and Gerry Haddix. It just so "happened" to be the same time that I had come home after losing my summer job in Pennsylvania.

At this unexpected meeting, we had an opportunity to renew our acquaintance and to get to know each other better. I rather quickly asked Anna Gay out on a date even though I didn't have any money. I took her to one of my favorite places, Camp Nathanael. We spent a nice afternoon together playing ping-pong in the Kentucky Building at camp. Believe it or not, I could play a pretty mean game of ping-pong even with the thick bifocal lenses in my eyeglasses. Over the years I had played many games in this recreation and store building at camp. Leslie Stone was a very good ping-pong player, but now I had a new competitor, Anna Gay Chapman, and she was great at the game. Between games, we chatted and shared our testimonies.

Well, so much for Anna Gay's visit with the Haddix family, and so much for me spending a lot of time with my family. Over the next couple of weeks, Anna Gay and I spent many hours together in my house, in the Haddix home, in my car, and at Camp Nathanael. Of course, we traveled to Hazard and camp in good old Black Moriah. Anna Gay did not seem to mind riding in my sometimes scary 1953 black Chevy. She didn't even mind my super thick bifocal glasses, and we really enjoyed each other's company.

Late one afternoon, we drove to a nearby state park and enjoyed a picnic supper together. As it began to get dark, we decided it was time to head back to Heiner. But we had a problem. I could not get Black Moriah into reverse to get turned around. The gear shift on the steering column seemed to be jammed. I didn't fancy myself much of a mechanic, but I looked under the hood to see if there was anything obviously wrong, trying to impress Anna Gay. I messed around with the shifting linkages and, believe it or not, freed up the locked gears. I was really grateful to get Black Moriah in the right direction headed for home. I was proud of myself, and I think Anna Gay was very impressed.

Anna Gay helped with the chores in the Haddix home. On one occasion, she made a batch of chocolate chip cookies, forgot to set the oven timer, and burned them to a crisp. She was so embarrassed that she dug a hole in the yard and buried them. That evening, when I went to see her, the Haddix family dog dug up the cookies and brought them to my feet, one by one! I was quite amused, but to say that Anna Gay was embarrassed would be putting it mildly! Another time she decided to make a peach cobbler. When we began to eat it, we quickly reached for our glasses of water. She had put in salt instead of sugar! She tried so hard to impress me with her "cooking skills." The way to my heart was definitely not through my stomach! One other thing she did was to put starch into the mop water instead of disinfectant. The floor had a dull slippery texture instead of a shiny appearance. Obviously, she was a girl in love!

And I was a guy in love! I thought Anna Gay was beautiful inside and outside; and I still think and know so!

We both acknowledged that God had brought us together in His divine plan for our lives. Anna Gay had planned to spend her summer in Florida, and I had planned to spend my summer in Pennsylvania. Instead, we found our plans had suddenly been changed, precisely at the same time when Anna Gay came north to

Heiner in the hills of Kentucky, and I went south to the very same place. Coincidence? Not on your life! God guided and directed us according to His plan, and both of us fell in love!

One thing did bother me a bit. Anna Gay was four months older than me. I always thought the guy was supposed to be older than the gal. Her birthday was November 15, 1940, and mine was March 17, 1941. Horrors! Yes, she was older than me but not that much, I rationalized, since she was actually born several weeks premature, and I was probably born a few days late. I also remembered that my mom was older than my dad. She was born on February 16, 1918, and my dad was born on March 13, 1918. My concern about this technicality was quickly forgotten as Anna Gay and I got to know each other better.

Anna Gay and I quickly established the fact that God was calling us into full-time missionary service. At this point, we did not know specifically where, but she agreed with me that a missionary radio ministry was the right direction to go. She did not necessarily want to return to the hospital for more nurses training. Rather, Anna Gay wanted to get some additional Bible and missions training.

We both had no doubt that God had brought us together, and we would follow His leading together one step at a time. So it was at this time, you could say we were going together. Anna Gay was willing to join me in my journey through the Myopic Zone!

We contacted Philadelphia College of Bible (PCB) about transferring Anna Gay's course credits from Appalachian Bible Institute (ABI) so she could earn a college degree. This would have required her to retake many subjects because the course requirements at PCB were different from ABI. Instead, she could take a year of missions subjects, enrolling as a special student. She would be studying at PCB while I was taking my classes at Philadelphia Wireless Technical Institute. She would stay in the dorm at PCB while I stayed with my grandmother.

Anna Gay needed to get back to Huntington for her mom's birthday on August 10, so I drove her home in Black Moriah. This gave me an opportunity to meet her parents, Mr. Andrew Chapman and Mrs. Billie Chapman. "Billie" is a good West Virginia name as well as a name like "Anna Gay" where the first and middle names are said together. This is also true for the names of some guys like the Deaton boy who lived up the hill from my house in Heiner. His first name was David, and middle name was Earl, actually the same as mine, David Earl, and he was always called "David Earl" by his family and friends.

But before heading to Huntington, Anna Gay and I wanted to make a birthday cake for her mom. With her cooking skills, Anna Gay baked the cake, and with my artistic abilities, I decorated it. Fortunately, Gerry Haddix was able to supervise the cake baking, and Anna Gay did a perfect job. However, the decorating part almost turned out to be a disaster. I was being so careful, or so I thought. I misspelled "birthday" and wrote "brithday" with the icing. We had to remove the icing, do some patch up on the cake, and rewrite "Happy Birthday, Mom." As we stood over the cake admiring our handiwork, I accidentally dropped the decorating tool smack dab on top of the cake. So we had to do some more serious doctoring up of the icing. Finally it was finished, with everything in place. We all had a good laugh at my expense. I felt justified in blaming the errors on my myopic vision.

I was happy that I could celebrate Mrs. Chapman's birthday along with Anna Gay and Mr. Chapman. The gifts Anna Gay's dad gave to her mom were quite unique. He gave her a neat little revolver hand gun (about the size of the Lone Ranger cap pistol I received for Christmas as a child) and a wheelbarrow. We knew that the gun was for self-defense and figured if anyone had to be shot, they could be hauled away in the wheelbarrow. That was really cool.

I enjoyed my brief stay with Anna Gay and her parents, and I was glad I could get to know them. They were really nice people, like most West Virginians. I knew that being from Kentucky, I was called a "hillbilly." I also knew that people in West Virginia were referred to as "mountaineers." But I also learned that a mountaineer is simply a dignified hillbilly. Anna Gay and I got this friendly understanding straightened out rather early in our relationship. All too soon I had to return to Heiner where I spent the next couple of weeks at home before heading back to Philadelphia and the new adventures that awaited me there.

As I look back on how the events of summer 1963 unfolded, I am amazed to see how God's hand guided in some major decisions that needed to be made. Anna Gay applied to PCB and was quickly accepted to begin classes in the fall of 1963. She had to pack her things in preparation for spending the next several months in the big city of Philadelphia, the "City of Brotherly Love," which was quite a contrast to Huntington.

I had to get back to Philadelphia, but I would not be traveling alone any more. Praise the Lord! We arranged for me to stop by Anna Gay's house in Huntington, spend the night there, and early the next morning I would drive us both to Philadelphia in Black Moriah.

Anna Gay's parents and my parents gave their blessings on both of us as our plans were quickly formulated and finalized. Raymond and Gerry Haddix were in total agreement and took credit and pride in their match-making abilities. Anna Gay considers Raymond and Gerry to be her mentors.

I said my goodbyes to my mom and dad, and to Dick, Johnny, and Barbara (and to Pudgy). The Lord provided just enough money to buy gas and meals for the trip back to Philadelphia. A new and exciting venture was unfolding in my journey through the Myopic Zone. I should say "our" journey through the Myopic Zone!

## 8

## BACK TO PHILADELPHIA, AGAIN (1963-1964)

---

*He keepeth the paths of judgment, and preserveth the way of his saints. Then shalt thou understand righteousness, and judgment, and equity; yea, every good path.* Proverbs 2:8-9

All too soon, it was time for me to return to my home in Heiner, Kentucky. I sure did enjoy my brief stay with Anna Gay and her parents in Huntington, West Virginia. Anna Gay had shown me many sights around the city including the beautiful Chesapeake and Ohio (C & O) Railroad passenger depot. I had traveled through Huntington during my two years of travel between Winchester, Kentucky, and Philadelphia, Pennsylvania. We visited the Owens Illinois glass manufacturing plant where Anna Gay's dad worked. We also toured through some glass-blowing facilities in the Huntington vicinity.

Now, I had to get my thoughts in gear for the long drive back to Philadelphia. This time, I would be going by way of Huntington, West Virginia, about a 120 mile journey from my home in Heiner, Breathitt County, Kentucky. The plan was to pick up Anna Gay and her things, and we would make the trip together in good old Black Moriah, my 1953 Chevy with its second gear machine gun-sounding transmission and its oil-burning engine.

I said my goodbyes to my mom and dad, and to Dick, Johnny (who I had nicknamed "Fuzzhead"), and Barbara (who I had nicknamed "Piltrin"). And I said goodbye to our pet boxer dog Pudgy, as well. I cleaned my thick-lensed bifocal eyeglasses, adjusted them on my face, and drove down the driveway toward the gravel road that would take me to the main highway.

My travel took me on Kentucky state highway 15 through Hazard, where I picked up Kentucky state highway 80 and headed through Hindman to Allen where I turned north onto U.S. highway 23. This took me through Prestonsburg and Louisa, to Cattlesburg (just a few miles from Ashland). At Cattlesburg, I turned right onto

U.S. highway 60, crossed the Big Sandy River into West Virginia, and proceeded to Huntington.

It was good to see Anna Gay again, as well as her parents. Her dad insisted that I park Black Moriah in the front yard up close to the house. We loaded Anna Gay's things into the trunk and on the back seat. Fortunately, I didn't have that much stuff so we were able to cram all of Anna Gay's things into the car, and we were ready to go first thing the next morning.

We had an early breakfast, and after a prayer asking for God's protection and safety, we climbed into Black Moriah, trying to be as quiet as possible since it was still dark outside at 5:00 in the morning. With Anna Gay's dad watching intently from the front porch, I eased the car across the grass to the curb. As the car's front wheels dropped off the curb, suddenly there was a tremendous tank-sounding roar from underneath the vehicle. I quickly got the back tires onto the street, parked beside the curb as fast as I could, and cut off the engine. The silence was deafening! By this time, Anna Gay's dad had rushed off the porch with a look of concern on his face. Now, what!?

Immediately, I suspected what had happened. The muffler had scraped the curb and pulled loose from the engine exhaust pipe. I was not surprised since I had used a coat hanger a few days before to hold the muffler in place. So much for my jerry-rigging!

While Mr. Chapman held the flashlight, I crawled under Black Moriah and reattached the muffler with the coat hanger wire. A quick check of the starter proved that the exhaust system was operating at its normal noise level much to my relief, and to the relief of Anna Gay's dad. The loud tank-sounding roar was gone! I assured Anna Gay's parents that everything was under control, but they weren't too sure about seeing their daughter depart for points unknown in a black 1953 Chevy with its second gear machine gun-sounding transmission and its oil-burning engine driven by a guy with thick bifocal lenses in his eyeglasses.

But we eased away anyway, heading north out of Huntington on West Virginia state highway 2 following the Ohio River. We continued to Point Pleasant, West Virginia, and there crossed the Ohio River to Ohio state highway 7, continuing to follow the Ohio River north all the way to Wheeling on the West Virginia side of the river. From there we turned east, drove into Pennsylvania, and joined the western end of the Pennsylvania Turnpike at Washington. We stayed on the turnpike all the way to Philadelphia in the eastern part of the state. It was a long, grueling drive with some unusual experiences, but Black Moriah got us safely back into Philadelphia. We thanked the Lord for His help and protection during the trip.

Our journey was not without moments of apprehension and excitement, to say the least. I had to add extra oil to the engine throughout the trip because the engine burned so much oil while on the road. I made frequent stops to check the oil level and added to it, as needed.

The roads we traveled took us up and down mountainous areas through large and small towns and cities on sometimes very lightly traveled highways to very congested city streets. It was sort of funny to see how the Chevy behaved as it was given more gas to get up the hills and then almost coasting down the other side. Most of the towns were at the base of the mountains where the main highway became the Main Street. As we came onto level pavement, I would accelerate as fast as I possibly could. At the end of the Main Street, we could look behind us and see a huge trail of gray-blue-black smoke as the exhaust shot out of Black Moriah's muffler and tailpipe that was held in place with my ingenious coat hanger. What a sight! What pollution! What an embarrassment! But what fun! It almost got to be a game to see how much smoke we could leave behind us on each Main Street. The engine of this car sure did burn the oil.

One situation we encountered was not too funny (at least at the time). As we were driving along enjoying a pleasant conversation, I glanced up at the rear view mirror and did a double take. All I could see in the mirror was blackness. Were my super thick bifocal-lensed eyeglasses playing tricks on me? I glanced over my shoulder and realized the trunk lid had popped open. We quickly pulled onto the shoulder of the highway and stopped. In the excitement, I almost lost my glasses, and Anna Gay could not believe her eyes. How long had we been driving with the trunk lid wide open? It couldn't have been too long because, like a good driver, I periodically checked the rear view mirror to observe traffic in the rear.

We checked to see what was missing in the trunk. Uncertain what had fallen or blown out, we secured the trunk lid, turned around, and rather slowly back-tracked, ready to pick up whatever we had lost. What a weird experience! What a serious dilemma! What an embarrassment (again)!

103

I felt sorry for Anna Gay. By now, I expected she was ready to head back home to Huntington. But she was resilient and determined to make the best out of a bad situation.

After retrieving what had fallen out of the trunk, we turned around and continued our travels into the unknown. What was going to be our next challenge as we journeyed together through the Myopic Zone? Needless to say, I had a serious talk with Black Moriah after that experience.

I had returned to the now familiar sights and sounds of big city life in Philadelphia. But for Anna Gay, it was a whole new world, moving from the lazy, beautiful West Virginia mountains and the city of Huntington to the hustle and bustle of downtown Philadelphia, Pennsylvania.

It was fun to see Anna Gay's look of amazement, and sometimes fear, as I introduced her to underground subways, noisy congested city streets with its array of sky scrapers, businesses, department stores, taxis, buses, trolley cars, trucks, cars, sirens, horns, and the chatter of pedestrians elbowing their way from one block to another. I had the joy of introducing her to the large salty, soft pretzels that were sold by vendors along the sidewalks in little food stands and from moveable carts. Philadelphia's hot pretzels slathered in mustard were hard to beat!

Anna Gay soon was settled into her dorm room at Philadelphia College of Bible, and she began to make friends with her classmates. She was considered a special student since she had classes with freshmen, sophomores, juniors, and seniors. This was quite an adjustment for her to make as well, but she did great. I considered her more than a special student at PCB; she was my special friend, my girlfriend, and I was proud of her.

With her nurses training, it was not too long before Anna Gay was able to get a part-time job at Doctor's Hospital located several blocks walking distance from PCB. She worked an evening shift, and, thankfully, PCB had an escort service where young men students would take turns meeting her at the hospital and walking her safely back to the college. The areas where she had to walk were not the safest places in the city.

I got situated at my grandmother's house and determined how best to get from there into Center City Philadelphia by public transportation (bus and subway which was actually the Frankford Elevated Train line). I had to get to Philadelphia Wireless Technical

Institute (PWTI) on Pine Street for my classes in radio electronics.

This was a whole new ballgame for me, studying in a secular institution, but I soon settled into a daily routine. My classes went until about 2:00 in the afternoon. I then had to get to my part-time job at the Franklin Institute, in the special lab areas of the museum. It just so "happened" that I had to walk from Pine Street over to Arch Street, and right past the side entrance of PCB on my way to the Franklin Institute. Who do you suppose I just "happened" to meet in the doorway as I went past PCB? Yes! It was Anna Gay Chapman!

We would be able to spend a few minutes together if Anna Gay was not in class. Then, I had to hurry on my way to get to work at the Franklin Institute just a few more blocks north on Arch Street. Whenever I could meet Anna Gay, it sure made my day!

The fact that I was studying in the technical field helped in getting the part-time job in the research section of the Franklin Institute. It was an interesting experience, working with the data processing for the Syncom satellite telecommunications links. The following description of the Syncom satellite was published in *Time Magazine*:

"The HUGHES/NASA SYNCOM
stands still at 6,875 MPH to talk to a billion people.

"Syncom is an entirely new kind of communications satellite. It is the first synchronous satellite – the first to *stand still* in space. Actually it is traveling 6,875 mph. But at its altitude of 22,300 miles, Syncom's speed matches the earth's rotation. Result: It is *parked* over the earth.

"From this vantage, above the mouth of the Amazon River, Syncom can see 40% of the earth. Thus it can beam signals to over one billion people in North and South America, Western Europe, and Africa. In fact, since Syncom's first month of operation, it logged more operating time than all other communications satellites had up to that time. Little wonder NASA has called Syncom a major breakthrough in the peaceful use of outer space.

"Syncom differs from other satellites in that it is precisely controlled in a high altitude orbit. It can be permanently *parked* while other types of satellites are in random, low-altitude orbits. The future Syncom system in development at Hughes requires just three telegraph, TV, and wire photo satellites to service all populated areas of the world."

Several offices in the research and development sections of the labs at the Franklin Institute, including the huge computer room, were devoted to the project of processing data from the Syncom satellite. Also the latest state-of-the-art magnetic tapes and IBM paper tapes and card punchers and readers were used.

One Saturday, a few of us were processing data as usual. I glanced out the window of our building adjacent to the museum and saw a man directing cars into our small parking area. He was showing people where to park and collecting money from them. We called security, and they chased the man away. He was a person off the street with an ingenious plan to put some money in his pocket. The people he was directing into the lot were coming to visit the museum, looking for a convenient parking place.

One of my instructors at PWTI was a Mormon. He knew I was a Christian and that I had graduated from PCB. He wanted to get me involved in Biblical doctrinal issues, and we had some interesting debates on several occasions. He wanted to engage in serious discussions to get me to become a Mormon, something I definitely was not interested in pursuing.

I remember on Friday, November 22, 1963, right in the middle of this same instructor's class, he was interrupted by the news that President John F. Kennedy had been assassinated. President Kennedy was traveling in a motorcade in Dallas, Texas, with his wife Jacqueline, and he was killed. All thoughts of electronics were replaced with conversations of disbelief that such a thing could happen. But it did, and classes were suspended for the rest of the day as we all tried to get up-to-the-minute news reports surrounding this tragedy.

After several days of non-electronic discussions, we were able to resume our courses of study. I was challenged by the technology and began to learn the theory of radio broadcasting, electronic circuits, and test equipment. One of our lab projects was to build a VOM (volt-ohm-meter) used for measuring voltage, resistance, and current. This also involved learning proper techniques for wiring electronic components (resistors, capacitors, and diodes) together and making good solder joints. I enjoyed hands-on projects like this, having to really utilize my thick bifocal lenses to see up close.

I was at a slight advantage since I had already studied the electronics theory required to pass the Federal Communications Commission (FCC) exam to get my Amateur Radio Operator License. I received my General Class License on January 24, 1963, with the assigned call: WA4DUP.

At PWTI, we learned how to use a slide rule, a device that preceded the scientific handheld calculators. The slide rule had to be kept calibrated in order to give accurate readings. Every instructor cautioned us students time and time again to be careful with the slide rule and, above all, "Do not drop your slide rule on the floor!"

Some guys weren't too careful, and more than once the classroom echoed with the clatter and crash of a slide rule hitting the floor. The one who made such a grave mistake was immediately razzed by the other students. Believe it or not, I never did drop mine!

By the time the lunch break rolled around, I certainly was ready to give my brain a rest and feed my stomach. A pretzel vendor knew exactly when to roll his hot pretzel cart right up to the front door of the school. Occasionally, I bought a pretzel and enjoyed the soft salty texture, without any mustard. We called this guy "The Pretzel Man," and he usually was shabbily dressed in not the cleanest clothes in the world. Every once in a while he would get some mustard on his fingers. No problem! He licked his fingers, wiped them on his coat, and grabbed some more pretzels for the next person in line. I never used mustard on my pretzels, that's for sure! This was just another daily typical activity on the streets of downtown Philadelphia!

On Sundays, I attended Chelten Avenue Baptist Church where I had moved my church membership in 1959 when I moved into the Philadelphia College of Bible dorm to begin my studies. Now I would take Anna Gay with me if her schedule and Christian service assignments at PCB permitted it. Sometimes, I would bring her back to my grandmother's house for a late dinner, then drive her back to the college in the afternoon.

Our friendship deepened over the months as she studied at PCB and I studied at PWTI. My next step was to propose marriage to Anna Gay, but first I had to get permission from the Dean of Women at Philadelphia College of Bible. I set up the necessary appointment, made my request in person and in writing, and was granted permission. This was supposed to be a secret, and I thought I had made that clear during my interview.

I found out later that the Dean of Women somehow accidentally "let the cat out of the bag!" She made Anna Gay promise her that she would not tell me or anyone about her slip up. Anna Gay did a good job in keeping this "secret" secret. So Anna Gay knew she was going to receive an engagement ring from me, but she did not know when, and this was to my advantage. It kept Anna Gay guessing about when my proposal would be made.

My grandmother helped me find a jewelry store in downtown Philadelphia where I might find a nice diamond ring at a reasonable price that I could afford. I bought the ring and had it put away in a secure place. My grandmother wanted to know everything that was going on between Anna Gay and me, but I realized she could not keep a secret, so I said very little about when I was planning to pose the big question.

Christmas 1963 was fast approaching. Both my grandmother and I began suggesting to Anna Gay that she really needed to have a good pair of boots since we still had a few months of cold winter weather ahead of us. All indications were that my Christmas present for Anna Gay was going to be a pair of warm, rubber boots.

During the Christmas break in both our schools, I planned to drive Anna Gay home from Philadelphia to Huntington, West Virginia, in Black Moriah. I would then travel on home from Huntington to Heiner, Kentucky, and spend Christmas with my family.

I met Anna Gay at PCB early on the Saturday morning of our planned departure for Huntington. She had her suitcase packed and was ready to go. Before leaving, however, I talked her into opening the Christmas present I had brought into the building with me. Most of the dorm students had cleared out after classes the day before, so all was pretty quiet on the first floor of the college. I carried my large Christmas-wrapped package into the empty student lounge as Anna Gay followed me, dragging her suitcase.

After wishing her a "Merry Christmas," I gave Anna Gay her present. The package was pretty big, but that is what one would expect when one wanted and needed a pair of winter boots.

Inside the first big box was another box nicely wrapped in brightly colored Christmas paper. After unwrapping the second box, there was another wrapped box. Pretty soon the floor was covered with torn wrapping paper and a dozen empty boxes. Each box had a smaller box inside it. It became obvious after several minutes that no boots would fit into the increasingly smaller boxes that Anna Gay was opening. At first, she was amazed at my talent for wrapping Christmas present boxes, but I could tell she was getting a bit perplexed. "Just keep on unwrapping and opening," I encouraged.

Finally, Anna Gay unwrapped a green rather used, thick,

battered-looking book titled "The Good Companions" by J.B. Priestley. She had such a disappointed frown on her face, and was just about ready to burst into tears. She said, "Well, I guess I should really thank you for this gift." I quickly took the book from her and thumbed through the pages, explaining what a great author J.B. Priestley was and how much she would enjoy this treasured used book that I had found in Leary's Bookstore in Center City Philadelphia. Then, I handed the book back to Anna Gay. I thought she was going to hit me with it, and knock my thick bifocal-lensed glasses clean off my face!

As she took the book and slowly opened the cover, without warning a little white box fell onto her hands. I quickly picked up the box, opened it, and presented Anna Gay with a diamond ring – her engagement ring!

Wow! Talk about a change of attitude! Anna Gay went from tears of frustration to tears of joy and happiness as she realized I was proposing to her. Thankfully, she said, "Yes!" And we entered a new phase in our journey together through the Myopic Zone.

We picked up all the boxes and wrapping paper, and discarded everything but the book, "The Good Companions," and her diamond ring which she immediately wore on her finger. We still have the infamous second-hand book that I bought for fifty cents in Leary's Bookstore. In fact, our son Philip proposed to his wife in somewhat the same manner as I had done with Anna Gay. Perhaps, someday, one of Philip's sons will propose to someone special using the same book. Who knows? The book was never meant to be read, and actually could not be since most of the pages have missing text where I cut out the opening for the ring box.

Our journey to Huntington, West Virginia, was uneventful. Except we did a lot of talking, discussing future wedding plans, and our missionary service together. After receiving approval from her parents concerning my desire to marry Anna Gay, I drove on to my home in Kentucky where my parents expressed their delight in our engagement.

What a great Christmas we all had with our respective families in Huntington, West Virginia, and in the former coal camp at Heiner, Kentucky. All too soon, it was time for me to return to Philadelphia, traveling by way of Huntington to pick up my Anna Gay. Our trip back up north went well, and our '53 Chevy seemed like it was driving on "cloud nine" with Anna Gay and me inside.

Our classes concluded about the same time in the spring of 1964. Anna Gay had done well with her studies in missions as a special student at Philadelphia College of Bible (PCB) and I was learning many new things in the field of radio electronics at Philadelphia Wireless Technical Institute (PWTI).

By this time, Anna Gay and I had set our wedding date for July 11, 1964. Neither one of us wanted a long engagement period since we were confident that the Lord had brought us together, and we were committed to serve Him in full-time missionary service.

My job at the Franklin Institute concluded as I finished my first year of classes at PWTI. So, it was natural for Anna Gay and me to return home for the next few weeks to make final arrangements for our wedding day. Before leaving Philadelphia, I put down a deposit on a little apartment in Melrose Park, a small community just outside the city limits of North Philadelphia.

I had also found a place in New Jersey where we could spend our honeymoon. It was a small resort coastal town called Stone Harbor, and I rented a small cottage close to the beach on the Atlantic Ocean. I tried to keep this a secret from my grandmother, who I was afraid would spread this news to others if she knew what I had planned. As it turned out, the receipt for paying the rental fee was sent to me at my grandmother's address. She met me at the door one evening waving an envelope in my face. She said with a big grin, "I know where you are going on your honeymoon!" Sure, she knew, since the printed return address on the envelope gave the name of the realty agent in Stone Harbor, New Jersey. So much for secrets!

Before heading south, I had one further item of business. That was to replace Black Moriah, my 1953 Chevy sedan, with its machine-gun sounding second gear, with a newer vehicle. Of course, I ended up at Reedman Used Cars in Northeast Philadelphia. I found a good deal on a metallic blue 1958 Chevy four-door sedan. It was a smooth-riding car that seemed to literally float around corners and curves. I forget what price I paid for it and what kind of a trade-in I got for Black Moriah. Of course, the Bill of Sale from the car dealer had stamped on it in big red letters: "SOLD AS IS."

The first thing I did was to have the oil changed at a garage close to where I was staying with my grandmother. The mechanic adjusted the lift under the frame of the car and began to raise it in the air. To my amazement, the right rear tire stayed on the ground even though the left rear tire was a foot or so off the ground. I thought my thick-lensed bifocal glasses were playing tricks on me again!

Upon a closer inspection, the mechanic discovered that the right rear shock absorber and mounting flanges were completely missing, somehow apparently ripped away. The right rear suspension was riding only on the coil spring, not a very safe arrangement. Fortunately, I was able to find a garage that could repair the problem by welding on a new flange and replacing the missing shock. I had the left shock replaced at the same time. The car handled much better, and there was no longer any "floating" around curves. I thanked the Lord that this matter was resolved on my "new-to-me" 1958 Chevy before an accident occurred.

I never did give this car a name but simply referred to it as "The Chevy." It got me home to Kentucky in fine order, and I had much more confidence in this "Reedman Special" than I did Black Moriah.

Anna Gay traveled from Philadelphia to Huntington, West Virginia, by train, and a couple of weeks later, I drove to my home in Kentucky in the Chevy. There was no problem with the trunk lid flying open and no trails of thick blue-gray exhaust covering the Main Streets in the towns and villages that I passed through on my way home.

Anna Gay and I were excited and happy. Our wedding day was fast approaching!

## 9

## MARRIAGE AND MOVE
## TO MELROSE PARK, PENNSYLVANIA (1964)

---

*But the path of the just is as the shining light, that shineth more and more unto the perfect day.* Proverbs 4:18

July 1, 1964, was a very hot, humid Saturday in Huntington, West Virginia. Anna Gay's pastor, Rev. Mel Efaw, was ready to perform the wedding ceremony. My mom had saved enough money to buy material to make a pretty dress to wear for the wedding. Anna Gay's parents could just barely afford to buy our wedding cake. Anna Gay's friends had arranged for us to use left over items from the receptions of weddings at Grace Gospel Church that had been held just prior to ours, one the week before and the other two weeks before. You might say that we were "married on a shoestring" since neither one of us or our families had much money.

Anna Gay made a beautiful bride in a plain, but pretty, wedding dress. I was nervous for some reason as the hour of our wedding approached. Even though the church was air conditioned, I perspired rather profusely as I usually did in summer weather. I learned to carry two handkerchiefs in my rear back packet. I should have had three! Of course, when I perspired, my unusually thick, heavy eyeglasses tended to slide down my nose. They probably would have fallen right off my face if I had not taken corrective measures like mopping my face and glasses every few minutes. Another issue was dealing with the steamed up lenses that required cleaning with one of my handkerchiefs. I don't know how many times I had to deal with these matters during the wedding ceremony. But somehow we succeeded and with great relief and joy, I heard the words of Pastor Mel, "I now pronounce you man and wife! You may kiss your bride!"

There was no turning back; now Anna Gay and I faced the challenges together of journeying through the Myopic Zone.

Following the reception, we rode away from the church in a Lincoln Continental owned and driven by a friend. A bit later we drove away from Huntington, West Virginia, in our blue 1958 Chevy. No offense to Black Moriah, but we were riding in style on that July eleventh evening, heading north to Stone Harbor, New Jersey, for our honeymoon.

Stone Harbor was a small town located on the Atlantic Ocean in the state of New Jersey. It was south of Atlantic City and just north of Wildwood. Both of those towns were rather large and were very popular tourist attractions. We wanted to go someplace that was a little quieter where we could enjoy the sandy beach and the ocean waves. I had rented a small cottage for the week that was just a couple of blocks from the ocean. We could walk over to the beach, swim in the ocean, and just have an enjoyable time together on our honeymoon there in Stone Harbor.

We took food with us, and Anna Gay had her first experiences preparing meals for the two of us. She had already learned how to cook and bake various recipes in the kitchen. Anna Gay wanted to impress me with her cooking abilities, and for the most part, she did real well with the meal preparations. We ate out a few times to keep her from having to fix every meal.

On one occasion, Anna Gay was preparing lunch for us. I was out in front of the cottage doing something on our 1958 Chevy car. All of a sudden, I heard a scream from the kitchen. I almost lost my glasses, but ran quickly inside to see what was going on. As I reached the kitchen, I saw a flaming pan on the stove. I quickly grabbed the pan and ran out to the front of the house the way I had just come in. I put the flaming pan on the curb to let the fire die out. Anna Gay was in tears and was somewhat mortified to think that I would put a pan of burning grease out on the curb for the entire world to see. She was afraid that our neighbors would know for sure that she was a new bride and was just learning how to cook. I assured Anna Gay that everything was all right and that she should not worry about the experience, but rather be thankful that the Lord allowed us to handle this emergency without burning down the cottage and without burning ourselves in the process of getting the pan outside. Neither one of us will ever forget that experience! Anna Gay had wanted to impress me with her cooking abilities, and she was preparing to make some homemade French fries. Somehow, potatoes did not make the lunch menu that day, and we enjoyed whatever other food Anna Gay had prepared. This was one of life's finer moments in our early days of marriage!

We really did enjoy our time there in Stone Harbor, and all too soon, we had to get back to the realities of our lives and return to Philadelphia. Actually, we moved into a duplex house that had been converted into a downstairs apartment in Melrose Park, Pennsylvania. This was a very small bedroom community located just outside the northern city limits of Philadelphia. Our little apartment had a living room, a bedroom, a kitchen-dining room area, and a bathroom. But that was all we needed as we began our lives together. Neither one of us had much to begin with. We were very appreciative for friends and family who gave us various pieces of furniture to make this little apartment livable. Some friends of the family had a sofa and chair that they had put in storage in their barn, and they gave these to us. We bought a nice oval braided rug which we put in the living room. Someone else gave us a bed and dresser set. My aunt gave us a buffet for our dishes. We had bought some used furniture for the kitchen which included a table with a couple of chairs. We found an old refrigerator for sale on the curb in front of a used furniture store. So we were set and ready to go. We were blessed and "as snug as two bugs in a rug."

Our apartment, located on Chestnut Street in Melrose Park, overlooked an open area in the back of the house that sloped down across a field, and in the distance we could see railroad tracks. This was the Reading Railroad that ran commuter trains from Center City Philadelphia up north through Melrose Park and on into several communities in the northern part of Montgomery County.

We both had very busy schedules in the early days of our marriage. Anna Gay worked as a nurse at the Doctor's Hospital in Center City Philadelphia on the 7 AM to 3 PM shift. She had to travel into downtown Philadelphia by public transportation, traveling on a bus which she caught at the end of our street. This took her to the northern terminus of the Broad Street Subway system. There she traveled by subway from north Philadelphia down into Center City and the hospital.

I had completed my first year of day school classes at Philadelphia Wireless Technical Institute (PWTI). After we were married, I transferred from day school to evening school which allowed me to work part-time in the mornings and study at PWTI in the evenings. It was a rather rough schedule for both of us.

My work at the Franklin Institute had concluded at about the same time the day school classes finished for the summer. I had been able to get a part-time job at Hess and Young, located on Second Street in Center City Philadelphia. George Hess was the proprietor of this business. George and his wife were close friends of the family and were members of Chelten Avenue Baptist Church. It is interesting to note that several years earlier my dad worked part-time at Hess and Young while he was attending seminary in Philadelphia preparing for the ministry. And now I was working in the same shop as I was preparing for missionary service. How's that for a coincidence!

The Hess and Young business actually provided a special service for regular print shops. Printed stock was sent to Hess and Young for applying gold stamping and hot embossing to the materials. The presses that we operated were the same that were used for applying ink during regular printing except, instead of ink, our presses were set up for doing the gold leaf stamping and the hot embossing work. We worked with all types and weights of printed stock from business letterheads and envelopes to greeting cards and record jacket covers.

At Hess and Young I operated a variety of presses. I learned how to set up the presses and do the make-ready for running stock through the presses for the embossing work. This was very interesting because heat was used on the platen and the make-ready had to be set to match metal dyes that were specially made for doing the embossing and stamping. The printed stock was fed into the press, an impression was made, and the printed stock was taken out of the press as the bed opened. Some of this press work was done automatically with the Heidelberg windmill-type presses. However, most of the Chandler presses had to be hand-fed because of the size and type of stock. One press was so large that it took two pressmen to operate it. The bed of this particular press was roughly three feet square, and it was referred to as "The Iron Man." One operator fed the rather large piece of stock into the press. Once in the press, the bed clunked closed to make the impression, and then as the bed opened, the other operator had to carefully and quickly pull the sheet out and stack it. Fortunately, we could adjust the speed of the presses to accommodate our dexterity in feeding in stock and taking stock out of the press. Each press had a safety release bar which could be pulled down to stop the impression.

It was fascinating work, and I really enjoyed the challenges to my artistic talents. The trick was to emboss the stock with just the right pressure using just the right amount of heat. If too heavy, the dye would cut into the stock, and too light a pressure, the embossing could not be seen. If too much or too little heat, the foil leaf would not adhere to the stock. Little did I realize that somewhere down the road in my journey through the Myopic Zone, I would have the opportunity to put this experience into practice. The shop had some smaller presses that were used to stamp names in gold leaf onto Bible covers, books, and things of that nature. It was a noisy place, and much of the time we had to wear protectors over our ears.

I would spend the morning working in the shop, grab a bite of lunch, and spend a few more hours there in the afternoon. Then I had to get over to PWTI for my evening classes. I generally took the subway to get to the school. Classes concluded about nine o'clock in the evening. Then, I had to make a bee-line for the Reading Terminal to catch the last commuter train from there to the Melrose Park station. I finally got home about 10:30 at night.

By the time I got to our apartment, Anna Gay would have had her supper and would be snuggled asleep in bed because she had to get up very early in the morning to be at Doctor's Hospital by seven o'clock AM. We arranged a schedule about how all this would work throughout the week. It was rather difficult, but we were young and doing fine with it. We had to earn enough money to pay for my schooling and to cover our living and traveling expenses.

We did have a bit of a conflict, however, in the winter time. Anna Gay loved to set the electric blanket to high when she went to bed. By the time I got home a good bit later, the electric blanket was really putting out the heat. It was usually too hot for me, and I had to turn the control back down to cool. If Anna Gay woke up during the night and discovered what I had done, she would crank the control back up to hot. So we had some interesting situations there trying to come up with a happy medium. Unfortunately, this was before someone got the bright idea of making these heating blankets operate with dual controls so that individuals could have their own setting without affecting the other person. But we survived, and we were really enjoying our journey through the Myopic Zone together during those busy days.

When Saturdays and Sundays rolled around, we both were pretty tired. Thankfully, we were able to recharge our batteries over the weekend even though we had become more active in my church, Chelten Avenue Baptist Church. About the same time we moved to Melrose Park, the church moved from its location on Chelten Avenue in Philadelphia to the small suburban community of Jarrettown. The Germantown section of Philadelphia was undergoing some dramatic changes, and many church members were moving out of the area into the suburbs. The concern was that the church building on Chelten Avenue be used by another church and continue to be a Gospel witness in that part of the city. A black congregation was very pleased to acquire the church and continued its ministry in Germantown.

In the meantime, the church members of Chelten Avenue Baptist Church began looking for a location in Jarrettown, or the surrounding areas, where they could purchase some property and build a church. At this point, this rural area was growing rather rapidly as families moved from the city to the northern rural outskirts of Philadelphia. With the move taking place, Chelten Avenue Baptist Church changed its name to Chelten Baptist Church and began meeting in a public school until a small chapel could be built. This actually was good for Anna Gay and me because our apartment was located much closer to Jarrettown. We did not have to travel the greater distance into Philadelphia to Chelten Avenue. I continued to keep my membership there at Chelten Baptist Church, and Anna Gay was accepted as an Associate Member. We both felt it best for her to maintain her membership in her home church at Grace Gospel Church, Huntington, West Virginia. As we faced the prospect of faith missionary service and the need to raise missionary support, we knew it was important to consider Chelten Baptist my sending church and Grace Gospel to be Anna Gay's sending church.

After living in Melrose Park for several months, we began having some difficulties with the landlord of our apartment on Chestnut Street. He was not making good on some major repairs and corrections that he promised would be made on the house. We began looking around for another place and found a small upstairs apartment just down the street on 501 Valley Road. This was also in a duplex house, and it was owned by Mr. and Mrs. Henry Burger, an older German couple. They were very nice landlords, and they made us feel right at home. It was a bit unusual arrangement, you might say, since we entered our apartment through the main front door on the first floor. The Burgers lived on the first floor, and we had the entire second floor. Not all of the rooms were connected, however, and this was quite an interesting situation. We could go into the kitchen and from the kitchen into the living room without going into the hall. But to get from the living room into the bathroom, we had to step out into the hall, and also the bedroom could only be accessed from the hall. This was a three story house and every once in a while Mr. Burger or Mrs. Burger would need to go from the first floor up to the third floor. They assured us that these times would be extremely rare. In order to get to the third floor, they had to come up the stairs, walk along the railing in the hallway, and then go on up the stairs to the third floor. So before Anna Gay or I went from one room to another, we had to make sure the coast was clear. This was not an ideal situation, but we learned to live with it, and we all made out just fine. We moved our used furniture from the Chestnut Street apartment to the Valley Road apartment with the help of Dick Seymour and Bob Fitzgerald, who were my classmates at Philadelphia College of Bible. We maintained contact with these guys after our marriage, and they were a big encouragement to Anna Gay and me. Dick was my best man in our wedding.

Both Dick and Bob were hams (amateur radio operators), and now I was a ham, as well. I had completed the electronics theory and Morse code requirements; I had successfully passed the FCC (Federal Communications Commission) examination; and I had received my General Class Amateur Radio Operator License with call sign WA4DUP.

Our new apartment had a very nice wooden deck off the kitchen. It was built on top of the roof of the downstairs kitchen. This was a great place where we could sit outside and enjoy the wooded area in back of the house. The deck was also a good place to eat our meals, if the weather permitted.

One morning, Anna Gay decided to make biscuits to go with our meal. Something went terribly wrong with the recipe, and the biscuits turned out to be as hard as rocks. We could not bite into them without doing damage to our teeth! Anna Gay was apologetic about the situation, and I assured her that it was no problem, but that, in the due course of time, she would learn how to make nice fluffy, mouth-watering biscuits. Well, now we were stuck with a plate full of hard biscuits. We had to dispose of them somehow, so I had the bright idea of throwing them into the woods behind the house. So here we are, standing on the deck outside our kitchen, throwing these biscuits into the trees. It scared the birds half to death; they did not know what was coming at them. It was interesting to hear the biscuits crashing through the tree limbs, tearing away leaves and branches as they fell to the ground. We wondered what Mr. and Mrs. Burger thought. They were a bit hard of hearing, so maybe they did not notice what was taking place upstairs. It was not too funny for Anna Gay at the time, but later, as we think back on that incident, we both have a good laugh.

This same deck was used for hanging out laundry to dry. There was a pulley arrangement with a line strung out to a tree back in the woods. Anna Gay had to secure the articles of clothing onto the line with clothes pins, continuing to move the line out to repeat the process in order to get all the clothes on the line to dry. On one occasion, we heard Mr. Burger's heavy tread on the stairs and knew he was coming up to our floor. He was carrying some underclothes that had accidentally blown lose off the line and dropped down into the yard below. He simply said, "Look what I found in the yard!" This was extremely embarrassing for Anna Gay, and it made her determined to make sure that everything was pinned securely to the line. This type of thing did not happen very often much to the relief of both Anna Gay and Mr. Burger.

Mrs. Burger enjoyed raising plants and flowers. As we walked through the front entrance doorway into the house to go upstairs to our apartment, we had to pass through the vestibule. There were a lot of beautiful flowers and plants all around the front window in that little room. One of the plants was a huge rubber plant that both Mr. and Mrs. Burger treated with extra special care. They decided to take a trip to Germany for a few weeks and left us in charge of the house. This also meant that we were in charge of taking care of all the plants and flowers inside and outside. No problem. We agreed to do this and determined to have everything in order when they returned from their trip. Several days after their departure, we began to notice a leaf or two lying on the floor in the vestibule. Horrors! They had fallen off the rubber plant! We also noticed that when we went in and out the door, opening and closing it as usual, the bump of the door resulted in a few more leaves from the rubber plant dropping onto the floor. From then on, we took special care when entering and leaving so that we did not slam the door, but closed it as gently as possible. In spite of our extreme caution, the leaves continued to drop from the rubber plant. There was nothing we could do but watch each day as more and more leaves hit the floor. Much to our dismay, by the time the Burgers returned from their trip, all that was growing out of this huge pot were several green stalks without any leaves hardly at all. We were afraid that the Burgers would be very upset when they saw this, but they just accepted the fact that the plant was either dying or trying to rejuvenate itself, and nothing further was said about the rubber plant. Eventually, they did replace it with a more robust and healthy plant which tended to keep its leaves on its stalk where they were supposed to be. What a relief!

We really did enjoy living in that apartment on Valley Road in spite of some of the challenges we faced with the landlords. They had agreed to rent the second floor apartment for $65.00 a month which we were able to afford at that time. The Burgers knew that we were newlyweds preparing for missionary service, and they were an encouragement to us, offering us words of wisdom and advice from time-to-time.

When we told people that we lived in Melrose Park, Montgomery County, Pennsylvania, they would look at us sort of strangely, wondering how we could afford to live in such a ritzy place as it was known to be. After explaining the fact that we were living in a small upstairs apartment in a duplex house, people understood more fully our situation. The apartment on 501 Valley Road was really ideal for Anna Gay and me as we continued to make preparation for missionary service. We began to explore in more detail ministry opportunities that were related directly to missionary radio. And my studies were progressing well at Philadelphia Wireless Technical Institute as I became more knowledgeable about radio electronics in the broadcasting field.

## 10

## PREFIELD EXPERIENCES  (1965-1966)

---

*Yea, though I walk through the valley of the shadow of death, I will fear no evil: for thou art with me; thy rod and thy staff they comfort me.*  Psalm 23:4

Anna Gay and I were very happy to be married and to be pursuing our goal of serving the Lord in full-time missionary service. It was not long before we settled down into a daily and weekly routine with our work, schooling, and church activities. I was so happy to have someone to share my experiences in journeying through the Myopic Zone. Our schedules were jammed pack full, but we were young, and we accepted the challenges that the Lord had placed before us. We knew that all of the experiences that we had, and that we were going to have, were planned by God for the future ministry that He had for us.

It was wonderful to see how God had prepared both of us to complement each other. I had artistic and organizational abilities while Anna Gay had musical and practical common sense skills. She had a beautiful alto voice and sang in trios and the school choir at Appalachian Bible Institute. Over a period of several years, Anna Gay saved enough money to buy her very own accordion, and she was an accomplished accordionist. Look out Lawrence Welk!

God gave us many opportunities to use our talents and abilities in ministry. Often, I would preach a message, and then illustrate it with a chalk drawing. While I drew the picture, Anna Gay played hymns on her accordion that followed the theme of my message and chalk drawing.

We knew for certain that our missionary service would be in some area of missionary radio. My "on the air" experiences as an amateur radio operator confirmed the practical applications and advantages of Christian radio broadcasting throughout the world. I could only use my ham radio license on a limited basis due to the logistics and difficulties of putting up a basic wire antenna that I needed in order to operate my home-brew transmitter. This was a real challenge because of our apartment layout and location. I was thankful that I could do some "hamming" from Melrose Park and our apartment on Valley Road. My time on the air, however, was also very much limited due to our extremely busy schedule.

Anna Gay continued her work at Doctor's Hospital where she worked as a nurse. I continued my part-time job at Hess and Young, operating various types of printing presses in this gold stamp and hot embossing facility. Then in the afternoons I would have to get over to Philadelphia Wireless Technical Institute to continue my electronic classes in the evening. I was learning more theory in the field of radio broadcasting and electrical circuits. We had regular classroom studies for learning the electronics theory, and then we had special classes in the lab where we were able to experience hands on applications by trouble shooting, wiring, and building electronic circuits.

By this time, I had been asked to serve on the Deacon Board of Chelten Baptist Church. I was pleased to serve in this way and felt it was a privilege for me to do so. This was a new learning experience for me, and I valued this opportunity to serve in the church.

In addition to this, both Anna Gay and I were asked to take over leadership of the youth group at Chelten Baptist Church. Talk about challenges, this was a huge one for us to tackle! The Lord gave us wisdom and strength to carry out the responsibilities that were required of us in this capacity. It was a real joy and blessing to work with the young people, challenging them to live for the Lord, teaching from God's Word, and accompanying them on social activities. Some of our activities with the young people included trips to bowling alleys, to roller skating rinks, and to other unusual fun activities for young people. One of the places where we took them on several occasions was located at Greenwood Diaries in a community not too far from the church. The specialty at Greenwood Diaries was the ice cream selections that they served. One of the interesting items was called the "Pig's Dinner." The ice cream was served in what looked like a pig trough and included three huge scoops of ice cream with all the trimmings. If a person was able to finish all of the "Pig's Dinner," he or she was awarded with a special ribbon stating, "I was a pig at Greenwood Diaries!" Usually, the guys had no problem in cleaning all the ice cream out of their troughs, but some of the girls could not eat all of the ice cream at one time, yet somehow they eventually cleaned out their troughs. Later, we discovered that a couple of the girls had eaten as much as they could, then excuse themselves, and went into the restroom. Apparently, they threw up half of the ice cream they had eaten, then came back and ate some more of the "Pig's Dinner." Finally, at some point, they were able to say they had eaten all of the "Pig's Dinner," and they were given the award. I do not believe that was the intention of the folks at Greenwood Diaries, and it certainly was not an acceptable practice in order to boast that, "I was a pig at Greenwood Diaries!"

During the months after our wedding on July 11, 1964, my mom's health began to deteriorate. About six years before, my mom was diagnosed with breast cancer and had to spend several weeks in a hospital in Lexington, Kentucky, following a mastectomy. She seemed to be doing well for several years and was counting the days when she would reach the seventh year anniversary mark without any reoccurrence of the cancer. But it did reoccur, and mom had to be admitted to Homeplace Hospital, Ary, Kentucky, the same place where my spleen was removed in 1958.

After several months, it became apparent that mom's cancer had returned with a vengeance, and her prognosis was not good. She would never be able to leave the hospital. We were all dismayed about this situation, but we took comfort in knowing that she was in the Lord's hands. Mom remained in good spirits even though confined to her bed. This was hard on my dad and my brother and sister (Johnny, age 15 and Barbara, age 12) who were living at home. At this time my brother Dick was a student at Letourneau College in Longview, Texas. (Dick was a freshman at Philadelphia College of Bible the same year that I was a senior there, and the following year he transferred to Letourneau.)

The family began discussing alternatives to making mom's hospital confinement more pleasant. Hospice care was not an option at that time. A plan was devised to move her from Homeplace Hospital in Kentucky to my grandmother's home in Philadelphia. A hospital bed was moved into the living room with nice view out the front windows, a much nicer arrangement than the four white walls of the hospital.

On September 7, 1965, mom was flown by private plane from the small airport in Hazard, Kentucky, to the Northeast Philadelphia Airport in Pennsylvania. My dad accompanied mom and the two nurses that helped during the flight. Johnny and Barbara stayed in Kentucky with friends. Anna Gay and I met the plane at the airport and followed the ambulance that carried mom to my grand-mother's house.

At this time, Anna Gay stopped her nursing job at Doctor's Hospital in downtown Philadelphia so that she could provide daily nursing care for my mom.

As we continued in our daily activities, Anna Gay and I began searching and exploring various mission organizations that were using radio communications in their ministries. During this time, I received a letter from my dad and family who were in Kentucky and who continued to receive the weekly *Grit Family Newspaper*. My dad came across an article in the *Grit* describing a mission organization that was constructing radio broadcasting facili-ties on a small island, called Bonaire, in the Caribbean. It was very interesting to read about Trans World Radio and to see how they had been broadcasting Christian programs in various languages from their first installation that was built in Monte Carlo, Monaco. At this loca-tion, Trans World Radio had secured the very building that Hitler used many years before which housed the transmitters that broad-casted propaganda around the world by shortwave radio. Now, the Gospel was being beamed to many countries from that very location using the very transmitters that had been used by Hitler. Trans World Radio was in the process of expanding their broadcasting locations and had been granted permission by the Netherlands Antilles govern-ment to construct super power transmitters on the island of Bonaire.

The *Grit* article went on to explain how that broadcasting had just begun from Bonaire, and that Trans World Radio (TWR) was in the process of expanding their operations and adding more transmit-ters and more antennas to the facilities on the island. There were several TWR missionaries on the island, but many more were needed to help in the expansion program. This included radio announcers, technical engineers, secretarial staff, and just about any other type of worker that could be used, including truck drivers, antenna riggers, and maintenance personnel.

This really interested us very much, and we began asking the Lord to give us direction and confirmation concerning TWR. We wanted to make sure we were following God's plan, and this facility could be something where we could use the training we had received.

I continued with my studies at PWTI and had gotten my

126

FCC, that's the Federal Communication Commission, Third Class Radio Broadcasting License. This was required for announcers and for personnel who would be doing on-the-air broadcasting in radio stations located within the United States.

The next step would be to get the commercial broadcasting license from the FCC. This was called the First Class Radio Telephone Operator License and was required by all technical engineers who would be operating or servicing the actual transmitting equipment in the United States of America. Since Bonaire was not under the jurisdiction of the Federal Communication Commission, this particular license was not needed for engineers who would be maintaining the facilities at a broadcasting station like of TWR on Bonaire.

It was not long after we received the article from the *Grit* newspaper that we learned Chelten Baptist Church had invited Dr. Paul Freed to participate in the upcoming missionary conference. He was the Founder and President of (you guessed it) Trans World Radio. Immediately we arranged to have lunch with Dr. Freed at some point during the missionary conference. Throughout the conference, Dr. Freed presented the challenges of Trans World Radio, and especially emphasized the facilities that were being used and expanded on the island of Bonaire in the southern Caribbean, about forty miles north of Venezuela, South America.

Anna Gay and I were really intrigued about this mission organization and about the challenges that were presented during the conference. We certainly enjoyed having Dr. Freed for lunch. (Actually, we did not have Dr. Freed *for* lunch; we had food for lunch that we had prepared for eating *with* Dr. Freed.) The time together gave us opportunity to ask specific questions about the ministry of Trans World Radio, its mission, its goals, its requirements for missionary personnel, and if this mission organization might be interested in considering us as missionaries.

Trans World Radio was a faith mission, which meant that all missionaries were responsible for securing their own missionary support team who would pray for them and also support them financially. This was a concept that was not new to us since Anna Gay was raised in a very missionary-minded church in Huntington, West Virginia. Grace Gospel Church emphasized missions, and Anna Gay dedicated her life to serve the Lord in full-time missions during a missionary conference. Faith missions were certainly not new to me, since my folks were faith missionaries, serving under Rural Evangel Mission in southeast Kentucky where I had the privilege of being raised as an MK and a PK.

As we concluded our personal conversations and time with Dr. Freed, he encouraged us to contact the Home Office of TWR which was located in Chatham, New Jersey. We were welcome to visit the headquarters and to contact the personnel there who would answer any other questions that we might have. Dr. Freed suggested that we fill out preliminary questionnaires or applications, submit them to the Home Office, and see how the Lord would lead. Anna Gay and I were continually asking the Lord for direction and guidance and to show us what His perfect will for us would be in our future missionary service. My rather thick-lensed eyeglasses did not seem to be an issue with Dr. Freed or for me. Apart from occasionally steaming up, I could see quite well through the thick lenses for reading dials on equipment or looking at schematics and identifying electronic circuits.

We did get in contact with the TWR Home Office and requested they send us Preliminary Questionnaires which we received quite promptly. We completed the paper work and submitted them to Trans World Radio. We also arranged to travel to Chatham, New Jersey, from Melrose Park, Pennsylvania, and personally meet with some of the staff there in the Home Office. In our discussions, we were told that it would not be necessary for me to complete the formal training at Philadelphia Wireless Technical Institute, since the broadcasting equipment on Bonaire was of a super-power nature, and that it was not necessary to obtain my FCC First Class Radio Telephone Operator License. The maximum medium wave transmitter power for a U.S. broadcasting transmitter was 50,000 watts. The medium wave transmitter on Bonaire was actually operating at 500,000 watts of power. Special high power circuitry was required in the transmitters for the super-power broadcasting, and much of the theory I had was practical and necessary, but the operating characteristics would be learned on location. This gave us a new perspective and timing of the practicality of trying to complete the course of study at PWTI. I figured that at some point I would want to complete the formal training and take the examination to get the FCC First Class Radiotelephone Operator License. But, that could be done at a later time. This would also mean that we could get to the field for missionary service sooner which was certainly appealing to us.

Our Preliminary Questionnaires were accepted, and we filled out the Regular Applications for full-time missionary service with Trans World Radio. Our applications were approved, and we were appointed in November 1965, as TWR Missionary Appointees. This meant that we could now begin our formal deputation ministry, and we began to secure a team of supporters who would pray for us and who would give monthly support for our missionary work. In addition to our monthly support, we had to raise money for our Equipment Fund which was needed in order to get us moved and established on the field. We were certainly excited to be now moving in a positive direction toward missionary service.

On one occasion, we were at the TWR Headquarters to receive deputation materials and instruction on this phase of preparation for going to the field. While we were in the Home Office, a telex message was received from Bonaire stating that one of the missionary staff, a transmitter engineer, had just died from a drowning accident. This was devastating news for the mission and for the missionary's wife and children. This also meant that there was now a great gap in the duties that this missionary had been fulfilling in the TWR broadcasting schedule. Right there in the office, we were presented with the challenge of getting to the field of Bonaire as quickly as possible to help replace the duties of this missionary. And so, right then, we were assigned to the field of Bonaire, Netherlands Antilles.

This gave us a specific target and goal as we began our deputation ministry. We began to make a contact list of family, friends, and churches where we could share the challenge that the Lord had given to us as Missionary Appointees with Trans World Radio. The Lord began to give us opportunities to share our missionary challenge and testimonies. We soon began to receive commitments from people in churches and friends and family who indicated that they would stand with us in prayer. Some of these also indicated that they would give financially to our Equipment Fund as well as toward our support on a monthly basis. These were exciting days as we looked to the Lord for His provision and as we presented our testimonies and the challenges of our missionary service.

We received invitations to share our testimonies and challenges in places beyond the Philadelphia area through personal friends who had family members in these other churches. It was amazing to see the Lord work and to see the interest that others began to show in our future missionary service. In some of our meetings, we used my chalk drawing equipment and Anna Gay's accordion.

Our very first deputation meeting was held in Kentucky at Camp Nathanael. This was such a blessing to see how the Lord had brought Anna Gay and me together at this very place, Camp Nathanael, several years before and how He had used our experiences at camp to challenge us for missionary service. And here we were, at Camp Nathanael, giving our testimonies and sharing how the Lord had led in our lives and how He was directing us to full-time missionary service with Trans World Radio.

Our next opportunity to share our testimonies was during a Sunday evening service at Chelten Baptist Church. The Missions Committee had warned us that the missions budget was full, and they didn't know how the church could take on support for us. After we spoke and told of our call to missions and to Trans World Radio, the pastor challenged the people to go above and beyond their current tithes and offerings and help with our monthly financial support. He said, "Don't rob Peter to pay Paul." Several folks accepted the challenge, and as a result, the church was able to take on a significant amount of our support. Of course, the pledges of folks to pray for us was greatly encouraging!

As we began to share our burden for missionary service, it became quite obvious that we would have to change our current activities so that we could devote more time to our deputation ministry. We had already discussed the fact that I would not necessarily have to complete my training at PWTI in order to be able to service in the capacity of a transmitter engineer on Bonaire. This was a relief, in some respects, since we were beginning to get worn out from Anna Gay working at Doctor's Hospital, me at Hess and Young and attending classes at electronics school, while serving as a deacon and as we both served as youth leaders at Chelten Baptist Church.

We felt that we could conserve expenses by not staying in the Melrose Park rented apartment but rather relocate during the remainder of our deputation. Anna Gay's parents had invited us to move to Huntington, West Virginia, and live in the upstairs apartment at their house which was available at the time. This would also put us in closer contact with churches in the Huntington, West Virginia, area and in Southeastern Kentucky where I was raised.

We prayed for wisdom from the Lord to know how to proceed, and we determined that it would be better to move to

Huntington, and this was scheduled to take place in February, 1966. Our family and friends encouraged us to proceed with our plans to move from Pennsylvania to West Virginia and complete our deputation ministry there before going to the field. Before leaving the Philadelphia area, my home church, Chelten Baptist Church, had made plans to ordain me into the Gospel ministry. I met with the pastor of the church, and he explained to me the procedures that would be followed prior to my ordination. I would have to prepare a lengthy doctrinal statement that would be distributed to an Ordination Council for their review. Following this review, I would then meet with the Council for a time of questions and answers regarding my doctrinal position and interpretation of various Scripture passages after sharing my testimony of how the Lord had called me into full-time Christian ministry and missionary service. I spent considerable time putting this information together, and then Anna Gay typed the material on our little portable electric typewriter. This doctrinal paper turned out to be quite a thesis with many, many pages. As I prepared the material, Anna Gay did the typing. Most of the typing had to be done in the evening when she was not working. One night, she was typing away on the paper, and we heard a knock at our living room door. It was our landlord, Mr. Burger, who said that the typing sound was so loud that he and his wife were not able to sleep. I was a bit surprised since both were somewhat hard of hearing. Apparently their bedroom was right underneath our kitchen, and Anna Gay was using the kitchen table for this project. Mr. Burger exclaimed, "Mr. Newell, the noise is so loud with the constant banging." Anna Gay was using the electric typewriter, and it was making a muffled noise, but we didn't think it was loud enough to disturb our landlord and his wife down on the first floor. We tried moving the typing project into the bedroom which was in the front of the house where Anna Gay had to use the small desk that we had. It was cramped and a little more difficult, but she continued night after night with the typing project. A few nights later, Mr. Burger came back upstairs again and complained about the noise again. Apparently, it was vibrating throughout the house even from the front room where Anna Gay was working. As a last resort, we folded up a quilt and put the typewriter on top of that to deaden the noise to an acceptable level. Finally, after a couple of weeks, the project was finished, and I had my doctrinal statement completed.

I presented this information to Rev. William J. Randolph, the pastor of Chelten Baptist Church, and he made copies and distributed the material to the pastors who would be serving on the Ordination Council. They were given a few weeks to review the material that I had prepared, and then the Ordination Council was scheduled to meet with me to verify that I would be a suitable candidate for ordination by the church. I appreciated this time together with the members of the Council, and it reinforced in my mind the position that I held in Biblical doctrine and Biblical teaching. The Council voted to proceed with my ordination, and a date was set for February 18, 1966.

While all of this was going on, Anna Gay and I were making our plans to move to Huntington, West Virginia. My dad had come to stay at my grandmother's house to be with mom whose condition continued to rapidly deteriorate. Anna Gay showed dad how to care for mom and how to give her injections for managing the pain she was almost constantly experiencing. Dad and I discussed the situation in light of Anna Gay and me moving to Huntington, West Virginia. He told us not to change our plans but make the move. Mom was in God's hands, and we knew in His time, He would call her home to Heaven. It might be a week, a month, or several months unless He performed a miracle and healed her from the cancer that was raging in her body. After prayful consideration, we felt led to make the move.

Before moving to Huntington, Anna Gay and I had a number of things that we had to sell or give away since the upstairs apartment in Anna Gay's house was furnished. The items of furniture that had been given to us and those who gave them to us were not interested in getting them back. So we were able to sell some of the things as used furniture which provided us with gas money to get us to Huntington. We actually paid for our last month of rent by giving Mr. Burger our refrigerator.

We packed things that we needed to take with us and had them in boxes ready to move out of the apartment. A good friend, and former classmate at Philadelphia College of Bible, agreed to let us use his dad's pickup truck and move our things to West Virginia. He would drive the truck, and we would drive our car. We needed a truck because by this time we had traded our 1958 Chevy for a smaller compact vehicle, a white 1962 Ford Falcon. We had limited space in the car, obviously, so we were thankful that Galen Brumbaugh would be driving the truck.

For some reason, we had to make all these arrangements fit

into a rather tight schedule. Galen would meet us at the apartment with the truck in the early afternoon of the evening when my ordination service was scheduled at Chelten Baptist Church. The plan was to load up our things from the apartment, travel to Chelten Baptist Church for the Friday evening service, and then head straight for Huntington, West Virginia, immediately following the service, traveling all night.

Well, things did not work according to our schedule, unfortunately. We were still loading the truck at the time the service was to begin at the church. I had called earlier and told the pastor that we were in a bad situation, and it appeared that we would be just a few minutes late for the service. He assured me that this would be all right, just hurry up with the packing, and then come as soon as possible to the church. Otherwise, we would have had to leave the apartment, go to the church for the service, then go back to the apartment, load up the truck, get in the car, and head for West Virginia. This would have required a lot of extra time back-tracking and would have put a kink in our master plan.

Anyway, we hurriedly got things wrapped up at the apartment, settled affairs with the landlord, changed for the service, and then headed for the church.

I hate to think how late we were for the service, but most of the people were still in their place, singing many, many hymns while waiting for us to arrive. It was rather embarrassing, to put it mildly, for us to march into the church over an hour late for the service. But everyone was very supportive of us and understood the challenges facing us at this point in our journey through the Myopic Zone. Somehow I managed to keep my glasses from steaming up too bad during the service. My dad, as a missionary pastor and member of Chelten Baptist Church, gave the Ordination message. I would have loved to have my mom there, too, but she had to remain in bed at my grandmother's house. Being ordained into the Gospel ministry was a humbling experience for me as I was introduced to the congregation as Reverend David E. Newell. What a blessing; what a responsibility! Anna Gay also had a part in the service; she maintained her composure as she sang a beautiful solo, "Master, Use Me."

We had already said our goodbye's to mom, although not realizing it would be the last time we would see her alive. So after the service, we had a very late start for our drive to Anna Gay's home and the apartment that awaited us in Huntington, West Virginia.

It was a long, tiring, and grueling journey, but the Lord kept us alert and safe as we traveled from Pennsylvania to West Virginia. Galen drove the pickup truck with all of our earthly possessions, and Anna Gay and I drove our compact 1962 Ford Falcon. Both vehicles were loaded to the gills. We traveled through the night and drove into Huntington shortly after sunup Saturday morning, February 19. We immediately unloaded the truck, and after a very brief cat nap, Galen began the long drive back north to Pennsylvania in the pickup.

We spent the next several days getting settled into our new apartment in Huntington. Then on February 25, we received the telephone call from my dad telling us that mom had been promoted to glory. This was a great loss to our family, but it was a great blessing to know that she was now free from her pain and suffering. Her body was made whole, and also she no longer needed to wear eyeglasses to correct her myopic vision. She could see Jesus perfectly! Anna Gay and I hurriedly packed some things and headed back to Philadelphia where Mom's funeral and burial would take place.

My brother Dick headed to Philadelphia from Longview, Texas, and my brother John and sister Barbara were driven to Philadelphia by friends of the family. After a moving memorial service at Chelten Baptist Church with family and friends, mom was buried in Sunset Memorial Park located in the suburbs outside the northeastern section of Philadelphia. It is the same cemetery where my baby brother Paul Richard was buried in 1943. Other family members are buried in this cemetery, as well.

Several days later, I dropped Anna Gay off in Huntington, West Virginia, and then accompanied my dad to our home in Heiner (Bulan), Kentucky. I'll never forget dad's comments as we both walked into the empty house. He exclaimed, "Dave, what am I going to do?" And he broke down, and we wept together. Dad had just lost his wife and the mother of his children. He was concerned about my brother and sister living at home as well as the ministry of pastoring the Bulan Community Church and serving as a missionary under the Rural Evangel Mission. We prayed together for the Lord to provide the answers to the many questions dad had as he was passing through "the valley of the shadow of death."

Some months later, dad's prayer would be answered when Hettie Adele Todd renewed her acquaintance with him. Years earlier, Hettie and my mom and dad, in their late teenage years, were members of the same youth group in a church in Philadelphia. Hettie had never married and became a missionary serving in the country of Peru. Eventually, the Lord brought Hettie into Dad's life as she accepted the role of wife and mother.

But here we were in Heiner in late February 1966 not knowing how the Lord would lead and provide in the future. I told dad that Anna Gay and I would put our deputation on hold and delay our missionary service so we could help with the immediate family needs. Dad said he did not want to see us change our plans but that we should proceed with the task of raising our support and getting to the field as soon as possible. Reluctantly, we agreed to move ahead with our deputation ministry.

It was just a couple of weeks later that Anna Gay's dad became sick with a gall bladder attack. He ended up in the hospital in Huntington with surgery scheduled to meet this medical emergency. Anna Gay and her mom and I waited at the hospital while the surgery was performed. The surgery was successful and after a couple of days it seemed that healing was taking place.

Late one evening, the doctor told us that Mr. Chapman was recovering and resting well. We all should go home and get a good night's sleep. We were thankful for this good report as we left the hospital. However, throughout the night there was a sudden turn for the worse, and Anna Gay's dad was ushered into the presence of the Lord. We received the news of his death by telephone early the morning of March 15, 1966. It was hard to accept, especially since we had received such a good report from the doctor the night before. And, again, Anna Gay and I and family members found ourselves walking through "the valley of the shadow of death."

Mr. Chapman was buried in Woodlawn Cemetery in Huntington, West Virginia. When things settled down after the funeral service and after visits from relatives, we told Anna Gay's mom that we would put our plans to go to the mission field on hold in order to help her during the next few months. Her response was the same as my dad, "Do not change your plans, but go to the field whenever your support has been raised; do not delay your missionary service."

We also sought the Lord's direction in this important decision. He confirmed that we should proceed, as He continued to open doors for us to share our testimonies with family and friends in churches in southeastern Kentucky and in the Huntington, West Virginia area.

I was able to get a part-time job with a small printing company (Franklin Printing) in Huntington. My experience at Hess and Young proved to be beneficial for this work. I also learned how to manually set type for jobs printed with the letter press equipment. This job helped to provide gas and grocery money for us while living in Huntington.

At times, we found ourselves very low on money even though we tried to be careful with our expenses. On one particular occasion, we had only a couple of cents between us. We didn't have a washer or dryer, and didn't have money for the Laundromat so Anna Gay was washing clothes in the bathtub. She recounts being frustrated and questioning how were we supposed to survive; "What are we going to do?" She remembers that I reminder her, "If we can't trust God to supply and provide for our needs now, how are we going to manage on the mission field?" This was a true test of applying the principle of "living by faith" which we were putting into practice during our days of deputation. Right then we committed this particular financial concern to the Lord, and we saw Him provide through unusual circumstances just what we needed, right when we needed it. Since that moment, we have experienced God's provision time after time in our forty plus years of missionary service.

The Lord continued to bring in pledges for our monthly financial support and Equipment Fund, as well as commitments from others to pray specifically for us. The Lord brought together a great team of supporters (family, friends, and churches) who promised to faithfully be a part of our missionary endeavourers.

By the first of May, all of our support was pledged, and we had about $3,000 in our Equipment Fund. The Lord brought in our needed support in just five months. We truly were blessed! Trans World Radio informed us it was time to order some furniture for our house on Bonaire and to secure our airline tickets for our flight from JFK Airport in New York City.

Furniture available on Bonaire was very limited and very expensive. The most practical approach was to buy wooden unassembled furniture and ship the items by crate to the island. We ordered a living room set, a bedroom dresser, a headboard, and a wardrobe, a kitchen table and chair set, and a roll of fiber glass screening for the windows. All of these items were selected at Sears, Roebuck, and Company where they were crated and sent to Bonaire by cargo ship.

We also secured several 55 gallon steel drums for packing and shipping personal items. Anna Gay packed many bags of soup beans, among other items like peanut butter and a variety of food items that were not available on the island. Anna Gay's mom watched in amusement as we packed the steel drums with toiletry items, clothing, food stuffs, tools, shoes, small kitchen appliances and my ham radio gear. This certainly was a new experience for all of us!

We found that the drums could be shipped for missionaries without cost to the port in New York City by Smith's Transfer. Friends hauled the packed drums to the trucking company, and they were sent on their way with the next load of goods bound for New York. We prayed that they would arrive in good order on Bonaire in a few weeks with nothing missing.

Before leaving for the field, we both visited the dentist for a final checkup and dental work. We also visited the eye doctor for a check of our vision. As expected, I needed to have a stronger prescription, and my very thick bifocal lenses had to be made even thicker. But, praise the Lord, I could see.

We had to secure our passports, and they were issued without any problems or delay. We received them well in advance of our departure date. We were ready to go!

On May 15, 1966, Anna Gay and I were commissioned for missionary service in Trans World Radio in a special service at Grace Gospel Church in Huntington, West Virginia. Anna Gay's pastor, Rev. Mel Efaw and a TWR Representative, Burt Reed, conducted the service. We were thankful that the church had already taken on a significant amount of our monthly support.

Our final order of business was to sell our little 1962 Ford Falcon. Newly appointed TWR Missionaries, Dave and Ruth Ann Arthurs, bought our vehicle and used it during their months of deputation. Later on, the Arthurs joined our Bonaire missionary staff. We were glad they got good use out of our Falcon. We drove the Ford Falcon from Huntington to the TWR headquarters in Chatham, New Jersey, as we prepared to depart for the field from New York City. The Arthurs picked up the car at the TWR headquarters a few weeks later.

Our departure date from JFK was scheduled for Memorial Day, May 30, 1966, with a morning flight on Trans Caribbean Airways. You can imagine we were excited and apprehensive at the same time. Neither of us had ever flown in an airplane, and here we were about to fly in a Boeing 707 from New York to San Juan, Puerto Rico, and on to the island of Aruba in the southern Caribbean. From Aruba we were scheduled to fly the short distance to the island of Curacao and then on to the island of Bonaire on smaller prop planes operated by ALM (Dutch Antillean Airlines). Wow! Our journey through the Myopic Zone was about to get very exciting indeed! What a Memorial Day it was!

## 11

# BONAIRE, NETHERLANDS ANTILLES (1966-1975)

*For the Lord God is a sun and shield: the Lord will give grace and glory: no good thing will he withhold from them that walk uprightly.* Psalm 84:11

My journey through the Myopic Zone took on a new dimension on Memorial Day, May 30, 1966, with our scheduled departure for the mission field. Anna Gay and I were greatly encouraged to have a few special friends join us in the terminal of the John F. Kennedy International Airport in New York City early that Saturday morning.

We had driven our Ford Falcon from Huntington, West Virginia, to the Trans World Radio (TWR) headquarters in Chatham, New Jersey, a few days before. We received some last-minute instructions from TWR concerning our flight and travel to Bonaire. We left our car at the TWR headquarters where Dave and Ruth Ann Arthurs would get it a bit later. Anna Gay and I spent our last couple of nights in the States with a former pastor of Chelten Avenue Baptist Church and his wife. Rev. John Fissel was now pastoring a church not far from the TWR headquarters and, in fact, his wife was a volunteer worker in the TWR office.

The Fissels drove us to the airport, and they were there to see us off. Also, Jack and Dorothy Keeney from Huntington, West Virginia, former youth leaders of Anna Gay and members of Grace Gospel Church, were also at the airport for our departure. Before boarding the plane, we all spent a few moments in a corner of the departure lounge and had a little prayer meeting. They committed Anna Gay and me to the Lord for our flights and for our missionary service with Trans World Radio. That was really a blessing and a wonderful send-off!

We were flying on Trans Caribbean Airways, which at that time had a direct flight to San Juan, Puerto Rico, with continuing service to Aruba, Netherlands Antilles. We were scheduled to transfer to a flight on Dutch Antillean Airlines (ALM) from Aruba to Curacao and connect with a flight from Curacao to Bonaire.

As we were leaving the plane for the stop-over in San Juan, the steward stopped us at the doorway of the plane when he saw the Trans World Radio lapel pin on my jacket. At his first glance, he thought that he saw T.W.A. The steward said, "Ah, Trans World Air...!" I told him that it did not stand for Trans World Airlines but rather, Trans World Radio.

During the brief discussion that followed, he stated that he was from San Juan and that he had listened to the medium wave transmissions from Trans World Radio, Bonaire.

We had already met a person who knew about Trans World Radio, Bonaire and who had listened to some of the broadcasts, and we had not even reached the island, yet. Wow!

The weather had been quite cool in New York, but it was a different story in San Juan. As I stepped out of the plane, my super-thick bifocal eyeglasses immediately steamed up, and water was literally dripping down my face. It was as if a steaming hot blanket had been thrown over me. Man, was it hot! After our brief layover, it was a relief to get back on board our Boeing 707 jet which had its air conditioning system working full blast.

Anna Gay and I had good flights from New York to San Juan and on to Aruba. I will never forget the landing on Aruba, a very small island. It seemed that our plane was going to set down in the Caribbean Sea. At the very last minute, we were over the runway and on the ground.

After going through immigration and customs, we checked in at the ALM counter. We learned that a special flight had been added going from Aruba directly to Bonaire to accommodate a group of boy scouts who were traveling from Bonaire to Curacao. So we were put on that flight which would take us directly to Bonaire without going by way of Curacao. This meant we would arrive on Bonaire well ahead of our scheduled time. I was able to make a phone call to the TWR office on Bonaire to give the mission folks our new arrival time.

We boarded the ALM Convair two-engine prop plane and soon were airborne, en route to Bonaire. By now, we really were getting excited about reaching the mission field. It was dark by this time, and as we were making our decent, preparing to land at Flamingo Airport, we were looking very expectantly out of the plane windows, looking for the obstruction lights from the radio antenna towers. Unfortunately, we had no idea what side of the aircraft these would be visible from as we looked out of the left side of the plane.

Some of the Antillean passengers on the flight saw our excitement and, apparently, suspected that we were joining the Trans World Radio staff on Bonaire. They were very helpful to us and suggested that we look out of the right side of the aircraft, which we did, and there before us we saw the red beacon lights on the curtain antenna tower, as well as the red beacon lights on the 760 foot tall medium wave antenna tower.

Needless to say, this was a great thrill for us, realizing that we were practically at our destination, on the field of Bonaire ready to begin our first term of missionary service with Trans World Radio.

Since we arrived on an unscheduled flight, it was understandable that some of the TWR missionaries were not at the Flamingo Airport to greet us. But that was all right. However, the entire staff made us most welcome over the next few days.

We were taken to the home of the Bonaire Dutch police chief where we would stay until our house was ready. The police chief and his family had gone back to Holland for several weeks, and he had asked TWR if someone could house-sit during the time they were off the island. This was a nice transition for us since the crate with our unassembled furniture had not yet arrived, and our barrels were on the high seas somewhere between New York and Bonaire.

Our permanent house, nearing completion, was of typical island construction built with cement blocks, a concrete floor, covered with terrazzo tile, a terra cotta roof, and jalousie-style glass windows. It was painted a pastel orange with white trim and was just the right size for the two of us.

The island of Bonaire is the second largest of the three islands comprising the western area of the Netherlands Antilles in the Caribbean Sea. Bonaire is located about 13 degrees north of the Equator and about 40 miles north of Venezuela. Bonaire is a small island of corral rock, sand, and cactus with divi-divi trees and scrub bushes scattered around. The highest elevation is 800 feet above sea level. From that elevation one can see almost the whole island surrounded by the beautiful clear waters of the Caribbean Sea. Also, one can feel the strong trade winds that constantly blew across the island ENE to WSW with a strength of 10-16 knots. The prevailing trade winds are so strong, that the knurled divi-divi trees with their branches would grow away from the winds. There are also a lot of colorful flamboyant trees and tropical plants and flowers such as hibiscus and bougainvillea.

One of the key distinctions of Bonaire was the great population of goats and flamingoes. The goats roamed all over the island while the flamingoes lived in the southern part of Bonaire where the salt flats were located. Bonaire is called "The Island of the Flamingoes." At the time of our arrival, the population of the island was around 7,000 people, and we were told that the goat population was five times more than that.

I soon discovered that while the trade winds blew refreshing breeze, they also blew dust and sand over everything, including my super-thick eyeglasses. It was a continuing battle trying to keep them clean. I also saw the effects these trade winds had on those who wore contact lenses. Their eyes were constantly watering, and it appeared that they were always crying, even while indoors and out of the wind. The only way for them to get relief was to pop out the contacts, clean them good, and put them back in place on their eyeballs.

Several times, I was encouraged to replace my heavy eyeglasses with contact lenses. But this did not appeal to me at all after seeing the distress that the trade winds caused to contact lens wearers. I decided to stick with my glasses and the trusty, reliable, heavy bifocal lenses.

We soon learned the location of key places like the fish market (where we bought local fish from the "Fish Lady") and the banana boats from Venezuela at the pier (where we bought fresh fruit and vegetables).

There was even a little snack-type shop, called "Super Corner" where we could buy French fries (cooked in peanut oil) and soft ice cream (that tasted like a combination of Saccharin and Brylcreem).

The Antillean people were dark-skinned and spoke the trade language, called Papiamento. The official language was Dutch, but many Bonarians could only speak Papiamento. Our landlady could not speak Dutch, and neither could we. She could not speak English, and we could not speak Papiamento. This was quite a dilemma for all of us, but we did our best to communicate with gestures, sign language, and grunts and groans. We quickly learned some key Papiamento and Dutch words that helped Anna Gay and me build relationships with the local people.

The location and composition of the island made Bonaire an ideal place for constructing the Trans World Radio transmitting facilities at the edge of the salt flats in the south part of the island. This enhanced the propagation of shortwave radio signals. Gospel programs were beamed into many parts of the world, including the Caribbean region, South and Central America, Europe, East Asia, and North America.

Trans World Radio (TWR) was literally "Telling the World of Redemption" utilizing super power transmitters designed by Continental Electronics of Dallas, Texas, (a medium wave 500,000 watt transmitter broadcasting at 800 kilohertz through a 760 foot antenna and a 250,000 watt shortwave transmitter capable of broadcasting on frequencies in the 16, 19, 25, 31, and 49 meter bands with directional antennas). An additional shortwave transmitter was broadcasting with 50,000 watts of power. The two larger transmitters were equipped with vapor phase cooling systems for the heat dissipation of the large electronic tubes.

The TWR studio and office facilities were located in Kralendijk, the capital of Bonaire, in the central part of the island. Initially, programming was sent to the transmitter site by way of telephone lines. Later, a multi-channel FM transmitter was used to send audio to the transmitter site. The studio equipment included six Telefunken M5 recorders, two EMT turntables, two McCarta Carousel cartridge recorders, and a multi-channel master console designed by Telefunken. Sub-control rooms were equipped with a console and with Philips, Telefunken, and RCA tape recorders.

The island power plant could not supply the huge amounts of electricity required to operate the super power TWR transmitters. TWR provided the needed power with two 16-cylinder Alco stationary locomotives with Westinghouse generators capable of producing a total of 3.2 million watts of electrical power. The diesel generating units weighed 45 tons each. In addition to these two, a 50,000 watt diesel generator unit was used for auxiliary power at the transmitter site during times that the transmitters were off the air.

The prefix for broadcasting stations in the Netherlands Antilles was PJ. The call letters for the Trans World Radio facilities were PJB. The Netherlands Antilles had a reciprocal agreement for amateur radio stations. In the United States, I was licensed as WA4DUP, and I applied for a Bonaire ham license. This was approved by the government, and I was assigned the call sign PJ5BG which a few years later was modified to PJ9BG. I could legally operate my ham equipment from Bonaire! After I got my ham equipment and antenna set up, I was able to make regular contacts with my dad back in the States who was operating with ham call sign WA4ZIZ.

Anna Gay and I were thrilled to be on the field and involved in the broadcast ministry of Trans World Radio. Of course, I was assigned to the transmitter site as an engineer and initially was put on a broadcast shift. This involved the technicalities of tuning and operating the two shortwave transmitters and the medium wave transmitter, assuring they were properly maintained and operated with maximum efficiency, closely monitoring critical parameters. This also involved maintaining and monitoring the operation of the two Alco diesel engines that supplied power for the transmitter site.

Anna Gay was also initially assigned to the transmitter site office to carry out the duties of secretary to the Chief Engineer, Richard Kennedy. She also assisted with other secretarial and filing work that was required by the transmitter site staff. She had a day shift while I initially had an early sign-on shift starting at 3:00 in the morning.

We had just enough money in our Equipment Fund to buy a used VW Beetle from a TWR missionary who was returning to the States. We also bought a new red Honda 90cc motorcycle which I used to travel from town to the transmitter site. Anna Gay drove our light green Bug to and from the transmitter building.

The fenders of our newly acquired VW Bug had been eaten through with rust. The continuously blowing trade winds picked up salt spray from the Caribbean Sea which attacked any exposed metal. We had a local Antillean man repair all four fenders. He made new ones out of 55 gallon drums and painted them to match the car. He did a great job! Operating a motorcycle was a new experience for me, and it was especially challenging because of my super-thick bifocal eyeglasses. With those on my face, I surely didn't need goggles. But I certainly did use my helmet.

I remember my first test of dexterity with my motorcycle was the very first morning that I was assigned to work the sign-on shift. Dick Kennedy was to meet me at our (the Police Chief's) house in plenty of time for us to get to the transmitter site and get the equipment (diesels and transmitters) functioning for the beginning of the morning broadcasts. The appointed time came and went; I was ready to roll in the pitch blackness, but no Dick Kennedy. Finally, I saw the headlight of his motorcycle coming down the road. He screeched to a stop and told me he had overslept, and we would need to take a "short cut" around the perimeter of the airport in order to make up for lost time. And away he roared, with me and my limited motorcycle operating experience trying to keep up.

The dirt track took us through the open fields (called "boonies") around rocks and cactus plants. A couple of times I missed a sharp curve in the track and went zooming off into the boonies praying I would miss rocks and cactus. As I bounced back to the track, my motorcycle headlight was pointing in all different directions as I tried to avoid the obstacles in the very rough and uneven terrain. Dick saw this in his rear view mirror and wondered, "What is the guy doing, and why doesn't he stay on the track?" Believe me, I was doing my best to stay on the bike while at the same time trying to keep my glasses from flying off into space.

Amazingly, by God's grace, we arrived at the transmitter site without having any wrecks. Then, we began the frantic attempt to get set for the first broadcast. We had to inspect the diesel building and start the diesel engines, inspect and power up the transmitter cooling systems, check the corner reflector antennas to make certain they were set to the correct meter band, confirm that the studio operator was ready with programming, and a host of other duties.

We had to synchronize the outputs of the diesel engines and put them on line before we could put the transmitters on the air. We generally had the transmitters on the air about five minutes before actual programming began. During this "idle" time, we broadcast the TWR signature signal (or "pingles" as we called them). This was a few bars of instrumental music and was "Stand Up, Stand Up for Jesus" played or repeated over and over again until it was time to officially sign-on. This signature signal helped shortwave listeners identify TWR and tune their shortwave radios to the correct frequency before the actual program started.

I think we had enough time for two pingles that morning before we began broadcasting to Brazil in the Portuguese language. It was very early in the morning on Bonaire, but in the target area of Brazil it was prime listening time in the morning.

What a thrill to realize the Gospel was being broadcast at that moment and that it was being a blessing and encouragement to listeners eager to hear the Word of God preached and taught. Even though we could not see our audience, we knew they were there listening to their radios as letters were received daily, not only from Brazil, but from all over the world. We claimed the promise of Isaiah 55:11, "So shall my word be that goeth forth from my mouth: it shall not return unto me void, but it shall accomplish that which I please, and it shall prosper in the thing whereto I sent it."

Not long after getting settled into our new home, we learned that the governor of the island was conducting a class for anyone interested in learning Papiamento. The word "Papiamento" literally means gibberish, a fitting description of a language whose words are composed of a mixture of Spanish, Dutch, Portuguese, and English. Papiamento is spoken only in the three Dutch Antillean islands of Aruba, Bonaire, and Curacao.

Anna Gay and I began learning the language and could soon carry on a very basic conversation with our Bonarian landlady and Bonaire neighbors. I had studied two years of French in high school and two years of Spanish in college. Anna Gay had studied Spanish. In one sense, this helped us with the Papiamento, but, on the other hand, it began to corrupt our Spanish, as we would learn later.

But for the present it was nice to be able to say, "Bon bini, con ta bai?" ("Hello, how are you?") And to reply to a greeting, we would say, "Basta bon; danki." ("Good enough; thank you.") We studied with the governor's class for several months. Then a year or so later, we continued to learn Papiamento with the help of missionaries who had been working in the Netherlands Antilles for several years.

A small Baptist church had been organized by the TEAM (The Evangelical Alliance Mission) missionaries and was pastured by an Antillean. Of course, the services were conducted in Papiamento, and Anna Gay and I began attending as my schedule shifts at the transmitter site allowed. We wanted to be a witness to our Bonairian neighbors and to people we met in the business community.

It was not long before word got around about my interest in drawing sketches, painting scenes with oils, and presenting chalk drawings with the special equipment that I had shipped to Bonaire. It was also noticed that Anna Gay had her accordion and that she had a beautiful alto singing voice.

This led to opportunities for us to conduct special services with Anna Gay playing and singing and me preaching and drawing, not only for TWR mission functions, but also for TEAM outreach ministries.

All of the transmitter site personnel had a variety of duties to perform during the times the TWR transmitters were not on the air. This included performing maintenance on the transmitters, the antenna systems, the diesel generators, and the buildings. One of my assignments was to use my drawing abilities to update the multitude of schematics for the equipment operated at the transmitter site. I had to work from notes and sketches that showed modifications of all kinds to the original circuits of the equipment. I needed to verify that the rough drawings and notes were accurate before drawing the final schematics that would be filed with the originals. I had to trace the wiring changes in the transmitters, power supplies, studio equipment, and other associated control panels. This involved climbing and crawling inside and outside the cabinets of all three transmitters.

I also helped to establish and organize an inventory of spare parts for all of the equipment used at the transmitter site and in the studio facilities.

Since Anna Gay and I had no children, we were able to adjust to our varied schedules without any major problems. I had to continually battle with my famous glasses due to wind and sweat.

Before we were married, Anna Gay and I discussed raising a family. I was concerned about our children inheriting my extreme myopic condition. My eyesight was worse than my mom's who was very nearsighted. I was afraid that the trend of worsening vision would automatically be passed on to our children. We committed this concern to the Lord and were confident He would take care of this and for us not to worry. We both agreed that it would be best for us to adjust to our new roles as husband and wife and adjust to living in a new culture before raising children.

Little did we realize that it would be seven and one-half years before the Lord would give us a child even though we were ready several years before that event took place. We had committed this to the Lord and trusted Him to answer our prayer for a child in His time and according to His plan for our lives.

In the meantime, we were happy to be serving the Lord with Trans World Radio. Then, in early 1967, TWR approached us about a short-term assignment at the mission headquarters in Chatham, New Jersey. The TWR broadcasting facilities and needed equipment was expanding, requiring a larger inventory of components and parts which had to be acquired in the United States and shipped to Bonaire. A better system was greatly needed, and I was asked to consider setting up a Procurement Department in the TWR headquarters. Anna Gay would be involved in secretarial work in the headquarters and would assist in my secretarial needs in this new project. After praying for the Lord's will to be done, we agreed to tackle this assignment. We explained this need and challenge to our supporting churches and friends, assuring them it was a temporary arrangement and that we would be returning to Bonaire by the end of the year.

We had a family house-sit for us and take care of our furniture, car, and motorcycle. And we headed for Chatham. The mission had just about completed a new office building a few blocks down Main Street from the original offices (a house and a part of a duplex building right across the street). The new building had an efficiency apartment upstairs where Anna Gay and I lived. We had the task and opportunity of choosing the furnishings, appliances, and furniture. It was very cozy, just right for us as a couple. This was a great advantage since we could be in the office by just walking down a flight of stairs, no fighting the heavy traffic in that busy New York Metropolitan area. Since we were right there, I was given the task of taking new TWR missionaries to the JFK Airport in New York. I also met TWR missionaries returning to the States for their furlough. Traffic in New York Metropolitan area was sure a lot heavier than what we had grown accustomed to on our small island of Bonaire!

It was interesting to watch passengers disembarking from their flights and passing through customs. On one occasion, a family of twelve came from Bonaire. It took two of us in two station wagons to collect them and their luggage at the airport and transport them to their destination in New Jersey. That was an all day event.

Putting the procedures in place for the Procurement Department was a major project which took me several months to accomplish. When I finished, TWR had a comprehensive list of vendors along with contact information. This would give smoother communications between the TWR fields (Bonaire and Monte Carlo at that time) and the TWR Headquarters. Our mission was accomplished, and we returned to Bonaire just before Christmas 1967.

It was great to be back on Bonaire and to be involved in our duties at the transmitter site. My responsibilities were expanded to include more than transmitter operation and maintenance. I was put in charge of overseeing the equipment in the audio racks. This equipment fed programming that was sent from the studio to the individual transmitters. Equipment in these racks was used to monitor the broadcast signals from the transmitters. I continued updating equipment, wiring schematics, adding electronic symbols and notes, using a drawing board and a tee square. I began spending some time in the Office/Studio Complex designing broadcast schedules and QSL verification cards for Trans World Radio.

Anna Gay continued to assist with secretarial duties at the transmitter site. In addition, she was assigned to be part of the music production team, playing her accordion and singing. All of the music selections were recorded and used throughout blocks of programming. The ensemble prepared selections in the English, Spanish, and Portuguese languages.

At a later time during a furlough, we were able to purchase a vibraharp and ship it to Bonaire. This musical instrument was kept in the large recording studio and used as accompaniment for musical groups. This was a great instrument, similar to a marimba. The bars were made of aluminum, and were positioned over horizontal tubes. Motorized paddles in the top of each tube gave the instrument a beautiful sustained vibrato sound when the individual notes (bars) were struck with the mallets. Anna Gay had never played this type of an instrument, but she learned fast, and had many opportunities to use the vibraharp in our ministry.

As the TWR staff on Bonaire grew in number so did the need for housing. The Lord made it possible for our mission to build several new houses, some of these close to the Caribbean Sea and some right by the water. As houses were available, staff had the option of relocating to one of the newer houses according to seniority. Moving days were experiences to behold!

Missionary A would move from house number one to new house number five. Missionary B would move from house number two to house number one. Missionary C would move from house number three to house number two. Missionary D would move from house number four to house number three. Then, one of the newest missionary families would be moved into house number four. The houses being moved out of and into were located in various villages around the island. So it was very hectic, trying to get all the moves done, usually in one day. Trucks, and cars (mostly VW Bugs) loaded with furniture and all kinds of stuff were being driven all over the place. If there was a piano in the back of a truck, there was usually someone playing the piano as the truck was being driven down the road! That was so funny to see! The Bonairians eventually figured out what was going on and just watched in amazement. They never moved from one house to another and sometimes could not comprehend what the crazy Americans were doing.

After returning to Bonaire from our temporary assignment at the TWR Home Office, we moved into a typical Antillean-style house in Terra Corra. The couple who had lived there was being transferred to the Home Office to work in the newly established Procurement Office that I had just set up.

A year or so later, we had the opportunity of getting in on one of these famous Trans World Radio staff moves. We moved from Terra Corra to a nicer house just outside Kralendijk across the road from the Flamingo Beach Club which gave us access to the beautiful sandy beach on the sea.

All the houses on the island used propane gas for cooking. The gas company, called OGUM, had a hard time keeping track of the gas tanks and the occupants responsible for them when they were moved from one house to another.

I decided to help this matter by going into the OGUM office just before our moving date to give them the serial number of our gas tanks. When I told Mr. Solomon that we were going to move, he was almost beside himself. He exclaimed, "Mr. New-well what am I going to do? With all this moving, how can I keep everything straight? Mr. New-well, you people keep moving all over the place, and I can't keep track of which tank belongs to who!" I assured him, I was only trying to be helpful and didn't want to create a problem. Eventually, he calmed down and gratefully took the tank information that I had brought for him and said, "Thank you, Mr. New-well."

Shortly after moving into our "new" house, we decided to give a small beagle-type dog a "new" home, as well. And so Amos became part of our family. It was Anna Gay, Amos, and me. That dog was very loveable, but he sure gave us a lot of grief on many occasions. Amos liked to pull clothes off the line and leave them laying all around the yard. More than once, our Dutch neighbors, Burt and Hilda, would gather the clothes from the ground when Anna Gay and I were not at home. One time, we tried to break Amos of his shenanigans by sprinkling hot pepper in his mouth. He merely licked his chops as if looking for more of the hot stuff which apparently he was enjoying.

Some of us initiated a little weekly tabloid paper, called *The Bonaire Feedback*, for the TWR staff with announcements, items of interest, news reports from the studio and transmitter sites, and a variety of other tidbits. I began drawing a cartoon strip, titled "Life with Amos," which depicted some of the funny and not-so-funny experiences we had with our little beagle. I did a total of 25 in the series back then. All of our work on *The Bonaire Feedback* was prepared on stencils and copied on a mimeograph machine. I enjoyed using my artistic abilities in this way. It was a challenge doing the artwork on the stencils using a stylus instead of a pen or pencil. It also was a challenge for me having to look through my super-thick bifocal eyeglasses which year after year became thicker and thicker as my journey through the Myopic Zone continued.

We had not been on Bonaire very long before we became aware of some bugs that were so tiny I could not even see them even with my bifocal lenses. These were little bitsy gnats that we referred to as "no see-ums." I had a saying for these little monsters, "no see-ums; big bite-ums; you feel-ums!" Their bites would raise large itchy welts. They must be first cousins to the chiggers that I experienced while growing up in Kentucky.

Other unwelcome critters were scorpions. Our house must have been built on a colony of scorpion nests. I had a three-foot pole that I called our "Portable Scorpion Smasher." I made a mark on the Smasher every time I killed a scorpion. In one year's time, I killed 99 scorpions!

During our first couple of years on Bonaire, my dad and his new wife, Adele, changed missions and moved from the Rural Evangel Mission in Kentucky to Source of Light Ministries (SLM) in Madison, Georgia. So during our furlough times, we made it a point to visit my folks at the SLM mission headquarters in Georgia. This gave us opportunities to learn more about the worldwide printing ministry of SLM and their use of Bible correspondence courses in several languages. Trans World Radio was already using SLM Portuguese materials to follow up listener contacts in Brazil.

On January 17, 1971, our little dog Amos experienced some real competition in the Newell family. This date was the arrival of our long-anticipated first child, Gaylene Anne Newell, who became the center of our attention! Gaylene was born in the little medical clinic on Bonaire referred to as the St. Franciscus Hospital operated by Roman Catholic nuns. The Dutch physician, Dr. Welvaart, handled the delivery along with one of the Catholic sister nurses. I was right there also, ready to assist, if necessary. I recorded Gaylene's first cries on a small portable tape recorder. Later in the morning, I had arranged to meet my dad on the air by ham radio, and I played Gaylene's cries for him and my step-mom to hear.

After waiting for several years, the Lord had given us a perfectly beautiful baby girl. This event certainly changed Anna Gay's ministry schedule, but she was still able to be involved part-time in the TWR music recording department in the studio.

Two years later, on March 2, 1973, the Lord blessed us with another child. Philip David Newell made his appearance into the world at the St. Franciscus Hospital on Bonaire. Dr. Welvaart, as usual, waited until the last minute to rush to the hospital. Anna Gay was more than ready to deliver, and the nurse kept telling her to wait, the doctor was on his way. She kept repeating, "Don't push; don't push!" At one point, it was just Anna Gay and me and one soon-to-be-born baby in the delivery room. I thought, I'd better adjust my thick-lensed glasses and get ready to deliver the baby myself! At the very last second, Dr. Welvaart came crashing through the door and took care of the soon-to-be-crisis! At last, Anna Gay could push!

Philip was a big handsome baby boy who was too long to fit into the little plastic tub that was reserved for newborns. His feet hung over the edge, but that was o.k. He was healthy!

According to the local custom, mothers who delivered babies were required to spend a full week in the hospital. And so was the case when Gaylene and Philip were born. My folks had flown to Bonaire a few days before Philip was born, and they were a great help to me and Gaylene during Anna Gay's stay in the hospital.

On a much different occasion, I had to spend a week in the St. Franciscus hospital following an accident on my motorcycle. I was taking some updated drawings to one of our TWR engineers who lived on the other side of Kralendijk. I drove past the house and had to make a u-turn. After making sure the road was clear, I turned my motorcycle around and was easing over to the left side of the road toward the house.

All of a sudden, a car had roared down the road, attempting to pass on my left, and ran smack into me. The car dragged my motorcycle and me a hundred yards down the road. The Antillean fellow in the car apparently hit the gas pedal instead of the brake, and he ended up in the boonies while I crashed to the side of the road with the motorcycle on top of me. I lost consciousness after the crash and woke up as I was being lifted into the island's only ambulance.

My glasses were smashed, my motorcycle was smashed, my helmet was cracked, and I was badly cut and bruised. But, praise the Lord, I was alive.

I suffered a cut on my left ankle, a bad bruise on my left buttock (which still has an indention at the site of the bruise), and multiple scrapes and wounds. Dr. Welvaart determined that I had experienced no internal bleeding but wanted to keep me under observation in the hospital for at least a week.

After being released from the hospital, I eventually was able to hobble around and resume limited work at the transmitter site. After several weeks of healing, I was able to replace the smashed parts on my motorcycle and began riding again, but to be sure, with a lot more caution.

Just about all TWR men missionaries owned a motorcycle. In spite of potential accidents, like I had, it was a very practical and inexpensive vehicle to operate and provided dependable transportation on the Bonaire roads, both paved and unpaved. Just don't run over any cactus plants or you'll end up walking beside a bike with a flat tire. It was fun to ride around the island during the day but especially at night under a full moon. Many times, if not on a broadcast shift, several of us would take our wives for a ride on our motorcycles. This was a way to have some leisure time and to take a break from the demanding pressures of the transmitter and studio operations. Thankfully, I never had an accident while Anna Gay was on board. We sure did enjoy those rides!

Friday afternoons were usually reserved for competitive sporting events for those who were not on duty. These co-ed events included volleyball and softball. In spite of my thick eyeglasses, I could play a pretty good game of volleyball. It did not take me long to work up a sweat and that always meant drippy steamy glasses that I had to continually clean with my large red bandana. I always carried at least two red bandanas in my right back pocket. I really enjoyed playing softball, as well.

On one occasion, we were warming up for a softball game. Two batters were knocking flies and grounders to the outfield. I was waiting to snag a grounder and failed to see the fly ball that was coming at me. The cry, "Look out, Dave!" came too late, and the ball hit me just above my right eye on the eyebrow. I felt pain; I saw stars; I heard my glasses shatter. Praise the Lord, no glass got into my eye, but I had a gash above my eye. I was driven to the doctor who sewed in a stitch or two and sent me home with a patch over my eye to begin my recovery. My journey through the Myopic Zone sure had its bumps and bruises!

Another favorite activity that we enjoyed on a day off was swimming in the crystal clear waters of the Caribbean Sea. At early ages, we had Gaylene and Philip in the water, and they loved it and learned to swim like fish.

I always had a problem, though, with snorkeling. I had to take off my eyeglasses in order to use the rubber mask for snorkeling. I could not see more than 12 inches in front of my nose. Eventually, I got the bright idea of taking the earpieces off an old pair of glasses and wedging the frame and lenses inside the mask. That worked pretty well! I could see the coral formations, all kinds of colorful fish, conch shells, sea cucumbers, star fish, and occasionally, a large barracuda.

One time, I put on my mask, started swimming, and then realized something was terribly wrong with my vision. Everything seemed so far away. What was happening to my eyes!? Finally, I discovered I had pushed the frames and lenses into the mask the wrong way, and I was actually looking into and through the front of the eyeglasses. At a later time, I solved this potential problem by having lenses ground to my prescription which I glued permanently onto the mask. That helped me see so much better! Then, I really began to enjoy snorkeling and spear fishing.

During our missionary service on Bonaire, Anna Gay and I had several opportunities for ministry apart from our regular transmitter and studio responsibilities. I preached and used my chalk drawing equipment many times, while Anna Gay played her accordion and vibraharp for special music at various events on Bonaire. During baptismal services on the sandy beach, the accordion proved to be very versatile. What a beautiful location and setting for such a service! One time we were asked to participate in a special conference with TEAM missionaries on the island of Aruba.

In November 1970, Anna Gay and I had the opportunity of participating in a radio rally that was conducted in the city of Velencia in Venezuela, South America. Also participating in this radio rally were Boyd and Kathy Griffith, and Jose Arauz. Anna Gay was involved with the music production, and I was on the engineering staff at the transmitter site. Boyd and Kathy did production work in the studio, and Jose produced the "Alianca en Marcha" program.

The idea originated of having a series of special meetings in Valencia, Venezuela, in connection with the Spanish broadcasts that were being daily beamed to South America from Bonaire on the medium wave transmitter, as well as those being aired on the short-wave transmitters.

Jose and another radio pastor from Ecuador were responsible for the preaching during these special meetings. Boyd and Kathy were helping with the special music that was presented, playing the trombone and the English hand bells. Anna Gay provided special music with the vibraharp. My contribution was to draw a chalk illustration during each service that depicted the theme of the message.

The meetings were well attended, and we saw some good results as many responded to the Gospel messages and were saved. Christians gave testimony to the fact that these special radio rally meetings were a blessing to them, and many of these people came to the services as a direct result of the invitation given over the radio. One man, in particular, traveled from a mountainous area quite some distance from Valencia to attend one of these meetings.

It was a tremendous experience for us to have a part in the series of radio rallies that were held in Valencia. Even though our Spanish was somewhat rusty from having studied Papiamento, we were able to communicate with the people and to feel a real part of the gatherings that met each evening for almost a week.

One of the highlights that occurred during our visit to Valencia was the occasion when we visited an Army Base outside of the city. We had the opportunity of going to Camp Carabobo and presenting a program of music, Bible message, and chalk illustration to a group of several hundred soldiers on this base. The question was asked whether or not any of the men listened to Trans World Radio, Bonaire, and it was thrilling to see that almost every hand in the meeting hall was raised.

At the conclusion of this special service, the invitation was given for those who would like to receive Christ to indicate this by the uplifted hand. Again, it was a thrill to see many, many hands raised in response to this invitation. This was certainly a unique opportunity for us to minister the Gospel in this way. As a final event in this service, I had the opportunity of presenting my chalk drawing to the Commanding Officer of the base.

It was rather interesting to travel from Bonaire to Caracas, Venezuela, by plane and then continuing on to Valencia by bus and taxi. We certainly were loaded down with equipment, carrying with us a trombone, a set of English hand bells with their tables, a vibraharp that was packed in two cases, and the chalk drawing equipment which was packed in a wooden case. However, the Lord undertook for us and made it possible for us to get the equipment to Valencia and back to Bonaire without any damage and without having to pay an excessive amount of overweight charges.

Our times of deputation in the States always proved to be very interesting and challenging. Our normal term on the field was three years, with a four month furlough. During this four month period, we visited our family, friends, and supporting churches in Kentucky, West Virginia, Pennsylvania, New Jersey, Delaware, Maryland, Tennessee, and Georgia. It was a busy schedule requiring a lot of driving and speaking engagements. It was not so bad when it was just Anna Gay and me. It became even more challenging when our family size grew from two to four with the addition of our first two children, Gaylene and Philip.

It was so neat to see how the Lord provided accommodations and transportation during our furloughs (now referred to as "Home Leave" by many mission organizations).

We generally made Huntington, West Virginia, our home base. One furlough, a man from Grace Gospel Church gave us a gas credit card and said, "Put all of your gasoline expenses on my charge card," and he handed me his card. What a blessing!

This was interesting since we still had not secured a vehicle to use during our traveling. We knew God had something for us at some point since we had a gas card, but where was the vehicle?

Several days later, a vehicle was delivered right to the door of our apartment. It was a brand new blue Chevy station wagon with eight miles on the odometer, perfect for our family of four. It was provided by a friend who told us, "Drive this station wagon wherever you need to go and when you return to the field, give it to another missionary family from our church to drive while they are on furlough." Little did he know that Anna Gay had prayed for a blue station wagon with air conditioning to use during our furlough. God indeed answered her prayer! We had a gas card, a beautiful Chevy station wagon, and were good to go! God's provision was certainly exceedingly above and beyond what we could ever ask or even think!

Several weeks later, the man who gave us his gas card, and his wife, took us out for supper to a town about an hour's drive up the

Ohio River from Huntington. On the way, he stopped to get gas. After filling up the tank of his car, he began fumbling around in his billfold to pay for the gas. After more fumbling, I whipped out my (his) gas card, handed it to him, and I said, "Here, use my card!" He did, and we all had a good laugh!

In early 1974, our Bonaire staff was informed about projected plans put forth by TWR to establish studio and transmitting facilities on the island of Guam in the Western Pacific. The mission was looking for a few Bonaire missionary staff members and families to consider being transferred to this new location to help build the new station.

After much prayer and consideration, Anna Gay and I expressed our desire and willingness to be reassigned to the TWR-Guam field. I had the engineering qualifications, and of real significance, was the fact that I now had my FCC First Class Commercial License, a requirement for transmitter engineers since Guam was a U.S. territory and came under the jurisdiction of the FCC (Federal Communications Commission) that regulated broadcasting facilities according to United States laws and regulations.

Prior to this, I had finally finished the electronics training I had started at Philadelphia Wireless Technical Institute through Cleveland Institute of Electronics (CIE). This technical broadcasting correspondence course normally took one year to complete, but it took me more than two because of my mission duties on Bonaire. On October 3, 1974, I received my diploma for successfully completing the First Class FCC License course.

The next step was to pass the FCC examination before I would be issued the FCC Commercial License. I had to take the examinations during furlough time when I could get to a U.S. Federal Building. My Second Class License was issued in Philadelphia on November 8, 1974, and my First Class License was issued in Hawaii on November 27, 1979. This gave me authority to maintain and operate the medium wave transmitter for KTWG and the two short-wave transmitters for KTWR on Guam.

Our family was one of those selected (in spite of my very myopic eyesight) and the wheels were put into motion for our transfer from Bonaire to Guam (after our scheduled furlough). This was an exciting time for us as we anticipated being part of the team that was going to construct the new broadcasting facilities on Guam located on the other side of the world.

It was with mixed feelings that we sold our furniture, appliances, and car, and packed our personal things to be shipped by boat to Guam. We said our good-byes to the TWR Bonaire staff; I adjusted my thick bifocal-lensed glasses; we headed to Huntington, West Virginia (our home base during furlough); and I prepared myself for continuing into a new chapter in my journey through the Myopic Zone.

## 12

## GUAM, WESTERN PACIFIC (1975-1984)

---

*If I take the wings of the morning, and dwell in the uttermost parts of the sea; even there shall thy hand lead me, and thy right hand shall hold me.* Psalm 139:9-10

From the time that we began our missionary service in 1966, every Christmas was spent on the field of Bonaire. Until now. Our family was being transferred from the island of Bonaire in the Caribbean Sea to the island of Guam in the Western Pacific Ocean.

As we began to make this transition, we also started our four-month furlough just before Christmas 1974. We made Huntington, West Virginia, our home base and moved into a missionary house provided by Grace Gospel Church, Anna Gay's home church. This house was located on Hughes Street in West Huntington.

Of course, we were in constant contact with Trans World Radio (TWR) as we prepared to move to Guam. At this point, the FCC (Federal Communications Commission) was still reviewing the proposed license application submitted by TWR to establish short-wave and medium wave transmitter sites on Guam.

Our furlough was extended, and our departure for Guam was put on hold pending the decision of the FCC. It would be counterproductive for us to move to Guam only to find out that a license would not be granted and have to return to the States and relocate on a different field.

This provided us opportunities to spend more time with family and friends in West Virginia and Kentucky and Georgia (where my folks had relocated with their missionary service at Source of Light Ministries).

Our family was not used to cold weather and did not have any winter clothes. Gaylene and Philip had never seen snow but soon learned how much fun it was to make snowmen and throw snowballs. We all borrowed winter coats and sweaters, hats and caps, and gloves and scarves to stay warm when outdoors. My super thick-lensed glasses were continually steaming up, as usual. We all survived the cold, snowy winter months in the Ohio Valley and were very happy to see the arrival of the warming Spring temperatures of 1975.

It was at this time that the FCC approved the Trans World Radio application and, the license was issued for the Guam medium wave and shortwave transmitting facilities. TWR set our departure date for late May, and we began preparing for our travel to the island of Guam. But we had encountered a problem with Anna Gay's health and soon discovered that she had contracted hepatitis. Our big question: "Will this mean our departure will be further delayed?" We committed our dilemma to the Lord for His will to be done. After several blood tests in the local hospital, the doctor figured that Anna Gay's health problem was in remission, and he gave his approval for us to depart in May with certain restrictions.

1. Break up the trip and do not fly all the way from the East Coast, to the West Coast, to Hawaii, and on to Guam.
2. Stay in an air-conditioned home for several weeks after arriving on Guam, and get plenty of rest.
3. See a medical doctor immediately after arriving on the island, and very carefully follow his instructions.

It was with eager anticipation, with apprehension for Anna Gay (and me), that our family of four traveled to Chatham, New Jersey, to receive our airline tickets and updated information concerning my responsibilities on this new TWR mission field. In late May 1975, we departed from Newark, New Jersey, headed to California, and on to Hawaii. I arranged to spend a couple of days and nights in Hawaii before continuing our flights to Japan and then on to Guam. It was a rough trip, especially for Anna Gay, but the Lord helped us.

A family from another mission on Guam had already left for furlough when we arrived, and we were able to live in their air-conditioned home for several months for Anna Gay's total recovery.

During our furlough time, I had gathered a good amount of information about the island of Guam. Guam is a strategic location with bases representing every branch of the United States military services. Agana, the capitol, is located in the center part of the island. Guam is one of five U.S. territories; its 209 square miles is one of the islands surrounded by the Pacific Ocean, and it is part of the Northern Mariana Islands. The Mariana Trench, the deepest section of ocean in the world (over 35,000 feet deep), is located just a few miles off the southeastern coast of Guam. Guam is about the same distance from the Equator as Bonaire, but it did not have the strong trade winds. Instead it is very hot and humid, is hilly, and is covered with dense jungle.

I soon discovered Guam was a place that would play havoc with my natural ability to perspire profusely, which translated to steamed-up and sweat-dripped thick-lensed eyeglasses. Yes, there was no mistaking the fact that I was continuing my journey through the Myopic Zone.

TWR missionaries, the Arthurs, had already arrived on Guam to do the preliminary groundwork for constructing the broadcasting facilities. The very day we arrived, the Navy Seabees brought earth-moving equipment to the Nimitz Hill location (overlooking the U.S. Naval ship base at Apra Harbor) where TWR had secured property for the studio building, the medium wave transmitter building, and antenna tower.

I began work immediately by sorting and preparing electrical cables that would be used to provide power to the transmitter building to be located about 800 feet below the ridge where the mobile home was placed that would serve as the TWR studio and offices. I also helped direct the bulldozing and grading operation that cut a road from the top of Nimitz Hill down to the site of the transmitter building and tower base. These areas had to be graded and smoothed. The terrain was pretty rough with gullies and ravines covered with sword grass.

Once the road was cut into the hillside, we could haul down the materials needed for constructing the cement block transmitter building. We also had to haul down the tower base insulator, the equipment for the anchor points, and the twenty-foot tower sections needed to erect the 1,000 foot antenna tower. By this time, several more TWR missionaries had arrived to help with the construction.

Before the tower could be erected, we needed to dig holes for the three concrete and steel reinforced anchor points where the cables would be attached to hold the tower secure. I spent many days operating a jack hammer to dig down into earth, rock, and coral. Of course, I sweat profusely in the hot, tropic sun and had to use my big red bandana handkerchiefs to mop sweat from my face and eye-glasses. Unfortunately, I could not see well enough to work without my thick-lensed glasses, and they kept steaming up and sliding down my nose, almost falling into the pit I was digging.

Fortunately, Anna Gay was recovering well from her bout with hepatitis. She was feeling good enough to help some of the other wives paint the twenty-foot tower sections. This was done on the ground before the sections were assembled. Even our young children, Gaylene and Philip, helped with the painting.

Erecting the antenna tower had its challenges. First, the base insulator had to be securely mounted on its concrete pad. Then a twenty-foot tower section was mounted on top of it which had to be temporarily guyed with cables. A special reinforced tower section, referred to as a "gin pole," was clamped to the side of this first section of tower. A cable was run through a pulley on top of the gin pole (which extended above the section) in order to pull the next tower section up where it could be maneuvered into place and bolted to the first section.

Temporary cables were attached to the second section, the gin pole was "jumped," and attached to the second section. This same procedure was followed until all of the tower sections were stacked on top of each other, making the 1,000 foot antenna tower. Permanent steel cables, with large insulators between sections, were attached to the anchor points and tightened to proper tension pressures.

TWR had secured a winch truck designed especially for pulling tower sections up the tower. The truck was not quite ready when we wanted to begin erecting the tower. Someone (no, not me) had the idea of using the rear hub of a Ford station wagon as capstan to raise the first sections of tower. After the vehicle was blocked up, a heavy rope was attached to the gin pole and run around the wheel hub. A couple of men had to hang onto the rope and pull with all their might while someone else gently stepped on the gas. This was a rather precarious procedure and, after raising two sections, it was obvious this method was extremely dangerous. So, the tower erection was discontinued until the winch truck was available for use. It worked so much better, and it certainly was a much safer operation.

The TWR facilities, located on Nimitz Hill, included the medium wave 10,000 watt transmitter housed in a cement block building, the medium wave broadcasting tower, the single-wide mobile home that housed the studios and offices, and an emergency generator.

I helped put the transmitter together, connecting the wiring, and carried out routine maintenance and electronic inspections. I also wired the studio equipment used for originating broadcasts and feeding programming to the transmitter. I was on call 24/7 in the event there was a problem. We wanted to keep any "down time" to a minimum.

The medium wave transmitter was issued the call letters KTWG by the FCC. The first morning we put KTWG on the air with regular broadcasting, Dave Arthurs and I were at the transmitter building to make certain all systems were functioning correctly. They were, and we began our trek back up to the studio. Half way up the hill, I turned to look down at the transmitter building and antenna and saw a beautiful double rainbow arched over the tower and thought of the promise in God's Word from Isaiah 55:11: "So shall my word be that goeth forth out of my mouth: it shall not return unto me void, but it shall accomplish that which I please, and it shall prosper in the thing whereto I sent it."

Anytime I needed to check the transmitter, the tower base insulator, or the guy cables, as a safety precaution, the studio operator had to stay in the building on the Nimitz Hill ridge while I made the trek down to the transmitter site. After shutting down the transmitter for the night, I announced, "I'm going over the hill!" and head out into the blackness of night with a powerful flashlight. I always ran into many spider webs as I fought my way down the path that was overgrown with tall sword grass. I had to clean the gooey, sticky webs off my eyeglasses when I got to the transmitter building.

My testing usually took an hour or so. Then, I headed back up the hill and, by that time, the spiders had re-attacked their webs, so I had to deal with the issue all over again.

When the missionaries who owned the house where we were temporarily staying returned to Guam, we moved to a house that we rented in the village of Santa Rita. This house was not air-conditioned, and we could sure tell the difference.

Our next door neighbors were Guamanians and made us feel right at home. Our house was located in a higher spot on the island that overlooked Apra Harbor. The house was constructed of cement block with a poured concrete slab roof that covered everything but the front room. That room originally was a porch and, at some point, it had been closed in with cement blocks, and a metal roof had been built over it.

At the house, I was able to put up a couple of ten-foot tower sections that had been discarded and abandoned by a communications operation. The tower sections were made available to ham radio operators. I mounted a vertical antenna on top of the tower and was back on the air. I had operated on Bonaire with call signs PJ4BG and PJ9BG. Now I was operating from Guam with my new assigned call from the FCC: KG6JFW.

As soon as we had the medium wave station, KTWG, on the air on Nimitz Hill, work on the shortwave facilities became top priority. The site for the shortwave transmitters and antennas was located at Merizo in the southern part of Guam. Everything had to be taken to Merizo by truck; this included the equipment for excavating; the materials for the transmitter building; the tower sections, cables, insulators, and wire for the antennas; the electrical components and wires for the transmitters; and eventually the two 100,000 watt shortwave transmitters.

We had to make many, many trips on winding, narrow roads up and around some pretty good-size hills (which we called mountains on Guam). Once again, the Navy Seabees were a great help to TWR. (They were happy to use these times as training exercises for the newer servicemen who lacked on the job training.)

Sometimes these training exercises resulted in near disaster. We were able to get the Seabees to bring heavy equipment back to Nimitz Hill. The project was to cut a road from the ridge down to the transmitter building. Apparently, the bulldozer operator did not understand the plan. He saw the building down over the hill and headed his bulldozer straight for it, not following the contour of the hill or the previously graded road. He plowed through tall sword grass, paying no attention to the terrain. The operator had to stop when he could no longer see what was ahead. It's a good thing he stopped when he did because had he proceeded just a few more feet, he would have dropped over a 10-foot embankment! The Seabees had to bring in another bulldozer to cut a road down to the stuck machine. They finally dragged it back to the top of the ridge, loaded it onto a trailer, hauled their equipment away, and didn't come back.

Later on during the site preparation in Merizo, a Seabee hauling a load of gravel for us hit a curve too fast and rolled the truck on its side. On another occasion, they hauled gravel to Merizo on two belly-dump trailers only to find that they could not figure how to dump the loads. So both belly-dumper rigs were driven all the way back to their base with the undumped gravel loads. In spite of these unusual and unfortunate situations, the Seabees were a tremendous help to TWR and our excavation and hauling projects as we constructed the medium wave and shortwave broadcasting facilities.

It was in 1976 that we experienced our first typhoon. Supertyphoon Pamela, as she was named, blasted Guam with winds of over 175 mph and torrents of rain! We lost half of a huge mango tree in the front yard of our house. It split in half and part of the tree hit the roof of our house and landed in the driveway where our vehicle was normally parked. I had moved it under the concrete roof overhang to within inches of the side of the house.

Our Guamanian neighbors had big breadfruit trees in their yard loaded with fruit almost ready for picking. All the breadfruit blew onto our roof along with limbs and branches. It was a real mess, but praise the Lord our family of four was unharmed. During the height of the storm, the wooden framework and the metal roof over the former side porch (now the living room) almost blew apart.

As the first half of the storm subsided, I found that metal sheets had begun to peel apart. During the eye of the storm, I climbed on the roof and securely nailed down the loose sections of metal. Then we waited, knowing the storm would again intensify and bring heavy winds and rains from the opposite direction. When the eye passed right over our village, we experienced perfect calm for over six hours. Then, the typhoon proceeded to gain strength and sounded like a dozen freight trains rumbling past our house. Again, the Lord protected our family and our house. We quoted Psalm 56:3 together many, many times. "What time I am afraid, I will trust in thee." Typhoon-strength winds continued for 18 hours.

Clean up took many, many weeks at home in Santa Rita and up on Nimitz Hill. Our studio building was tied down with anchors and did not sustain any major damage, and the cement block transmitter building remained intact. The guy cables kept the antenna tower from falling, but it was twisted slightly. We corrected this by retensioning the guy cables at the anchor points to straighten the tower.

Our main problem was the destruction of the island's power grids and water supplies. Dave Arthurs and I dragged a 2,500 watt generator over the hill to the transmitter building. We were able to get KTWG back on the air with about 1,000 watts of power, enough to provide broadcast coverage to Guam and give emergency information and announcements. At various times KTWG was the only local station on the air. We back-fed power up to the studio so essential equipment could be used for broadcasting. Dave and I just about killed ourselves, hauling gasoline down through the sword grass to our emergency generator at the transmitter building. I managed to keep my glasses on my sweaty face during those grueling trips up and down the hill.

Our village was without electrical power for six and one-half weeks, and we had no water to our home for four weeks. We used candles for light, a hibachi grill for a stove, and a cooler for the cups of ice that were given to us by Navy friends. (The Navy base at Apra Harbor and the other bases had backup generators for power and desalination plants for producing drinkable water.) The Navy base opened its gates so civilians could go to the galley for food and meals. What a blessing that was!

It was a miracle that only one person on the island was killed during the typhoon, but mass destruction could be seen everywhere with palm trees blown over, downed power poles and lines, and wood frame homes demolished. Only concrete block structures with con-crete roofs remained intact. Property damage was estimated to be more than 400 million dollars. Power crews came from Japan, Hawaii, and other countries to help with the power restoration.

Relatives of our neighbors stood in line for eight hours to buy a 100-pound block of ice from the ice plant when it was able to resume production. They chopped off a chunk and gave it to us. Wow! It was as if they had given us a piece of gold!

While living on Guam, we experienced many tropical storms, typhoons, and earthquakes. Fortunately, none were as potent as Super-Typhoon Pamela.

In September 1977, we were able to begin broadcasting with the two 100,000 watt shortwave transmitters from Merizo. KTWR was on the air! The KTWR facilities had been dedicated by the President, Dr. Paul E. Freed. Island dignitaries were also on hand, including the Governor, U.S. Representative A.B. Wan Pat, and a U.S. Navy Admiral, who represented the military community.

The KTWR facilities included huge curtain antenna arrays that could be slued to direct the broadcast signals to various parts of the world. Initially, broadcasts were directed to Mainland China, Japan, Korea, the Philippine Islands, Vietnam, and Kenya in East Africa.

I helped build and wire the cabinets of the two shortwave transmitters. I also manned several broadcast shifts at night in

Merizo that ended at midnight. This required driving home to Santa Rita in the blackness of night, a real challenge with the myopic condition of my eyes.

I was driving home very late (actually very early) one New Year's Eve after we signed off at midnight. As I approached the small village of Umatac, I saw mobs of revelers milling around on the main street where I had to drive. People were beating on metal garbage cans and lids, making all kinds of racket to welcome in the New Year. Even the police jeep was driving up and down the street dragging a half demolished garbage can.

I inched my way up the street, attempting to not run over anyone. Suddenly, a man appeared right in front of my little Datsun pickup truck and forced me to stop. He held a plate of gross-looking chicken in his hand and insisted that I take some. I did, and ate some while he stared at me. He then moved aside and let me pass. I was sure glad to get out of there and leave the mass confusion behind where many were having a great party of eating and drinking (not water, but tuba, an alcoholic beverage made from fermented coconut milk).

All in all, the Guamanian people were very friendly. They always wrongly assumed that since we were from the U.S. Mainland that we were either school teachers or military-type people.

The island public and private schools had a good number of teachers from the United States, the Philippines, as well as from the Mariana Islands. It was the same for the University of Guam (UOG) where students came from Guam as well as from many of the outlying islands such as Truk, Ponepei, Saipan, and Tinian. We became good friends with the missionary couple who ministered at UOG through the Southern Baptist Student Union.

As we began to explore the churches on Guam, we discovered that there were three Southern Baptist Churches located in Tamuning, Agana, and Santa Rita; a Conservative Baptist Church located in Agana; and several other denominational churches. Guam had a Seventh Day Adventist (SDA) church that also conducted a private school. The SDA had a very good medical facility on the island, as well. Guam was predominately Catholic, and each village had its own priest and Catholic church. The main Catholic cathedral was located in Agana, the capital of the island.

We attended Marianas Baptist Church in Santa Rita. It was strange to hear the pastor ask each Sunday, "Who's leaving the island this week?" Many of the folks in the church were involved with the military, and sooner or later, they would be transferred from Guam to other parts of the world. We could sense some discouragement on the part of the pastor as he began to lose some faithful members and workers in the church. Our situation was different, and we could add some stability to the church so we got involved in Sunday school classes and helped with the youth activities.

In 1977, Gaylene, our oldest child who was born on Bonaire, started grade school. We found that the Guam public schools were not the greatest, so we enrolled her in the SDA private school. Other missionary kids attended this school as well as many Guamanian kids. First, though, Anna Gay and I made certain that only regular school subjects were taught, and no mention was made of SDA principles and practices, and no such classes of this nature were taught either.

Two years later in 1979, we enrolled Philip, our second child who was born on Bonaire, in the SDA school, as well. On many occasions, Gaylene and Philip brought some weird-spelled words home from school. They picked these up mainly from their Filipino teachers who spoke with a unique accent in their pronunciation of English words.

We welcomed our third child into the world on March 21, 1979, when Holly Beth was born at Guam Memorial Hospital. Anna Gay was in extended labor, as usual, and for many hours we paced the hospital halls together. A call had been placed to her doctor who had his office at the SDA clinic.

While waiting for the big moment, we kept hearing a Dr. Segesie being paged over the hospital PA system. We had seen him and heard his high-pitched, squeaky voice several times as we passed each other in the hall as he hurried from one seemingly emergency to another.

In the meantime, Anna Gay's doctor still had not arrived for the delivery, and we kept on walking up one hallway and down another, always within close proximity to the delivery room. Suddenly, it was time! "Where's our doctor?" Nobody knew! Soon Anna Gay was being rushed to the delivery room. I had permission to be present for the birth of Holly, and I was tossed a gown, a mask, and a covering for my head (that looked like a shower cap) and coverings for my shoes. I was frantically trying to get all this paraphernalia on without losing my eyeglasses while running down the hall behind the orderly who was shoving Anna Gay on the gurney behind a nurse who was clearing the way! I never did get the shoe thingies on but followed the procession into the delivery room anyway. While all this was going on, I remember hearing the urgent pleas blaring over the PA system: "Dr. Segesie, report to the delivery room stat!" "Dr. Segesie, will you please get to the delivery room immediately!" "We have an emergency in the delivery room!"

Dr. Segesie came roaring into the delivery room like a run-away freight train! That's right, the Filipino doctor with the high-pitched voice delivered Holly Beth into the world. He did a great job, and so did Anna Gay, and so did I!

Just as the excitement in the delivery room died down, Anna Gay's SDA doctor came rushing into the room dressed in his scrubs. All he could do was congratulate everyone and tell Anna Gay she did a good job. He also thanked our newly acquainted Dr. Segesie for standing in for him. Holly Beth was our third and final child, our caboose.

By this time, our family had moved from the tiny village of Santa Rita to a nicer house located beside the road leading to and from the Naval Magazine Base (where bombs, rockets, ammunition, and weapons of all kinds were securely stored for ships, planes, and submarines). On many occasions, convoys of military vehicles escorted by police on the road and helicopters in the air, passed by our house either going to or coming from the Naval Mag. We never knew if it was a training exercise with empty trucks or if the convoy consisted of trucks loaded with deadly ammunition.

Guam experienced a lot of destruction due to intense military action during World War II. The island was eventually liberated from the Japanese forces after fierce bombardments by the United States military from sea, land, and air. On several occasions, especially after brush fires, I would take our son Philip into the jungle ("boonies") to look for war relics. We had to fight mosquitoes and sword grass, and I had to protect my very thick-lensed glasses. But we really enjoyed those expeditions together.

We found clips of bullets that were very unusual in that they could be used in both the Japanese as well as in the American rifles. We found a huge tank wrench, a smashed mess kit and canteen, some fragments of batteries, some gun cleaning tools, hand grenades (which we did not disturb), and three mortar rounds (which looked safe enough since the powder had become crystallized). I found out later, these had to be destroyed at the Naval Magazine as a normal procedure and for safety reasons.

Live bombs were sometimes unearthed around the island during excavation projects. These were always treated with great respect and carefully taken to the Naval Magazine where they would be safely blown up. On more than one occasion, we heard a blast come from down the Naval Mag Road and would say, "Well, there goes another one!"

At special times throughout the year, the U.S. military bases opened their gates to let civilians inspect various pieces of equipment (that were not considered top secret at the time). We have taken our family inside a floating dry dock, to ride on a Navy harbor tugboat, on a tour inside a Polaris nuclear-powered submarine, to ride in a Navy helicopter, inside an Air Force B-29 jet bomber, and to see other Navy planes and ships, as well as Air Force planes.

Every year, just before Christmas, the civilian and military communities joined forces to collect items for people living on the Northern Mariana Islands. These donated items included canned goods, assorted tools, canvas (for their sailing boats), flashlights, nails and screws, cooking utensils, toys for the kids, and many other useful things. The military packed everything into wooden crates, secured them with parachutes, and designated which crates were to be delivered to which island. These crates were then transported to the outer islands by C-130 Air Force planes. These particular transport planes were used to fly missions into typhoons as well as to perform air drops. Two representatives of the news media were permitted to fly on each of the Operation Christmas Drop missions.

I represented KTWG on one such mission after receiving the necessary clearances from the Air Force. Everyone on this flight was given a boxed lunch to eat en route. After strapping ourselves into the seating harnesses toward the back end of the aircraft, the C-130 Hercules plane headed north from Andersen Air Force Base. The flying time for this mission was just over two hours before we reached our destination. Of course, there was no runway on the small island so the crates had to be shoved out the back of the plane. The parachutes were automatically deployed which set the crates some-what gently down on the beach.

In preparation for this exercise, the plane made several diving passes over the island as the loadmaster leaned out a door on the side of the aircraft and threw out rolls of toilet paper. This helped him determine how the wind currents were blowing and at what approximate speed as the streams of white toilet paper unfurled. By observing this, he was able to direct the pilot on the correct course to fly. Then, it was fascinating to watch as the crew opened the back doors of the aircraft. As these opened, the crew (who were securely strapped on tether harnesses) positioned the first crate on the back ramp of the plane. The loadmaster gave a signal as the plane pulled out of the dive over the beach, and the crate was shoved out. This was done for each crate. It was neat to see the parachutes open and the crates drop down onto the beach, avoiding the water on one side and the palm trees on the other.

This is one of the most memorable experiences I have had in my journey through the Myopic Zone. I did not lose my eyeglasses, but for some reason my stomach became upset with all the dives, climbs, and banks, and I brought up a good bit of my boxed lunch and deposited it into a convenient air sickness bag. Enough said about that!

Another memorable experience was enjoyed by our whole family during a planned special commemoration of the Navy's 201st birthday. School children were encouraged to draw and submit posters depicting the event. More than 1,000 posters were submitted, and our Gaylene's poster was awarded second place in her grade level. (I did not help her; she did the drawing all by herself!) As a result, our family was invited to be a part of the birthday bash hosted by Rear Admiral Kent J. Carroll and his staff at the Navy Command Center on Nimitz Hill (ComNavMarianas). The other winners and their families were also invited. The Admiral presented Gaylene with a nice certificate and a U.S. Navy cap. The kids (12 in all) who won first, second, and third place in their grade levels received the same. A huge cake in the shape of Guam had been prepared, and on it were placed 201 candles. All 201 candles were lit and then blown out by the kids. Then the Admiral proceeded to cut the cake with his sword. That was really impressive. This event certainly was a most unusual and unforgettable experience.

Holly Beth was about to outgrow her crib which we had to put in the hallway of our house on Naval Mag Road. It was apparent that we needed a bigger house, with more bedrooms. So, we moved into a four-bedroom house in Hyundai (a housing development in another part of Santa Rita) where some other TWR missionary families were now living. In fact, at this time, TWR was using one of the houses as a recording studio. The rooms held a lot of recording equipment (microphones, turntables, amplifiers, mixers, tape decks, and recording tapes).

Since TWR had valuable equipment in this house, I felt it needed to be protected, so I set up a motion alarm system connected to a bull horn on the roof. I finished the installation, and that very night it proved to be invaluable! In the middle of the night, the signal alarm blasted away. A nearby TWR missionary heard it and called the authorities. I was called, as well. The front door was discovered wide open, but nothing was missing. Further investigation showed the small bathroom window had been pried open. It followed the same MO of previous burglaries in the neighborhood. The bathroom window of an unoccupied house would be pried open, a child would be lowered into the bathtub, and he would then go into the living room and unlock the front door from the inside. It was a quick snatch, grab, and leave with as much loot as possible. However, in our case, the siren on the roof began blaring as soon as motion was detected, and this scared the would-be robbers off without taking anything. That was a rather rude awakening for them, but praise the Lord, it was a blessing for us. It was such an evidence of God's perfect timing in me being able to get the alarm system operational at just the right time!

As the TWR ministry continued to expand with more broad-casting hours with more languages, the staff continued to grow. We began planning for the construction of a permanent larger office and studio complex on Nimitz Hill to replace the original modular house that was used from the beginning. I helped design the new two-story building which contained several studios, control rooms, and offices, including a tape and record library room, kitchen and lunch room, and a shop for testing and repairing the electronic and studio equipment. I did a lot of drafting work on the plans prior to actual construction.

All of us TWR men missionaries, and even some of the women, helped with the building construction in addition to maintaining our current studio and transmitter programming and broadcasting shifts. This really was a major project! I had to use several big red bandanas to wipe away the sweat from my face and eyeglasses, especially while working outside in the sun.

About this time, I was given a new assignment. I was appointed to take over the position of Program and Frequency

Coordinator. I was now responsible for the operation of the studios and control rooms that were used to produce new programs and prepare blocks of broadcasts in the various languages that were aired from the KTWR shortwave transmitters in Merizo.

We received programs that were produced by nationals in recording studios located in Japan, Taiwan, the Philippines, Hong Kong, Korea, and Vietnam. These programs, which were recorded on regular-size tape, had to be copied onto other larger-size tapes and prepared in language blocks. These long-play tapes were taken daily to the shortwave transmitter site in Merizo and fed to the transmitters on the tape decks on site in the transmitter building.

I began producing a new shortwave program in English called "DX Listeners' Log." This program was especially geared to those who listened to shortwave broadcasting stations in all parts of the world. The listeners would write down ("log") information about a specific shortwave radio station such as the station call letters, time of the broadcast, content of the broadcast, and a request for a station QSL card (a verification card with the station's call letters, and transmitter specifications, and operating frequency). If the listener's information about the KTWR broadcast was correct, we would send him or her a TWR verification card.

My program included current frequency changes made by international shortwave broadcasting stations, tips and hints to help shortwave listeners in their listening and logging, and a devotional-type challenge from the Word of God. I really enjoyed doing the research, writing, and recording for "DX Listener's Log." KTWR received many comments about the program from listeners who would always be sure to request a KTWR QSL verification card. I also designed new QSL cards for KTWG and KTWR, and I enjoyed those challenges, as well.

Another interesting aspect of my new position had to do with planning and coordinating the meter bands and frequencies that would be used by KTWR in order to avoid interference from other international shortwave broadcasting stations. All of this advance coordination had to be filed with the FCC (Federal Communications Commission) in Washington, D.C. I worked with a scientific engineer in England who projected which meter bands would provide TWR the best propagation for future frequency periods. I depended on his prediction charts for the work that I needed to do. This was quite a technical challenge to say the least.

Trans World Radio began receiving mail from listeners to the shortwave broadcasts almost immediately after KTWR became operational. Some told of receiving Jesus Christ as their Savior. Others had spiritual questions that required a response. Still others sent reception reports requesting a KTWR QSL card. It was not too long after we began the shortwave broadcasting that we put in place a Follow-up Department.

Anna Gay and I were familiar with the materials printed and distributed by Source of Light Ministries (SLM) since my folks were now serving with that ministry. During our furloughs, we spent time with them at the mission headquarters in Madison, Georgia. I introduced the concept of using SLM English Bible correspondence courses with TWR listeners. In 1982, TWR began offering these Bible study lessons to listeners as a follow-up tool. This gave the staff who worked in this department a direct, personal ministry with radio listeners, and it was a real blessing to both our TWR missionary staff and the unseen listeners in many parts of the world.

A bit later on, TWR produced an English program called "Shortwave Bible School" that was based on SLM printed Bible study lessons. As this was developed, we changed the program name to "Source of Light Bible Studies."

While serving on Guam, Anna Gay and I began a personal ministry with military men and women. Every Friday evening, we opened our home to anyone who wanted to come for a home-cooked meal prepared by Anna Gay. Following the meal, we enjoyed a time of singing with Gaylene playing the piano. Then, I conducted a Bible study which concluded our evening fellowship time. We had military men and women coming from the Naval Air Station, the Navy Band, the Apra Harbor Navy Base, the Seabee Base, and other military installations around the island.

A major highlight while serving with TWR on Guam was the opportunity to assist in planting a church. We encouraged veteran missionaries that we had known for many years to come to Guam and establish a church. It was thrilling to finally have the first service of Pacific Independent Bible Church. Anna Gay and our kids were on hand for this service, but I was actually in Mainland China at the time in connection with our TWR Chinese broadcasts and underground listener follow-up.

The shortwave broadcasting continued to expand, and as Program Coordinator, I had to travel to the various locations where program blocks were being recorded. This required trips to Hong Kong, Taiwan, Japan, and the Philippines. It was during one of these trips to Hong Kong in 1977 that I was able to take a day trip with two other TWR leaders. We traveled from Kowloon, through the New Territories, to the Mainland China border town of Lowu.

Construction of the shortwave facilities on Guam was just about completed and soon KTWR would be "on the air." At that time, no foreigners could cross the railroad bridge from the New Territories into the Mainland. But we could look across the river and see Chinese people in the countryside where our broadcasts would soon be reaching with the Gospel. Wow! We prayed and wept together as we saw this great country with its people who needed to hear the Good News of Salvation in the Chinese language. China was one of our primary target areas!

It would be about a year later that I again made the journey to the border of Mainland China at Lowu. This time I was able to walk across the railroad bridge and set foot in the closed country of China which at this time was beginning to allow a limited number of foreigners across the border into the towns and cities of southern China such as Canton (now called Guangzhou), Shekou, Shenzhen, and Foshan. What an experience! Since then, I had the privilege of traveling in Mainland China nine times and Anna Gay three times.

During one of our furloughs, we were traveling across Pennsylvania on the Pennsylvania Turnpike en route to Philadelphia. After riding for a couple of hours on the turnpike, we decided that it would be nice for the children, as well as for us parents, to have a change of scenery. So we left the turnpike at the Breezewood interchange.

We left Breezewood, traveling through the mountains, heading toward our destination in York, Pennsylvania. As we were traveling down the highway, we passed a mailbox beside the road that had big letters on the side that sort of caught my eye as we whizzed along. As we continued down the road, I was trying to fit the letters and words together, because there seemed to be something very familiar about the name. After contemplating on this for several seconds, it dawned on me that the name I had seen on the mailbox was J. Otis Yoder.

After spending the last three years on the island of Guam, where we were involved with the construction of both the KTWG medium wave station and the KTWR shortwave station, I had remembered this name belonged to one of our broadcasters. We were airing "Hope For Today" which was being produced by Heralds of Hope, Inc. with the speaker being J. Otis Yoder. I knew that he was giving his address as Breezewood, Pennsylvania, and so this had to be the same person.

So I turned the car around and headed back toward the mailbox where we saw this familiar name. We pulled into the driveway of this very large, old, frame farmhouse. We went to the door and introduced ourselves, and were received very warmly by the staff who were working in the house when we arrived. We were thrilled to have the opportunity of meeting Dr. Yoder, his wife, and several of the staff members who were involved in the "Heralds of Hope" ministry.

The Lord's timing in all of this was perfect, since the moment of our arrival was about the only time that particular day that we would have found the Yoders present. We had a wonderful time of fellowship with them, and were able to tell them firsthand about the ministry of Trans World Radio on Guam. We were also able to give them some helpful suggestions and information regarding their follow-up program and for the procedures that they were using in mailing letters back to listeners who had written in response to their radio broadcast.

Just a few days prior to our visit there, they had received a letter from Norm Olson in the TWR International Headquarters, telling them of some recent letters (in English) that had just been received from listeners in Mainland China who heard their radio broadcasts from KTWR Guam. I believe that these were some of the first responses that came to Trans World Radio from Mainland China since the regular broadcasting began in September 1977.

Our visit with J. Otis Yoder took place in June of 1978. At that time they were in the process of completing a new building which was located just across the highway from the present farmhouse that they were using for their headquarters. It was great for us to be able to meet one of our broadcasters personally and to spend a brief time visiting with him and with his staff. The Lord really used that "chance visit" to encourage both Dr. J. Otis Yoder and his staff, as well as ourselves, as we were preparing to proceed with our furlough ministries in the York and Philadelphia areas of Pennsylvania.

Journeying through the Myopic Zone on the island of Guam certainly had its challenges. Since the island was located 13 degrees north of the Equator, the weather basically was hot and humid, with very little breeze (except when typhoons passed close or right over the island). I stayed drenched in sweat most of the time. This also had a negative affect on my super-thick bifocal-lensed eyeglasses. The heavy glasses kept sliding down my nose, and I had to keep pushing them back up so I could see.

Someone raised the question, "Why don't you get contact lenses?" This time, unlike on Bonaire, I began to seriously "look into" this possibility. There were no trade winds blowing; there was not much in the way of dirt and grit to get into my eyes. A couple told me that they would cover the cost for me to get my first pair of contact lenses. That clinched it!

During the initial appointment with our SDA optician, I almost passed out when the eye doctor placed a contact on my eyeball. Good grief, he was placing a foreign object in my eye! I got over the initial shock, and after further examinations, the doctor determined I would need hard contact lenses because of my extreme myopic condition. Soft lenses could not be made for my super-nearsighted eyes.

I finally learned how to properly use the contact lenses after weeks and weeks of practice putting them in and taking them out, using the correct wetting and soaking solutions. Basically, they were the first things to go into my eyes in the morning and the very last things to come out before going to bed at night.

Believe it or not, I used the same pair of hard contacts for 13 years. Many times, I came awfully close to losing one or both, but praise the Lord, I always found them. The right contact had a tendency to slide off my pupil if I sneezed or if I made a sudden movement with my head. It would not fall out, but instead would move way back in the corner of my eye. (It felt like it was touching my right ear!) When this happened, the vision in my left eye remained normal, but naturally out of focus and fuzzy in my contactless eye. When it dislocated, I had to have Anna Gay take a small plunger-type device and gently reach way back in the side of my eye and lift the contact out. Thankfully, it remained stuck to the plunger, and I would remove it, clean it, and stick it back on my pupil where it was supposed to be.

Those contact lenses really improved my vision. I no longer had the distortion in my peripheral vision that the thick eyeglass lenses caused. Things appeared more natural, and that was great.

Since the hard contact lenses tended to maintain the shape of my pupil, they stabilized my vision. Normally, my eyeglass prescription had to be made stronger each year in order to keep my vision close to 20/20.

Eventually, my myopic condition got to the point that even hard contact lenses could not be made to the strength of the prescription I needed. But in the meantime, I rather enjoyed journeying through the Myopic Zone with my hard contact lenses instead of my heavy, super-thick bifocals.

One time I was traveling in Asia. I was at the Hong Kong International Airport waiting to board my flight. I moved my head too quickly, and suddenly my right contact disappeared. I knew immediately where it was (way back in the side of my eye). And Anna Gay was not with me! Panic! And a prayer: "Lord, please help me get this contact out and back in place without losing it."

I slowly made my way to the nearest restroom, spread out my handkerchief on the sink (to catch the contact if it fell out), and pulled out my little plunger. Very carefully, I touched the side of the contact with the plunger, and slowly slid it back onto the pupil (something I had never done before even though I tried many times). Praise the Lord! He guided my hand, plunger, and contact safely back into place. And I could once again see normally! And I happily continued my journey and flight.

As our children grew older, Anna Gay and I sought the Lord's direction in making a change in our field of ministry with Trans World Radio. We were concerned about the allergies that Holly, our youngest was experiencing. The allergy doctor ran a series of tests and discovered Holly was allergic to molds and mildews. Our house did not have central air, and we could not afford to run the window units continuously. Due to high humidity levels, green mold began to grow inside our closet doors. Our oldest daughter, Gaylene, as a teenager, was maturing into a beautiful young lady and the Guamanian boys were beginning to eye her. Our middle child, Philip, was a preteen and thoroughly enjoyed the outdoors and island living.

After consultation with TWR leadership, it was determined that a transfer to another location was in order. Moving to the Monte Carlo studios was not an option for us since our kids would have to attend boarding school in Germany. So, I accepted a position in the Trans World Radio International Headquarters in Chatham, New

Jersey. I would serve as Assistant Candidate Secretary and not as a transmitter engineer. Actually, this was fine because during the past few years on Guam, I moved out of the technical work and was involved more and more in administrative duties.

As we made some personnel changes on Guam, I began training a co-worker to take over my responsibilities of Program Coordinator, and another co-worker to take over the production of the program "DX Listeners' Log." But I retained the duties of Frequency Coordinator for KTWR.

We had to sell most of our furniture and appliances. We did keep our teak dining room table and chairs, as well as the teak china cabinet. The kids sorted through their things to determine what we would be able to ship back to the States.

I placed all of the things we wanted to keep in the middle of the living room and calculated the size of the wooden crate we needed. Everything fit nicely inside the crate as we packed and closed it with the help of fellow-missionaries. This was shipped to the New York City harbor.

We would need a vehicle in New Jersey, and I found we could purchase a Subaru station wagon on Guam and ship it to New York for less than it would cost to purchase it in the United States. So, I arranged to have the Subaru shipped inside a container. Our family actually saw the cargo ship leave Apra Harbor that was carrying our earthly household possessions and vehicle away from Guam, bound for the harbor in New York City. And we prayed that all would arrive safely, including our family as we prepared for the long journey from the Western Pacific to the East Coast of the U.S.A.

My journey, our journey, through the Myopic Zone was about to take on a new dimension, and we eagerly anticipated seeing how the Lord would help us in this major transition from the slow island-pace of living to the fast-paced hustle and bustle of city life.

And so our family of five departed from the tropical island of Guam on September 29, 1983. At that time Gaylene was twelve and three-quarters; Philip was ten and one-half; Holly Beth was four and one-half; and both Anna Gay and I were forty-two.

## 13

# TWR - CHATHAM, NEW JERSEY (1984-1987)

---

*Behold, the eye of the Lord is upon them that fear him, upon them that hope in his mercy; to deliver their soul from death, and to keep them alive in famine.* Psalm 33:18-19

A major transition was about to take place that would affect our entire family. Our move to the Trans World Radio International Headquarters in Chatham, New Jersey, meant new responsibilities for me; a change in the role of missionary, wife, and mother for Anna Gay; and the need for Gaylene, Philip, and Holly to meet and make new friends. This also meant the need to attend new schools for Gaylene and Philip. Holly would be starting school in about a year.

Anna Gay and I, and our kids, drove to a vantage point overlooking Apra Harbor the day I knew the cargo ship carrying our personal effects, furniture, and Subaru station wagon would be headed out to sea. As the ship passed from our view, I prayed for the Lord's protection during the long sea voyage from the island of Guam to the harbor in New York City.

Yes, our family was just about to experience many new adventures in my journey through the Myopic Zone.

Now that our earthly possessions were en route to the United States, our thoughts turned to packing suitcases and preparing for our airline reservations for mid-September 1983, which included Korean Airlines flight 008 from Gimpo International Airport in Seoul, Korea, to John F. Kennedy International Airport in New York City, with a stopover in Anchorage, Alaska. We would first fly from Guam to Tokyo, Japan, and then on to Seoul for our flight to the States.

Then, on September 1, 1983, the news quickly spread around the world that Korean Airlines flight 007 was shot down over the Sea of Japan. All 269 passengers and crew were killed. The Boeing 747 jumbo jet was en route from New York City to Seoul via Anchorage, Alaska. It reportedly had strayed into Soviet airspace around the time of a scheduled missile test.

What a tragedy this was! I took special note that our scheduled flight to New York was on flight 008, flying the same route only in the reverse direction. I asked the Lord for wisdom in what to do about our flying that reverse route in less than two weeks after the incident. It was too late to change reservations to another airline. Korean Airlines offered a lower rate than Northwest Orient and Pan American for our travel. Some strongly suggested that I cancel our reservations, but it was not practical to begin trying to make new reservations with new international flight schedules. Besides, I felt that flight 008 would most likely be one of the safest flights with all the international outcry against the drastic actions that the Soviets had taken. The Lord gave us peace to proceed with our plans, and we were assured that many of our family, friends, and supporters were praying for our safety.

There were a few moments of apprehension now and then throughout the long flight from Korea to Alaska. Then, as we landed in Anchorage without incident, a loud cheer and applause erupted inside the aircraft. We were safely back on United States soil! Praise the Lord! There was an even greater response as we landed at JFK International Airport, the final destination of Flight 008.

Trans World Radio (TWR) owned a couple of houses in Chatham, New Jersey, and we arranged to rent the spit-level one that was located at 82 Woodland Road, just a few blocks from the TWR Home Office. I especially liked this house because there was a pair of railroad tracks situated right behind the backyard fence! I could not believe my good fortune!

The New Jersey Transit operated commuter trains from points west, through Chatham, and into Hoboken, New Jersey. This rather busy line was electrified so a good many of the trains were electric passenger cars or cars pulled by electric locomotives. Some of the passenger cars were pulled by diesel engines, as well. Every so often, loud diesel engines pulled freight trains past our back yard.

It did not take long for me to realize how different the pace of living was in Chatham, in this New York Metropolitan area, compared to the slow pace of living on the island of Guam. Here it seemed like we were in a constant rat race, and, boy, it certainly did take some major adjustments for all of our family! We were experiencing reverse culture shock for sure!

It was not long after our arrival in Chatham that we were able to collect our Subaru station wagon from the New York City port.

Then, it was time to have our furniture delivered. Our crate was consolidated with other items and was scheduled to be delivered to our house on Woodland Road. On the set date, I received a call from the forwarders stating our crate was too large for the truck they had planned to use, and the delivery would be delayed. Finally, a new delivery date was set, and we were looking forward to getting our stuff. When the truck arrived, I discovered they did not even bring the crate. Instead, it had been opened at the port and the contents unloaded into the consolidator's truck. I was not too pleased to learn this, but after our personal effects and furniture were unloaded in the house, we found that nothing was missing and nothing sustained any damage. It surely was great to get our stuff unpacked and put into place in our "new" home. The only thing missing was my Guam crate wood that I had planned to use for a number of projects.

One of the first orders of business was to enroll Gaylene and Philip in the Chatham public school. They made the transition well and soon developed friendships with kids in their classes and kids in our neighborhood.

At the time of our arrival in Chatham, Trans World Radio made a move of their own from the headquarters building in town (which they had outgrown) to a new, larger office facility in the county (referred to as Chatham Township). In 1967, Anna Gay and I were involved in setting up the new headquarters building on Main Street, and now in January 1984, we were on hand to help with the move from the Main Street office to the new, larger building in Chatham Township. This is also when I began my new responsibilities as Assistant Candidate Secretary. This involved working directly with new TWR Missionary Appointees and with prospective TWR Missionary Candidates. I wrote letters, made telephone calls, set up appointments, and conducted meetings with those who expressed interest in missionary service under Trans World Radio.

Not long after "learning the ropes" in the Candidate Department, I traveled with a couple of other TWR staff to the Urbana Conference in Illinois. Many mission organizations were represented at this huge convention which was held every few years at that same location. We set up a TWR display board and handed out a lot of information and spoke personally with many who were exploring various avenues of missionary service.

I also continued my work begun on Guam as the Frequency Coordinator for the KTWR shortwave broadcasting schedules. This involved occasional trips to Washington, D.C. to meet with FCC (Federal Communications Commission) officials concerning the TWR proposed frequency assignments.

On one occasion, I was returning to Chatham by way of a flight from the National Airport in Washington to JFK in New York City. After being patted down, I walked through the security scanner and set off the alarm. "What caused that?" I thought. It couldn't be my eyeglasses with the super-thick bifocal lenses because I was now using hard contact lenses. After several times of going back and forth through the detector, each time setting off the alarm and being patted down, the officer finally told me to go on (and stop holding up the line). Later, at home, as I was handing the kids the souvenirs that I had gotten for them at the airport, I discovered an oversize metal coin I had purchased for one of them which I had stuffed into my shirt pocket. Aha, that was the mystery item that was causing the alarm to go off before my flight!

My ministry in the TWR Home Office was certainly different from what I had been doing on Guam. It was even more unusual for Anna Gay. Her primary responsibilities at this time were to our children (and to me, as her husband), but she still wanted to be involved in some area of ministry in the TWR office. However, there were no available TWR assignments. Some other mothers who had served overseas in TWR fields faced the same situation when their husbands were reassigned to duties in the TWR Headquarters.

It was not too long before I realized how much higher the cost of living was in the New York Metropolitan area compared to the island living on Guam. Our missionary support was not quite adequate for our newly-figured monthly budget. Just as some of the other missionary wives had to do, Anna Gay also had to find a part-time job while the kids were in school to supplement our support.

She found part-time secretarial work at a business right there in Chatham that handled billing for a shipping company. Believe it or not, this company was associated with the production of salt on the island of Bonaire! She met some executives who spoke Papiamento, the Antillean language we had learned during our service on Bonaire with Trans World Radio.

Another order of business was to find a church. We were introduced to Evangel Baptist Church, a Conservative Baptist Church, located a few miles away in Springfield, New Jersey. We soon learned that in this New York Metropolitan area, which included many towns and cities of all sizes, no one referred to distances in miles, but rather in "drive time." This was because of the masses of people and vehicles, and the congestion on the roads and highways, especially during rush hour.

As we tried to find our way around the congested traffic, it took a while to get used to the way the names of roads and streets changed from one side of an intersection to the other. Many motorists were impatient with us as we drove a bit slower than they did. As they blasted their horns and made faces at us, I simply smiled and waved, trying to contain my frustration. But, it was not long before I knew the roads (not necessarily their actual names) after following a co-worker to Evangel Baptist Church, turning at this light, going past that landmark, and making a jog down another side street.

Our family became active associate members of Evangel. (Anna Gay maintained her membership at her home/sending church, Grace Gospel in Huntington, West Virginia, and I maintained my membership at my home/sending church, Chelten Baptist in Dresher, Pennsylvania.) I began working with Boys Brigade, and Anna Gay began working with Pioneer Girls. Our kids were active in these groups, as well as in their Sunday school classes.

Anna Gay and I also joined a group in Evangel referred to as "Dinner for Eight." Every month or so, we would go to one of the couple's homes for a meal. We were scheduled to go to a home located in Plainfield, New Jersey, an area not familiar to us. I had been given directions to the house, and with those in hand, we drove away from our home in Chatham. As we headed south on this road, turning onto one street, then onto another street and crossing a major intersection, it began to get dark, and we could not see the names on the street signs. I knew where we were going, so I kept going, but Anna Gay insisted that we were hopelessly lost. By this time, it was totally dark, and I had to admit we were totally lost. And worst of all, it was past the time when we were supposed to begin our "Dinner for Eight" meal. Fortunately, I had the home telephone number of where we were going. This was before the advent of cell phones, so I had to find a pay phone at a service station. And I could tell we were not in a very good neighborhood, but I had no choice but to stop and call. The folks were concerned about us and were relieved to hear from me. They said we had made a wrong turn and gave us directions from our precarious location to their house. Needless to say, I heaved a sigh of relief as we pulled into the driveway and saw six faces peering out the front window. And needless to say, Anna Gay and I were very embarrassed to be one and one-half hours late for the dinner. Everyone was very gracious, and we tried to enjoy a rather cold meal. Somehow, we found our way home later (much later) in the evening without getting lost again, thanks to Anna Gay's superb memory and my defensive driving skills. I was sure ready to take out the contact lenses and give my strained and tired eyes a long rest.

Our family continued to settle into our responsibilities in Evangel Baptist Church. It was located in an area of Springfield that was heavily populated by Jewish families. There were several Jewish temples within just a few miles of the church.

Before too long, I was asked to serve on the Elder Board, and I accepted this opportunity. I had served years before as a Deacon in Chelten Baptist Church, and now I found myself serving as an Elder. Sometime later, the pastor resigned and I was asked to serve on the Search Committee. That was quite a challenge, especially since my assignment was to make certain we had someone to supply the pulpit for the Sunday services.

Our next door neighbors in Chatham were very helpful to us, unlike the neighbors on the other side. We began learning more about this New York Metropolitan area where we were now living. Our good neighbor offered to act as our tour guide on a trip from Chatham right into downtown New York City, and we accepted.

On the set morning, we caught the train (New Jersey Transit) in Chatham and rode it to Hoboken, New Jersey. Next, we traveled under the Hudson River on the PATH subway. We saw Times Square and the Radio City Music Hall and eventually ended up in Chinatown where we found the Hung Fat Restaurant. This was just a "hole in the wall" that opened into a dingy-looking eating area. I honestly felt like I was back in China. The looks and smells were very much the same. Most important, the food was delicious, and the Chinese proprietors were warm and friendly. This actually was the first of several trips our family made over the next couple of years as we occasionally treated ourselves to a train ride to New York City and to a meal at the Hung Fat Restaurant.

On one of these trips into Chinatown, our family ran into a sort of parade with a mass of people milling about in the streets. We were curious to know what this was all about so I asked a policeman what was going on. He very sharply and rudely replied, "It's Saint Patrick's Day!" Well, I knew for sure that it was not anything related to Saint Patrick here in Chinatown, especially on this June afternoon. People carrying long, colorful dragons were leading the parade, weaving from one side of the street to the other. There were people with musical instruments, followed by a woman and a man who, I now could see, were the bride and groom. Then came more people who were the well-wishers. The whole street had been blocked off to allow the procession to proceed to an apartment building that was decorated with streamers.

I urged our family to move closer to the apartment building so we could see what was going to happen next. As we made our way through the mass of people, I could see a cabbage hanging from one of the windows. But then, I almost lost my contacts when I realized the streamers up and down the building were actually fire crackers! Immediately, I urged our family to quickly go back before the fire crackers were lit. Suddenly, the long strings of fire crackers began to go off. The sound was deafening, and I'm glad we were able to get back away from the building. The blasts continued for at least fifteen minutes and, of course, they were accompanied by massive volumes of smoke that settled onto everything and everyone in the immediate area. It sounded like gunfire and looked as if a war was in progress. We got to see and experience a most unusual ceremony in New York City, one that is so typical in Mainland China.

Now that we were living and serving in the United States, we no longer had the normal four-month furlough (or Home Leave) after a three-year term on the field overseas. Instead, I was able to leave the TWR office for limited periods of time to visit with and report to our supporting churches and friends (and family). This certainly was a lot easier on everyone in the family by being away from home for just a few days or a couple of weeks compared to being uprooted for a four-month stretch.

Thankfully, our supporting churches and friends, and family were located in New Jersey, Pennsylvania, Delaware, Maryland, West Virginia, Kentucky, North Carolina, Georgia, and Texas. Other than Texas, none were located west of the Mississippi River. Some of our missionary co-workers had to travel all the way from Maine to the West Coast during their furlough times, and this was very time-consuming, costly, and tiring for them and their families.

I remember visiting one of our small supporting churches in Southeastern Kentucky, not too far from where I grew up. I had gotten a slide program from the Audio/Visual Aids Department in the

TWR office. Normally, I always checked the slide carousel and accompanying narration on the cassette tape. I ran out of time but had been assured that everything was in order and ready to go.

All went fairly well in the first part of the service. Then it was time for me to preach a message, give a report of our missionary activities, and thank the folks for their prayer and financial support. However, as I began talking from the pulpit, I was interrupted by a rather big woman who stood up and said, "David, would you please speak louder so we can all hear you?" I said, "Yes, Ma'am," tried to collect my thoughts, and continued preaching (with more volume).

The last part of my presentation was to show the slide program with the taped narrative. I was glad to finish my speaking since by this time I was almost hoarse from having to talk so loud. Five minutes into the 15-minute program, I was horrified to see a slide pop on the screen that had the image on its side! How could this happen? Then, after another three slides in their correct position, another one was upside down! Of course, everyone in the audience noticed the problem, including my lady friend who stood up and exclaimed, "David, why are some of the pictures on their sides and some are upside down? Are we supposed to stand on our heads?" I had no reply. Boy, was I embarrassed! And the lady was just speaking her mind, (in love) which she had always done in her faithful missionary service at Camp Nathanael (Scripture Memory Mountain Mission). I had known this lady ever since I attended summer camps as a camper, then as a junior counselor, and then as a summer worker and counselor while a student at Philadelphia College of Bible. Anna Gay also knew this lady and her co-worker who were members of this church. Oh, brother! Somehow I finished the slide program (with another three or four scattered slides in their incorrect orientation), apologized for the problems, sat down, and mopped the perspiration from my face with my handkerchief. My contact lenses stayed in place during the ordeal, and I was sure thankful for that. At least something worked correctly!

One Sunday, in the Fall of 1984, after the evening service at Evangel, I had to stay for a meeting of the Elder Board. Tim Walker, a Trans World Radio co-worker, was also on the Elder Board. So we arranged for Anna Gay to take Tim's family and our family home to our house in Chatham. Tim would bring me home after the meeting and collect his family. After the meeting, we left the church parking lot and headed toward the town of Summit on our way to Chatham.

Tim was driving a small, compact car. As we approached an intersection, we heard several sirens but could not tell from which direction they were coming. We had the green light, so Tim decided to go through the intersection, turn left, and then move over to the curb until we could identify from which way the emergency vehicles were coming. However, little did we realize that we were turning right into the path of a car that was fleeing from the police. The driver had crossed into the opposing lane of traffic to avoid stopping behind the vehicles that were waiting for the light to change.

I remember hearing the blare of sirens, the screech of tires, and the bone-jarring jolt as our vehicle hit the other vehicle in a head-on collision. I momentarily lost consciousness as I was jammed into the seat belt with my knees and legs smashing into the dash board. I couldn't catch my breath, and all I could hear was the constant blare of the sirens. Finally, the sirens were silenced, and I tried to make sense out of what had happened. Tim had slammed into his seat belt, but his head still hit the windshield, which resulted in a bad cut. Miraculously, I did not lose either contact lens during the accident!

The driver in the other car was slightly injured and was arrested on the spot for eluding police at high speeds, drunk and reckless driving, and possessing drugs and a fire arm.

Overlook Hospital was just a few blocks away, and emergency personnel and ambulances arrived on the scene within just a few minutes. All three of us who suffered injuries were quickly taken to the emergency room for observation and treatment. Of course, the offender was taken into custody by the police and hustled off to jail from the hospital.

Tim and I called our wives, and they immediately came with our kids to the hospital. We were able to leave after medical treatments and interviews with the police. I was required to have an ultrasound a few days later to make certain I had not suffered any damage to my kidneys and other internal organs. I was able to assure the medical people I was certain that I had not experienced any damage to my spleen (because I did not have one, since it was removed when I was in high school).

After we all got back to our house, we prayed together, thanking God for His hand of protection. Even though we both received multiple injuries, Tim and I were alive! It could have been much worse following that head-on collision and its impact that totaled the vehicle. I thought back on my two previous accidents when I could have been killed. My bicycle accident in Kentucky and my motorcycle accident on Bonaire, and now this head-on collision, were all reminders and proof that God had more missionary work for me to do and that He was protecting me in an unusual way as I continued my unusual journey through the Myopic Zone.

After living in Chatham for about a year, we found ourselves faced with another move. It had become necessary for TWR to sell some of its assets, including a couple of houses to help with its financial situation. One of those houses was ours on Woodland Road beside the railroad tracks.

With the help of friends and co-workers, we began looking at houses in neighboring towns and communities. I had already discovered that the cost of living in this New York Metropolitan area was much higher than it was living overseas. While living on Bonaire and Guam, we did not have the option of buying a house, so we had been paying rent ever since our marriage in 1964.

Now that we were back in the States, the option to buy was something I wanted to consider. The problem: we had no equity, no savings for even a down payment. A life insurance policy that was initiated by my home church when we went to the field in 1966 had earned some value. My church agreed that I could cash in the policy and that a new, better life insurance (annuity) policy would then be issued which could be used for retirement later on in life.

All of this transpired about the time that Anna Gay and I found a house in the small city of Plainfield, New Jersey. The city had experienced racial tensions and rioting in the 60's, and it was slowly growing out of the stigma which that had caused. We were able to find more house at a lower price in Plainfield than in some of the surrounding towns.

During a three-day window, the down payment requirement was extremely low for those who qualified. Somehow, we qualified for a mortgage loan, and we were able to make the minimum required down payment, thanks to the cashed-in insurance policy. It was a new and scary experience, but we clearly saw the hand of the Lord opening this opportunity for us to buy instead of rent. Everything was approved, the bank issued us a mortgage, and we became proud first-time homeowners of a two-story house with a basement and an attic at 1375 Belleview Avenue, Plainfield, New Jersey. We were in a quiet, mixed neighborhood not far from Scotch Plains and North Plainfield, and the Muhlenberg Hospital was just around the corner.

I knew the house needed some repairs, painting, and remodeling, and that is why we were able to get it at a much lower price then usual. I had to learn a new route of travel going north from Plainfield through several small towns to the TWR Home Office in Chatham, typically a 45 minute drive.

Our "new" house even had an above-ground swimming pool that had not been maintained for a couple of years. The water was a deep pea-soup green color. Our "new" neighbor told me how to "shock" the pool and filter out the crud. Philip and I shocked the tar out of the pool after pulling chunks of wood, tree limbs, and bricks from the bottom, but we never could get it to a crystal clear color. We swam in it anyway, and tried to enjoy it. Eventually, the sides rusted through, the liner tore apart, the water drained out, and it was no longer useable. I had more important challenges, though, which included cleaning junk out of the attic, basement, and garage. We threw stuff out the attic windows into the yard, dragged debris out of the basement, and cleaned out the garage. I had to have everything hauled away in a large dump truck. What a job!

Some of the needed renovations in the house included replacing the heavy claw-foot tub with a shower, and finishing off the attic to make it into a bedroom for Gaylene. Unfortunately, I had to do this work during the hot summer months. What a challenge, trying to cut Sheetrock and insulation while keeping dust and sweat out of my eyes. I had to use many bottles of wetting and cleaning solutions for my thick contact lenses. I did most of the work myself in the evenings and on Saturdays. After completing the attic project, each of the kids had their own room, and they were very happy about that.

We had known that the city public schools were not good, but we were able to make arrangements to send our kids to Timothy Christian School in Parsippany, New Jersey, about 20 minutes drive-time from our house. This was possible because Anna Gay was hired at the school as a Teacher's Aide, which meant we did not have to pay tuition. It was amazing to see how the Lord made this great provision at just the right time. (The Headmaster of the school was also the choir director and song leader at Evangel Baptist Church where we had been attending since moving to Chatham in 1984.)

Winters in our area of New Jersey were most interesting and unpredictable. I had learned how to drive in snow, and I considered myself a very good driver. It's the other guys who caused the traffic tie-ups because they didn't have the driving techniques needed for snow-covered streets. Most businesses closed down if severe, snowy weather was in the forecast. This allowed motorists to get home and off the streets before they became impassable. I am thankful that Trans World Radio followed this practice.

Snow was predicted to start falling late one morning. Several inches of the white stuff was expected throughout northeast New Jersey. TWR planned to close the office in the afternoon, but those of us who lived outside Chatham were encouraged to leave shortly after lunch. I knew I had to go over some moderately steep country roads, and so I left. It had already started to snow heavily and after driving about 10 minutes, I discovered the cold wet snow was sticking to everything, even the streets.

As I approached one of the hilly roads, I saw some vehicles with wheels spinning away, but going nowhere. I was able to maneuver around the stranded cars while maintaining traction and climbing to the crest of the hill. Eventually, I came to another section of road that descended rather steeply with an intersection at the bottom of the hill. By this time the snow was deeper and icy patches were beginning to develop on the roadway. I watched some vehicles ahead of me slip and slide down the hill. One or two had real trouble keeping on the road and almost ended up in the ditch. Each motorist waited at the top until the vehicle ahead got to the bottom and continued on through the intersection. I prayed again for the Lord's help and protection as I eased over the crest and began my downhill journey. It was tricky, but I reached the bottom intersection safely and continued carefully on my drive home.

By the time I reached our house on Belleview Avenue, there was already about three inches of snow covering the yard and driveway. I figured Anna Gay and the kids were on their way home from school, and I wanted to get the driveway shoveled before they arrived. I had the driveway cleared, but no Anna Gay and kids, and the snow was continuing even heavier and thicker. After an hour and a half, the driveway had another two inches of snow on it. And I began shoveling again, trying to keep ahead of the accumulation.

By now, I was really getting concerned. (We had no cell phones at this time.) I had called the school much earlier and got no answer. Anna Gay had not called me at the house, and there were no messages on the phone. I called the New Jersey State Patrol to inquire about any reported accidents between Plainfield and Parsippany. There were none. I could get no information concerning my family. I prayed for the Lord's protection where ever they were in our blue Subaru station wagon.

Now, it was dark and the driveway was covered with another two inches of snow which I just left to accumulate. I needed to stay by the phone! I could not go looking for them since there were about six different ways to get from our house to the school. All I could do was commit them to the Lord, and wait.

Finally, I saw headlights through the window. It was Anna Gay and the kids slowly coming down the snow-covered street. What a relief! Praise the Lord, they got home safely. After getting everyone inside the house and warmed up, I learned that the school had closed early, and Anna Gay and the kids left immediately. Some snow was already sticking to the streets, but our front-wheel drive Subaru could handle this with no problem and so could Anna Gay, who is an excellent driver. However, they had gotten tied up in a traffic jam when a tractor-trailer truck jack-knifed and totally blocked the road on which they were traveling. All other vehicles had to stop; they could not turn around; they could not go forward; they were stuck. They had to wait for a wrecker to somehow get through the congestion and clear the road. Added to this was the fact that they had to go by a business park, and due to the amount of snow falling, these businesses had released all their employees early resulting in much more traffic than usual, and gridlock.

The normal drive-time of 25 minutes had turned into a drive-time of more than 5 hours. Wow! That is one experience we will never forget! Gaylene, Philip, and Holly did great during this ordeal. Not one of them complained about needing to go to the bathroom. The kids had a little bit of food left from their lunches and snacked on this. There was enough gas in the car for Anna Gay to periodically turn on the engine to get the heater going. Needless to say, though, everyone was happy to be finally home in our nice warm house. Now, let it snow! Let it snow! Let it snow! And it did, for several more hours. We sure had a bunch of snow to shovel the next morning. School was closed, and the TWR office was closed for the next couple of days, as well.

Even though I do not think it was related to the auto accident on April 7, 1986, I could hardly get out of bed one morning due to severe back pain. I had to literally crawl on my hands and knees before being able to pull myself to a standing position. Somehow, I was able to drive to the TWR office later in the morning, but was in almost constant pain that shot from my back, down my lift leg, to my foot. Some of my TWR co-workers convinced me to make an appointment with a chiropractor in a neighboring community near Chatham, which I rather reluctantly did. (I remembered going to a chiropractor who had come to Bonaire to be of medical assistance to the TWR staff. I was not totally pleased with the diagnosis and the few treatments I had before bowing out of the program.)

At the time of the scheduled appointment, Anna Gay had to drive me in our Chevy Astro van from Plainfield to the town near Chatham, which was a good 45-minute drive. I was in sheer agony the whole time as we drove to the doctor's office. I couldn't sit on the front passenger seat and had to kneel in front of the middle seat, pleading for Anna Gay not to hit the pot holes so hard. I wanted her to drive slow and easy, yet at the same time wanting her to speed up and get the traveling over and done.

The treatment was what I had dreaded with a crunch here and a tweak there on my poor, sore back and side. Then, I faced the challenge of our return 45-minute trip back to Plainfield and the resulting agony. Somehow, with the Lord's help, we got back home, and I immediately popped out the contact lenses and tried to find a relatively comfortable position in the bed. I told Anna Gay that I was not going back to the chiropractor in two days for the next treatment. The next day I called to cancel the follow-up appointment and very politely said, "Doc, I realize that I have not given you a fair chance to treat my back, but I have determined that this just is not the treatment for me, and I am canceling my appointment." Thankfully, he did not try to twist my arm about the appointment. That actually would have added insult (pain in my arm) to injury (pain in my back).

I ended up going back to our family doctor who prescribed some pain medication for my aching back. The back pain gradually subsided and the sciatic nerve pain in my leg eventually departed, as well. I thought for a while that this might remain with me in my journey through the Myopic Zone. Quite thankfully, I have never experienced this type of problem since then.

However, I was about to experience a different type of problem that not only affected me, but my whole family, especially my son Philip.

One Saturday afternoon, I was tackling a project of some sort at the house. Anna Gay was doing her housecleaning; Gaylene and Holly were working on some activity; and Philip was riding his bicycle at a nearby park. Our neighbor's son Carl was riding his own bike with Philip.

Our world was suddenly thrown upside down when Philip came running up the street with his buddy fiercely pedaling his bike in front of him. They were screaming at the top of their lungs, "A big guy robbed Philip of his bicycle!" Carl's dad and I finally calmed the boys down enough so they could tell us what had happened. Somebody had forcefully yanked Philip's bicycle from him and took off with it down a path in the park.

Immediately, I yelled for Anna Gay to call the police and have them meet me in the park. Our neighbor hopped in his car, and with his son, headed to the park. I jumped into our van with Philip right beside me, and we made a bee-line for the park. We drove along the roads in and around the park, as did our neighbor. Believe it or not, we spotted Philip's bicycle in the weeds where it had been hurriedly and unceremoniously ditched. About the same time, Philip saw the guy who took his bike trying to hide in some bushes. Then the police arrived, caught the young man, and put him into the back of a police car. Philip identified the person and confirmed that he was the suspect who had robbed him of his bike. I felt it was necessary to press charges, so the fellow was taken into custody.

A few days later, I had to take Philip to the courthouse in Elizabeth, New Jersey. We had prayed that the matter could be settled quickly without Philip having to testify in court. This would have been a very traumatic experience for both of us, but especially for Philip who had already been traumatized by the robbery. Thankfully, the case was settled without Philip being put on the witness stand since the fellow, who already had several run-ins with the law, admitted to the crime. We retrieved Philip's bike from the police station, and he was able to ride it again after I repaired the damages it had sustained during the ordeal. Needless to say Philip and his buddy were not permitted to ride their bikes to and in the park unless accompanied by one of us parents, and that was certainly all right with them.

When the incident was fully resolved, I wanted to talk with the young fellow, but was unable to do so. I believe he was sent off to a reformatory camp of some sort. We prayed that someone could reach out to him and that he would not continue in a life of crime.

After I finished the remodeling projects in our home in Plainfield, we arranged for Anna Gay's mom to come from Houston,

Texas, to live with us. She was no longer able to take care of herself and her apartment in Houston, and was at this time living with Anna Gay's brother and family. We wanted to help care for Mrs. Chapman, and we were now able to do that since our Plainfield home had a small room downstairs that we could use for a bedroom. There was also a half-bath downstairs which made the new arrangement possible. Our kids were a big help to us as we tried to make Granny Chapman feel at home in her new surroundings. This was a major adjustment for all of us, but the Lord gave us the grace and strength to make this work.

Granny wanted to help Anna Gay with housework and cooking, but she was limited due to her frail physical health. One time, Anna Gay instructed Granny to put a meat loaf in the oven for our supper. She must have put it in to bake too early in the day, and by the time Anna Gay and the kids got home from school, the poor meatloaf was charred and had shrunk in the pan to one-quarter its original size. But there was no fire, praise the Lord, just the smell of burned meatloaf.

It was always a relief when we all got back home in the afternoon and evening, and found Granny Chapman to be all right and the house to be all right. A major adjustment for Granny, as it was for our family, was the faster pace of living and all the congested roads and streets. This was quite different from what she was used to in Huntington, West Virginia, and the suburbs of Houston, Texas.

By now, some major adjustments and changes were taking place at the Trans World Radio Headquarters. In a measure to conserve mission expenses, several staff members who were being paid a salary by TWR were let go. Staff members, like myself, who were receiving missionary support, were retained, and some were moved into other positions of responsibility.

I was moved from the Candidate Department to the Accounting Department. I was trained to take the place of the man who was hired to handle work with the mission finances in this department. My new responsibilities included cash management and involved receipting and making bank deposits. I also paid all TWR bills and transferred funds from headquarters by electronic wire to all the TWR overseas field locations.

Managing the mission finances was a real challenge for me. Daily I had to determine the bank account balance, figure in the day's donor receipts, make a deposit, and make sure there were sufficient funds to cover the checks that I needed to issue. If funds were short, I had to transfer a sufficient amount from the money market account to the checking account. It got to the point where I had to hold sending out payments to vendors until we had sufficient funds in the account. All of the accounting and check processing was done through computer software, and I had to learn all of the procedures needed to do the cash management job efficiently and correctly.

I had to prepare paychecks, payment checks, and financial reports under the supervision of the Chief Financial Officer. Over a period of time, I became more comfortable and proficient in my new assignment. I also became increasingly aware of the stressful situation this was creating for me. I finally had to make the determination that this just was not my "cup of tea." I enjoy challenges and working with figures, but this was a massive undertaking where mistakes, even the seemingly smallest ones, could have bad consequences. The Lord helped me to do the job correctly, but I began discussing a possible change in my responsibilities and field of service with TWR leadership.

Since there were no positions available in the Home Office, I had the options of either serving as an area representative for TWR or being transferred to a TWR field in an overseas location. Both Anna Gay and I felt that our first priority was to consider our family and children. As an area representative, I would be required to travel a good amount of the time. Serving overseas would require a major change and adjustment in a foreign country if our family was to leave the United States. As we prayed and committed these matters to the Lord, it was soon apparent that none of the options offered to us were acceptable.

We wanted to be associated with a mission agency that was involved in international ministries. Of course, we were somewhat familiar with Source of Light Ministries, and we knew they had an international outreach.

I did not necessarily want to switch to another mission agency, so I presented the possibility of being seconded from TWR to Source of Light Ministries (SLM). I also approached SLM about this arrangement. Source of Light leadership was open to the idea, but TWR leadership felt at that time that the two mission agencies were not that closely aligned since SLM printed and distributed Bible teaching correspondence courses while TWR produced and broadcast Bible teaching radio programs.

We then explored some other mission agencies, but the Lord kept impressing upon us to seriously consider serving with Source of Light Ministries even though this would mean severing our missionary service with Trans World Radio.

After much prayer and many discussions, Anna Gay and I determined that the Lord was definitely leading us to apply for service with Source of Light at the mission Headquarters in Madison, Georgia. We also discussed this matter with the pastors and missionary committees of Chelten Baptist Church (my home/sending church) and Grace Gospel Church (Anna Gay's home/sending church). Both gave favorable impressions that this move would be good for us, our children, and our continuing missionary service.

Anna Gay would have more of an opportunity to serve as a missionary, something she was unable to do at the Trans World Radio headquarters due to their staff structure. Of course, Anna Gay's primary responsibilities was to me as her husband and to our children, and then be involved in ministry as she was able. She would rather be doing this, anyway, than to continue working as a Teacher's Aide.

We were accepted by Source of Light Ministries (SLM), and so I began a transition in my journey through the Myopic Zone along with the rest of the family. This meant relocating from New Jersey to Georgia.

It was hard to say goodbye to our co-workers and to the mission under which we had served for 21 years, but we knew that God was leading us as He indicated, "this is the way, walk ye in it." Even though Anna Gay never worked in the Home Office, she was still a TWR missionary. At Source of Light (SLM) she would have a place to serve in the SLM Headquarters as it would fit her responsibilities as a wife to me and a mother to our children. My journey through the Myopic Zone was now taking a southern approach with our move from Plainfield, New Jersey, to Madison, Georgia.

Before that could happen, however, we needed to relocate Granny Chapman, put our house up for sale, sort and pack our personal effects, arrange for a moving company to transport everything to Georgia, and establish a place to live in Madison near the SLM office.

In rather record time, all of the above matters were favorably resolved. Granny Chapman would return to Houston to live with, then later close by, Anna Gay's brother and family. Our house had appreciated about 75 percent since we purchased it, and it sold quickly at a price just below the appraised amount. Our kids did very well in determining what things they wanted to keep and what they wanted to sell at our pre-moving yard sale. From the sale of our house, I paid off the mortgage and used the remaining funds to cover the cost of a moving company and to make a good down payment on a home in Georgia. I had traveled to Madison a couple of times prior to our move and was able to stay with my folks who were also serving at the SLM Headquarters. My dad was a great help in gathering information about our housing.

Source of Light had some one-acre lots available for its missionaries to use that were located just about a quarter of a mile down the road from the mission compound. I was able to secure an undeveloped lot from SLM where a spot could be cleared for setting up a double-wide pre-manufactured home. I checked out several mobile home dealers in the area and found just the right size and floor plan for our family of five. I conferred with Anna Gay by telephone, described the home to her, and took pictures of a similar home. She trusted my judgment, and after selecting the wall decor, lighting, and floor coverings, I signed the papers to have the house built. It was constructed by a company in Gainesville, Georgia, where I had visited with my dad. Later, the pre-manufactured home was moved to our lot on Mission Road.

We all looked forward to moving south closer to my stomping grounds in Kentucky, as well as Anna Gay's in West Virginia. Our kids were excited, too, since the fast pace of living in the New York Metropolitan area was not their "cup of tea" after living on islands from the time they were born. Our missionary service was going to take on a new dynamic as we laid down the tools of "missionary radio" at TWR and picked up the tools of "the printed page" at SLM.

Before we headed south to Georgia, our TWR co-workers gave us a reception. Some of the staff put their heads together and prepared the following summary of our missionary service in Trans World Radio which was read during the farewell activities. It is titled: "Dave and Anna Gay Newell, This is Your Life!"

"Many years ago, when boys were boys and girls were girls, two young lovers, Dave and Anna Gay, married. They dedicated their lives to the Lord and to missionary service with Trans World Radio. The year was 1965.

"By May of 1966, they were commissioned and arrived for their first term on the small, but beautiful, island of Bonaire. Dave maintained the transmitters and worked transmitter shifts. He even drew up revisions in the circuits for the three transmitters and the diesel generators. And, amid his active schedule, managed enough time to teach junior boys in Sunday school and to occasionally preach.

"Meanwhile, Anna Gay was filling an important role as secretary to the engineers. She also taught a young teens class.

"Their second term on Bonaire brought a wave of excitement. Gone were their days of peaceful co-existence and nights of relaxing to the rhythm of the waves. A giant pink flamingo, native to this Caribbean island, directed its flight path over the Newell household and dropped a precious bundle of joy, named Gaylene, into the arms of Anna Gay. January 17, 1971, marks the day.

"During their second term Dave continued his faithful tasks which included working on audio equipment and operating the transmitters from three in the morning until 12 noon. This time around, Dave did chalk drawing presentations in his spare time, and Anna Gay, naturally had her hands full with her bundle of joy. They can remember eating sweet corn, brought to Bonaire by two TWR MK's, and the arrival of the Bjorkmans. About halfway through their second term, the flamingo once again flew over their abode, only this time he was blue, if you can imagine a blue flamingo! Again, he zeroed in on Mama Newell's arms, bringing a bouncy little boy, henceforth referred to as Philip, born March 2, 1973.

"The end of their second term also brought an end to the aqua waters of the Caribbean and replaced them with the deep blue of the Pacific. They were transferred in May of 1975 to the U.S. Territory of Guam, a 209-square-mile island known as the "Pearl of the Pacific," for their third term with TWR. Here, Toto birds and iguanas co-inhabit the island with the U.S. military. Dave, Anna Gay, Gaylene, and Philip substituted the salt-savored 87 degree climate of Bonaire for the muggy 87 degree temperature of Guam. Instead of

Papiamento, it was now Chamorro. Anna Gay brought with her a good case of hepatitis, but she recovered to go on to bigger and better accomplishments, such as helping to paint 66 twenty-foot-long shortwave tower sections. No wonder TWR women stay in shape with that kind of physical labor!

"In addition to tending to the needs of her family, she squeezed time to type daily program logs, do some secretarial functions, direct a children's choir, help in Sunday school, and teach a Good News Bible Club for military children. Near the end of 1977, Anna Gay worked in the mail department, processing mail from shortwave listeners.

"Meanwhile, Dave managed to keep his schedule full by being in charge of the studio equipment and assisting in the engineering of the transmitters. Eventually, he became technical supervisor of KTWR, TWR's shortwave station, and shortwave Frequency and Programming Coordinator. He never lost sight of the importance of Sunday school and would faithfully transport 15 to 20 children to church in his '69 Volkswagen bus.

"By their fourth term, beginning in September of 1978, the Newells were pretty well settled into their home in the village of Santa Rita. Caught up in the rigors of battling typhoons and hosting dinners and Bible studies for military personnel, their busy lives were going to become busier. It was March 21, 1979, when a pink B-52 Bomber, a vintage model left over from World War II days, took off from the U.S. military base and spread its wings toward its bombing target. Yes, at the precise moment, the pilot, probably a woman, released the hatch button and dumped a pink bombshell on the Newell household. Holly Beth had arrived!

"All three children were active during their time on the field; Gaylene with her Brownie Troop and piano lessons; Philip with his soccer, piano lessons, and pastime of watching military vehicles.

"But soon they needed to learn to readjust to life in the U.S. and the U.S. school system. The Newells completed their fifth term in December of 1983. Their years on Guam had been interspersed with special trips to Manila, Hong Kong, and Taiwan. They enjoyed riding double-decker buses, cable cars, trains, and ferries. But now it was time to take up residence once again in the United States and to join the TWR International Headquarters Staff. Ah, the bliss of working in Chatham! Or was it? Especially, when you have to deal with the likes of Cliff Floyd and Jean Hagmann in the Candidate Department. They liked Dave so much that after having him work with them from 1984 through 1986, they shipped him up to Finance. Actually, they really did work well as a team! This past year or so, Dave handled Accounts Payable. Whether it was transferring Mission funds to Sri Lanka or paying New Jersey Bell, Dave was the man to see. He also served as the liaison between TWR and the FCC, managing Guam broadcasting frequencies.

"Meanwhile, Anna Gay participated in a prison ministry to female inmates at New Jersey's only prison for women. Accompanied by the pastor of their church and a few other dedicated ladies, Anna Gay toted her accordion along to provide music. She also worked as a Teacher's Aide at Timothy Christian School.

"Over the years, the Lord has protected Dave and Anna Gay, as well as their children. Not only through the difficulties and hazards of field living, but also through a near-death tragedy in the States. That fateful night of April 14, 1985, brought Dave and Tim Walker to a near encounter with eternity. A drunken driver ran a red light and collided with them. But the Lord's protection encircled both men, and they both survived to tell the story.

"We will remember you, Dave and Anna Gay, as dedicated servants of the Lord as you leave us and assume your new responsibilities with Source of Light Ministries. But the heartbeat of Trans World Radio will always be with you. You have invested your lives in us, and we in you. Every piece of equipment you have repaired and every listener letter you have answered will not be forgotten by the Lord. Etched into the sands of time, and into the sands of Bonaire and Guam, will be the memory of your service. The Lord richly bless you and your family."

## 14

## SLM - MADISON, GEORGIA  (1987-2004)

---

*The Lord gave the word: great was the company of those that
published it.*  Psalm 68:11

Before transitioning from Trans World Radio to Source of Light
Ministries, Anna Gay and I made personal contact with our supporting churches and friends to let them know how the Lord was
directing us in this stage of our missionary service.

Some were a bit surprised but understood our situation and
our need to change mission agencies.  They were pleased that we
would still be associated with a mission agency that had a worldwide
ministry outreach.  However, there were a couple exceptions.  One
was a church in Pennsylvania that had begun supporting us from the
very beginning in 1965.

This particular church had unchangeable guidelines for
situations like ours.  The missions committee looked at us as if we
were just beginning our deputation as brand new missionaries rather
than veteran missionaries with twenty-one years of service.  Also,
they did not feel that Source of Light Ministries (SLM) was reaching
third-world countries.  Even though Anna Gay and I met with the
missions committee on two separate occasions and explained how
SLM had branches in over a dozen countries, with most being recognized as third-world countries, the committee decided that the church
would have to drop their financial support (about $500 a month) and
to remove us from their missions program.  This was very disappointing since this church was the very first one to contribute to our
Equipment Fund in the early days of raising a support team.  I am
thankful that God knew all about this, and I knew He would provide
through others to make up this deficit, and He did!

We resigned from our duties at Evangel Baptist Church
as the date of our departure drew closer.  One member of the church
confronted Anna Gay, and said, "Traitor!" and walked away.  This
was another one of very few exceptions where we were not

encouraged to make the change from Trans World Radio to Source of Light Ministries.

Some people are used to living such a sheltered life and are not open to any sort of change. This can be said of church folks and missionary folks, as well. During one of our furloughs, a lady in my home church felt that it was not right for us to raise our children on the mission field. She said, "I will never let my daughter go into missionary work, especially outside the United States!" What an awful attitude! What a way to hinder God's blessing!

I found that it is so important to follow God's leading in both the small and the great decisions in life. I continued to rely on the promises of Proverbs 3:5-6: "Trust in the Lord with all thine heart: and lean not unto thine own understanding. In all thy ways acknowledge him, and he shall direct thy paths."

During our furloughs, and while living in New Jersey, our family had visited my folks (Earl and Adele Newell) in Madison, Georgia. They were missionaries serving in the Headquarters of Source of Light Ministries (SLM), and we had learned more and more about the SLM ministries and were becoming more familiar with the areas around Madison.

Madison is a small, beautiful town located on US highway 441, just north of I-20, a major interstate highway connecting Atlanta with Augusta. Madison is smaller than Plainfield, New Jersey, and is situated in a rural section of Northeastern Georgia. It is completely different from the jam-packed streets and roads of Plainfield and the New York Metropolitan area. We all looked forward to leaving the fast-paced, congested living of the north and moving to the quiet, peaceful living of the south.

The SLM Headquarters consisted of administrative offices, a print shop, and a Bible correspondence department. At this time SLM had established Branch offices in 25 U.S. and foreign countries. Bible study courses were being printed in English and several foreign languages. These lessons were used in the Madison School, as well as in the Branch Schools. Associate Schools were developed through the Home Office and through various branch locations. The Bible lessons were provided at no charge to the students who were enrolled and learning more about God and His Word.

My first assignment was in the print shop. There was a need for a person to operate one of the Gazette web-fed printing presses, and I was "pressed" into service. I had previously operated a variety of presses at Hess and Young after graduating from Philadelphia College of Bible. Those presses were used for hot embossing and gold stamping jobs (using no ink), and now I found myself operating a press that was actually using ink to print Bible lessons. I was happy to be learning how to operate an actual printing press.

This was totally different from operating super-power transmitters, which was all right with me. Actually, I had been moving away from technical duties in Trans World Radio and was handling more administrative duties. I continued to maintain my interest in the amateur radio hobby, and this did require some technical electronics know-how.

I was now back in the south, and my original call sign of WA4DUP fit right into my new location in Georgia. It wasn't too long after moving that I was able to put up an antenna beside our house and get back "on the air." My dad was also "on the air" from the mission Headquarters where he had set up his ham radio station in his office. He was operating with call sign WA4ZIZ.

As time permitted, Anna Gay was able to get involved in the SLM office, doing secretarial work while the kids were in school. It was great that she could put her skills to use in our new missionary venture in the Myopic Zone.

During the past years on Guam and in New Jersey, I always had my annual eye checkup. Every year my vision continued to be stabilized by the hard contact lenses; I was grateful that my prescription remained unchanged. By this time, I found that for close-up work, such as writing, reading, soldering, and drawing, I needed to use an inexpensive pair of reading glasses along with my contacts.

It was a blessing to now be living closer to our families. We not only lived within a mile or so of my folks, we also worked with them at the SLM mission Headquarters. My sister Barbara and her family lived in a neighboring community; my brother John and his family lived in Southeastern Kentucky and worked at Camp Nathanael (Scripture Memory Mountain Mission). Some of our family did live a bit farther away. Anna Gay's brother and his family and her mother, lived in Houston, Texas. My brother Dick and his family lived in Laurel, Maryland.

Our kids were soon involved in church and school activities and began making new friends. (Morgan County had an excellent public school system.) We all were happy to be establishing our lives in Northeastern Georgia. This was definitely more our style of living! However, wherever the Lord took us in our missionary service, we learned to be content. Wherever that location would be, we were happy and counted it a privilege to be missionaries in the Lord's service. We could say with the Apostle Paul, ". . . for I have learned, in whatsoever state I am, therewith to be content" (Philippians 4:11).

Our family had been associated with Bethany Baptist Church (where my folks attended) since our move to Georgia. We had visited Sandy Creek Baptist Church on a couple of occasions, one of which was a service where the chorale from Appalachian Bible College (Anna Gay's alma mater) presented a concert. Several Source of Light missionaries and their families attended this church, and we learned that there was a strong, active youth program for kids of all ages. As our kids grew older, Anna Gay and I wanted to make sure that they were involved in youth activities.

Eventually, we moved our associate memberships from Bethany Baptist to Sandy Creek Baptist, and this is where Anna Gay and I currently have our associate memberships. I missed attending services with my folks, but our kids were glad that we made this change, and they became very active in the youth group programs.

Sandy Creek is located in the country about 12 miles north of Madison. The pastor was on the board of Neighborhood Gospel Missions (NGM), and we began learning about this mission organization and its goal of one day establishing a camp and conference center on its own property. At this time NGM was conducting summer camps at rented facilities in the Northeastern part of the state. The mission was also using Source of Light Bible study courses with its summer campers.

In 2002, I was invited to serve on the Board of Neighborhood Gospel Missions, and I counted it a privilege and blessing to have a part in the NGM ministry.

Our ministry with Source of Light varied over the next eighteen years (July 1987 through December 2004). The following will summarize the responsibilities that Anna Gay and I had during those exciting and challenging years of missionary service at the SLM headquarters.

### July 1987 - September 1988

I began training in the Print Shop to meet the urgent need for another pressman and also to gain an understanding of the overall production and distribution of the lesson materials. I operated one of the large Gazette presses. I also had the responsibility of inventory control, reviewing the inventory twice a month; of scheduling lesson materials for printing; and of processing all printing orders in the Print Shop office.

Anna Gay began assisting as part-time Receptionist and Secretary to the Home Director.

### October 1988 - February 1990

I worked in the Print Shop 3 days a week operating the Gazette press printing Bible study lessons and training a new missionary to take over the inventory and clerical work in the shop. I worked in the Graphics Department 2 days a week helping with layout and design, processing film in the darkroom, and burning metal plates for the printing presses. (By September 1989, I was working full-time in the Graphics Department.)

Anna Gay continued assisting as part-time Receptionist and Secretary to the Home Director.

### March 1990 - May 1991

I was working in the Publications and Graphics Departments and was appointed Publications Coordinator, responsible for overseeing the work done in preparation of materials to be printed, including design, typesetting, layout, proofing, lithography, and masking. I began serving on the Administrative Council and supervising the Chinese translation projects.

Anna Gay continued assisting as part-time Receptionist and Secretary to the Home Director.

### June 1991 - March 1993

I was appointed Field Director, responsible for the SLM worldwide ministry through 12 overseas Branches. I coordinated Field ministries and Branch projects with the Assistant Field Director. (At this time over 1,500 Associate Schools were using SLM materials in nearly 85 countries.) I continued serving on the Administrative Council and supervising the Chinese translation projects.

Anna Gay continued serving as Receptionist and Secretary to the Home Director. Her additional duties included ordering materials and supplies for the SLM Office and Print Shop, and supervising the Mail Room operations. She initiated and organized the Ladies Auxiliary, supervising the newly established mission hospitality and social committees.

### April 1993 - March 1996

I was appointed Assistant General Director in March 1993, responsible for all Administrative Council members. My new duties included receiving departmental reports and recommendations, chairing the Administrative Council meetings, reviewing financial reports from each department, maintaining an accurate organizational chain of command, and assisting the Field Department staff. I also began editing *The Reaper* (the official mission periodical) and all other mission publications. I continued to supervise the Chinese translation projects.

Anna Gay continued serving as Receptionist and Secretary to the Home Director, ordering materials and supplies for the Office and Print Shop and supervising the Mail Room operations. She also continued as Ladies Auxiliary Supervisor.

### April 1996 - February 2001

I continued my responsibilities as Assistant General Director with additional duties which included serving on the Executive Committee of the Board of Directors and chairing the Policy Review Committee. I was also appointed Editor of *The Reaper* and coordinated the work in the Publications and Graphics Departments, as well as coordinated the Chinese outreach ministry.

Anna Gay was appointed Assistant to the Home Director along with her continuing duties as Receptionist and Secretary to the Home Director, Mail Room Supervisor, and Ladies Auxiliary Supervisor. She also ordered materials and supplies for the Office and Print Shop.

### March - December 2001

I continued my duties as Assistant General Director, serving on the Executive Committee, the SLM Board, and chairing the Policy Review Committee. I also served as Editor of *The Reaper*, edited all mission publications, and supervised the Chinese outreach ministries.

Anna Gay was given new responsibilities as Secretary to the Director of Human Resources and continued with her duties as Receptionist, and the Ladies Auxiliary Supervisor. She also continued ordering materials and supplies for the Office and Print Shop.

### January - December 2002

I continued as Assistant General Director and the many responsibilities associated with that position. In addition, I was appointed Director of Outreach Ministries to coordinate the Outreach Ministries (Field) Department and Regional Field Directors. I also served as Regional Field Director for Asia, and continued to supervise the Chinese outreach ministries. By this time, my plate was full (really too full); it was affecting my administrative abilities.

Anna Gay continued as Secretary to the Director of Human Resources, as well as her other duties of ordering, as Receptionist, and Ladies Auxiliary Coordinator. She was given the added responsibility of Publications Expediter, preparing job tickets for the printing presses, reviewing stock inventories, and maintaining Print Shop records.

### January 2003 - December 2004

I continued as Assistant General Director, Director of Outreach Ministries, Regional Director for Asia, Editor for all mission publications, and Coordinator for Chinese outreach ministries. I also chaired the Policy Review Committee, coordinated the Outreach Ministries (Field) Department and Regional Directors, and served on the SLM Board and Executive Committee.

Anna Gay was appointed Regional Director for Central and South America and the Caribbean. She continued her duties as Secretary, Receptionist, and did the ordering for the Office and Print Shop.

Since being appointed Field Director in 1991, I have had the privilege of traveling somewhat extensively overseas to visit many Source of Light Branches. I had to travel by myself on many trips, so it was always a real help and blessing when Anna Gay could travel with me. It was so much easier to relate to female missionaries and staff in the various Branches when Anna Gay was at my side.

Most of the foreign SLM Branches were directed and staffed by nationals from the particular country where the Branch offices and Associate Schools were located. It was very important to visit our national leaders from time-to-time and to let them know that they were not forgotten by the administration leaders and staff at the mission Headquarters in Madison.

Our purpose was not to spy on them but to learn first-hand about their culture, to understand the ministry challenges they faced, to pray with them, and to encourage them. We could then communicate what we had learned to the SLM Board, the SLM leadership, and the missionaries in the home office. During these trips, I was humbled and encouraged as I saw the faithful, sacrificial service that our national missionaries were performing.

The primary mission of the SLM Branches was to use the Bible study materials as a foundation for their outreaches. This included establishing Associate Schools within their country, culture, and language. It was exciting to see how the worldwide ministry of

SLM was growing. As Field Director, I witnessed missions in action. I also witnessed many obstacles that were continually being put up by the enemy (the devil) and his demons. You can be sure that where God is blessing, there will be opposition, but we have the promise in 1 John 4:4, ". . . greater is he that is in you, than he that is in the world."

I faced the usual challenges of traveling on these trips through the Myopic Zone with my trusty hard contact lenses (which I tried to wear from the time my feet hit the floor in the morning until my head hit the pillow at night). I also had to carry my super-thick lensed eyeglasses for use when the contacts were not in their places on my eyeballs.

Each overseas journey had its own unique times of dangers, frustrations, ministry opportunities, awkward situations, and tremendous blessings. I tried to be as economical as possible in planning itineraries and flights to foreign countries. The following condensed report describes my 48-day journey that took me into 10 countries and was included in the March/April 1992 edition of *The Reaper* (the bi-monthly magazine published by Source of Light Ministries).

"Around the World in 48 Days"

From January 3 through February 19,1992, I visited our SLM Branches in Korea, the Philippines, India and Kenya. I also made stops in Hong Kong, China, Singapore, Malaysia, Holland, and Germany. I was hoping Anna Gay could accompany me on this trip, but sufficient funds were not available, so she remained in Madison this time (until I traveled from Kenya to Holland).

The Lord answered prayer concerning my health and safety during the more than 25,000 miles of travel. I rode on every type of transportation imaginable, including bicycle, motorcycle, auto rickshaw, jeepney, double-decker bus, pickup truck, subway, train, boat, plane, etc. The climate ranged from winter snow in Korea and Holland to tropical heat in the Philippines and Singapore.

I had the privilege of speaking in 34 church services, prayer meetings, special staff meetings, and fellowship groups (many times through an interpreter). I also had 22 appointments with SLM missionary staff members and with missionaries from other agencies.

The primary purpose of this field trip was to visit our SLM Branches in the Far East and Kenya, to encourage our co-workers, to review Branch projects, to gain insights into our overseas ministries, and to survey areas of potential expansion.

## Korea

Our National Director, Rev. Paul Bahn, had an extensive weekly schedule that involved pastoring, counseling, discipling, teaching, and preaching. I traveled with him January 4 through 9 and had the opportunity of speaking on various occasions. We had to spend many hours driving from one meeting to another because of the crowded streets and roads in Seoul and the surrounding areas. This was very tiring and frustrating. We were able to meet with three of the Korea SLM Board members and review some of the financial matters concerning the ministry. Two rather unique ministries were conducted weekly by Paul. Many sales clerks and employees from the Sampoong Department Store attended Sunday morning worship services. The Department Store Church met in a nicely furnished room adjacent to the furniture department. After the service, the people went to their designated work areas in the store. This store was huge, with five levels above ground and two levels for parking underground. Another ministry was held in the Hyundai Corporation Facility for Research and Development where 25-35 Hyundai employees met each Wednesday at lunchtime for a Bible study.

## Philippines

It was a great joy to travel with the Philippine Source of Light (PhilSOL) National Director Dr. Luz Nacionales, and missionary Rev. Pio Deniola throughout the Philippines January 9 through 17. We visited the Region IV-A office directed by Dexilie Alcon. Tina Hidalgo was working in this office and was responsible for Regions IX-XII (the Mindanao area in the south). We visited the cities of Iloilo and Bacolod in Region VI (the Visayas area) under the direction of Sally Espinas. I had the opportunity of speaking at many prayer fellowship meetings during our travels. These were attended by students, Bible lesson distributors, pastors, and PhilSOL staff. Many pastors stated that they found the Bible study materials a great help in their ministries.

It was a delight to spend time with the PhilSOL staff in the Main Office. I could sense their spirit of joy in serving the Lord. I was saddened, though, when I saw several boxes containing over 5,000 Bible study lessons that were addressed but could not be mailed because no funds were available for stamps. We were looking to the Lord to provide the needed funds for postage.

One of our PhilSOL Board members took us into a squatters village inhabited by thousands of people who had come to Manila from all over the Philippines looking for work. There was no electricity, running water, or sanitary facilities. People lived in shacks made from scraps of wood and cardboard. We visited a pastor and his wife who lived there in a small, crude church. Plans were being formulated to use this church as a distribution point for an Associate School to reach throughout this village with our Bible study lessons. Also, plans were being made to expand the SLM ministry throughout the Philippines. Rev. Deniola, would be traveling throughout the Visayas Region, representing PhilSOL in churches and other meetings. I appreciated the opportunity of meeting with the PhilSOL Board Members during a meal we shared at Max's Fried Chicken. The Board expressed their desire to see more funds coming from within the Philippines to support the PhilSOL ministry.

## Hong Kong

My next stop was Hong Kong where I spent a few days meeting with missionaries from various mission agencies. I met with Rev. Linton Smith (Chinese Baptist Mission), Mr. Stephen Lee (Gospel Fellowship), Rev. Peter Shek (Lighthouse Baptist Church), and Rev. Samuel Chiang (Christian Nationals) to discuss the printing of our first lesson series in Mandarin Chinese.

We had a great challenge before us in printing and distributing the New Life in Christ, Course 1 lessons. All twelve lessons will be printed in one volume along with a self-guided answer sheet for the question pages. The first printing would consist of 3,000 lesson booklets in the simplified script (for use in Mainland China) and 3,000 in the traditional script (for use in Hong Kong and Taiwan). We estimated that our lessons could be printed in Hong Kong for the cost of one U.S. dollar per booklet, which has twelve lessons in each booklet.

## Mainland China

Before leaving Hong Kong, I was able to take a trip into China accompanied by a missionary couple. By pre-arrangement, we met with a young Chinese lady who had recently received Christ as her Savior. We ate with her in a crowded, noisy restaurant. The joy of the Lord was evidenced on her face as she eagerly shared some of the truths she had learned from reading her Bible. We were able to answer the many questions she asked. It really struck me as I realized that this new believer had no Christian fellowship and no place to worship. How I wish I could have slipped her a copy of NL-1 to help her spiritual growth! She wanted to be baptized, and this would be arranged to be done secretly at a future time. She wanted to share Jesus with her family and friends, but this had be done carefully and discreetly because of the authorities. We continued our encouragement to this young lady as we walked through the darkened streets toward the train station. Meetings like this often take place in parks where there is more liberty to share the Gospel and the Bible in an inconspicuous manner.

**Singapore**

It was a blessing to stay with former TWR co-workers Dan and Rose Ellen Blosser while in Singapore, January 22 through 26. One of the reasons for visiting this country was to evaluate the practicality of establishing an office or Branch there for handling our Chinese materials. I met with representatives from several different mission agencies. After evaluating their comments related to printing and to establishing an office in Singapore, it became evident that this location was too far removed from Mainland China. The real pulse of what was happening in China could be better felt in Hong Kong, and also it would be more economical to print our lessons in Hong Kong. It would also be a better distribution point. These advantages still outweighed any potential restrictions that might be imposed when China took over Hong Kong in 1997.

Singapore is surrounded by Muslim countries and is in a somewhat precarious position religiously and politically. The Singapore government is very sensitive to any missionary activity that reaches beyond its borders into Malaysia, Indonesia, Thailand, and Mainland China.

**India**

During the 17 days I spent in India, January 26 through February 12, our National Director of Amar Jyoti India, Rev. Pramod Das, traveled with me. Solomon Peter, director of the work in the South Zone, met us in Cuttack on January 30, and the three of us traveled together throughout the country. Also, it was great to have Sangram Naik and Christo Dan accompany us on various segments of our journeys.

The dedication of the Amar Jyoti staff, including our evangelists and volunteer workers throughout the country, was very evident everywhere I traveled. At that time, there were 65 national workers in the centers located in Cuttack (East Zone), Delhi (North Zone), Jeypore and Bangalore (South Zone), and the many outlying districts.

We had the unique opportunity of visiting several remote tribal villages deep in the mountain regions of Orissa. Only recently, these tribal people wore very little clothing and had no blankets. They were very primitive, but the Gospel was being received, and now there were several believers. In one village we dedicated a prayer hall that the tribal people had built. In another village we saw an abandoned church that was built over 100 years ago. The missionaries had gone long ago; the building was falling apart, with cows and other animals going in and out. The village had fallen back into paganism.

We spent a few days in Hyderabad with Brother Wilson. On February 6, I had the privilege of dedicating the Nachuram Grace Gospel Church to the Lord during a two and one-half hour service in which Pramod and Solomon also participated. I even laid a couple of bricks for the baptistry that would be dug in a corner of the property. The believers in this Hindu village of Nachuram were a living testimony of the Lord's saving and sustaining grace.

Another highlight in India was participating in the cornerstone laying ceremony for the new center in the village of Manchenahalli on February 10. Several believers from the village and the pastor, Evangelist Nagaraj, met with us on the one-acre property. Just a few days before, the permit and signed documents were issued by the village authorities for the construction of this prayer hall. After Pramod laid the cornerstone, he and Solomon visited in the home of Nagaraj while I stayed with the group. It was felt that my presence in the center of the village might jeopardize my safety and might create some threat to the believers because of the strong anti-Gospel and anti-government factions there.

We had many other unusual meetings in the villages and cities that we visited which included a Seekers' Conference in Dhenkanal, a presentation of sewing machines in the fishing village of Puri, an Amar Jyoti Board meeting in Cuttack, traveling by Jeep to the tribal village of Karanjaguda, the presentation of awards to children at the center in Jeypore, a fellowship meeting on an Army base in Hyderabad, a Bible study in the home of a Hindu doctor in the village of Keesara, the baptismal service in Bangalore at Sanky Tank, and teaching a Bible study class at a girls' school in Bangalore.

In India, the challenges were great, the potential of ministry was staggering, the funds and resources were limited, and persecution of believers continued as Satan tries to hinder the work of Amar

Jyoti. The Lord wonderfully provided funds for a diesel van which would be a tremendous asset to the South Zone office. Plans were being formulated to establish a recording studio in Cuttack for developing audio materials that would provide new methods of presenting Bible truths.

## Kenya

From Bombay, India, I flew to Nairobi, Kenya, to visit our newest Branch that was established by my folks, Earl and Adele Newell. Because of government regulations, Source of Light had to be organized under the umbrella of an existing agency. Jack Stiles, director of In Touch Kenya, had already established a large SLM Associate School with close to 5,000 students. He agreed to oversee the ministry of In Touch Kenya/Source of Light. Jack had been appointed to direct the Branch until a National could be trained to take over the ministry there. I had good discussions with Jack and my dad as we developed and agreed to the working relationships needed for the ongoing of the SLM ministry in Kenya.

One of the goals of the Kenya Branch was to conduct seminars for training and educating pastors and lay leaders who are interested in establishing Associate Schools. Already, over 25 Associate Schools had been established through this Branch.

The door for using the Bible study materials in Kenya was wide open. We had concerns that the present stock of lessons would not be sufficient to meet the demand. Until this situation could be corrected, the expansion of Associate Schools was limited. The immediate goal was to build up the stock in the office. We met with a missionary couple who had arranged for the use of our lesson materials in the public schools in the Maasi Region. The curriculum included a class of Protestant Pastoral Instruction. The District Education Officer had approved this project. There were 289 elementary schools with 57,800 students who would be taught the SLM Bible lessons. The goal was to introduce the course in 150 schools that year and expand into the remaining 139 schools the next year. What an opportunity! I was very impressed with the commitment of Jack Stiles, his wife, and the Kenyan staff to the Branch in Kenya. The Lord helped my folks complete their project of establishing the Branch during the six months that they spent in Nairobi.

## Holland

My flight from Africa to the United States was routed through Amsterdam, permitting a stop-over there. Anna Gay was able to fly to Amsterdam a few days before I arrived from Nairobi. After arriving at the airport, I traveled 2 ½ hours by train to Hengelo. It was a wonderful meeting on February 16, right there on the train platform! Anna Gay and I spent the next few days together with our Dutch friends, Harry and Nora Stoker. We had first met them on Bonaire almost 25 years before, and now they were showing us many parts of their country.

We rode by car to Noordhorn in Germany. There were no checks by border guards. The gates were wide open for unrestricted entry into Germany and the same was true on our return into Holland. This apparently was typical of the wide-open borders throughout Eastern Europe, a reminder of the wide open doors of opportunity that the Lord had given the ministry of Source of Light worldwide!

I am thankful for the things that I experienced and saw during my adventure of going around the world in 48 days! I wish you could have gone along to receive the same challenges and blessings of seeing the power of the Gospel in the lives of people who have been redeemed from many kindreds and tongues and peoples and nations.

"And they sung a new song, saying, Thou art worthy to take the book, and to open the seals thereof: for thou wast slain, and has redeemed us to God by thy blood out of every kindred, and tongue, and people, and nation; and has made us unto our God kings and priests: and we shall reign on the earth" (Revelation 5:9,10).

In 1990, I was given the task of coordinating the development, translation, and printing of the SLM Bible study courses in the Chinese language. I was very happy to assume these responsibilities since, while serving with Trans World Radio, the Lord had burdened my heart about the masses of people in Mainland China who needed to hear the Gospel and who needed Bibles and Bible study materials.

Some translation work was in progress at this time, but there was no coordination. One group in Hong Kong was translating a course into Traditional Chinese while another group in Singapore was translating the same course into Simplified Chinese, and yet another group in Taiwan was translating another course into Traditional Chinese.

Over a period of time, I was able to set priorities for which course to translate and which group or groups would be best equipped to do this work. We wanted to concentrate on the Simplified Chinese language and get the first course translated, printed, and distributed. Also, I introduced the concept of preparing a bilingual version in both English and Simplified Mandarin Chinese that would be printed with all lessons in one book, rather than in the typical individual lesson booklet format. The Lord helped with this ongoing project, and we saw translations completed and Bible study books printed by a partner in Hong Kong.

Next we were able to print individual lesson booklets in the Traditional Chinese language. These were printed and distributed in Hong Kong and Taiwan.

I had the privilege and opportunity of traveling to Singapore, Taiwan, Hong Kong, and into Mainland China on quite a few occasions in connection with my Chinese outreach responsibilities. Anna Gay was able to accompany me three times into Mainland China, and it was always an added blessing for her to travel with me. I prepared the following report, "Flight into China," after traveling to Zhengzhou in north-central China.

"It's Friday, April 18, 1997, and I am at Hong Kong's airport with Cathy Yang (not her real name), just about ready to board China Southern Airlines 737. Our destination is a city in east-central China. I just prayed that the Lord would protect us and the things carefully packed in our luggage: Bibles, Bible reference books, and Source of Light Chinese Bible study courses! As we boarded the plane, I have peace in my heart that everything is going to be all right.

"I am grateful for this Chinese staff member of a ministry in Hong Kong who is traveling with me. The day before, we had sorted the precious materials we are carrying to believers in China. Now, we are on our way after a one-hour delay in departure.

"We are an hour or so late arriving at our destination. We separate after getting off the plane as a precaution to lessen any suspicions. The first hurdle is to get through immigration control. The officials are really scrutinizing my passport, but no questions are asked as it is handed back to me. 'Thank you, Lord!' Now to claim my luggage. Cathy has already gotten her suitcase and is moving out of my view into the customs area. 'Lord, please keep her safe.' I have my suitcase and am getting in line with some of the other passengers. But I can't understand the Chinese on this paper that an official is handing to everyone. She's looking for someone who can deal with me but now is moving on to other passengers. (I was to learn later that it was a customs declaration form.)

"Uh-oh, now in the customs hall, I see the customs officials are directing some passengers to take their luggage to the x-ray machine for inspection. 'Lord, I do need your protection!' That customs agent is motioning to me. He wants me to go on through the door into the greeting area. Praise the Lord! I found my friend who had already passed through the crowd. She gave me a big smile as I joined her with my unopened luggage. We're safely in China with our goods intact! I smiled, too!

"It is later in the evening, and we are unpacking the Bibles, reference books, and Bible study courses (including New Life in Christ, course 3, just printed a couple of days before in Hong Kong). I wish you can see and hear the expressions of joy and appreciation from these who will use what we brought. I even have two pounds of Folgers coffee and a couple of packages of chocolate chips in my bag.

"That morning, knowing it was the day of our flight into China, I had asked God for some special verses from His Word. He gave me Psalm 89:20-22. God is saying in these verses that David (His servant) would be anointed for a special purpose (to be Israel's second king) and that He would be with him. God would give David strength and boldness, and the enemy would not alter God's purposes for him. The 'son of wickedness' would not be able to harm David.

"My name is David, too. And I am also God's servant and have been set apart for this special opportunity of taking much-needed Bibles and Bible lessons into China. I had the assurance that God was not going to permit Satan to create problems by hindering or harming us.

"The things we brought will be carefully used in this house church (and others) to disciple new believers, and they will be used to share the Gospel with unbelievers. Even the chocolate chips were put to immediate use. Following the Bible study on Sunday afternoon, a meal was prepared by and for the twenty or so people who will attend the evening church service. A huge batch of chocolate chip cookies was served, and they disappeared fast!

"On May 12, the day after I returned to the United States, I met some good friends from Florida who stopped by the offices of Source of Light. They told me that on Friday, April 18, between 8:30 and 9:00 AM, a group of 250 missionaries at Bradenton Village in Florida was very concerned about me and specifically prayed for my protection. The time in east-central China is twelve hours ahead of the Eastern United States. The time that Cathy and I were going through immigration and customs at the airport in China was Friday night between 8:30 and 9:00 PM, **exactly the same time they were praying!** I had assurance that others were praying, too. God certainly did answer prayer! 'The Lord is my light and my salvation; whom shall I fear? The Lord is the strength of my life; of whom shall I be afraid?' (Psalm 27:1)."

As I journey through the Myopic Zone, my interest in trains and railroads continued. In May of 2003, I planned to visit the SLM Branch office in Las Cruces, New Mexico. (In January of the same year, I took Anna Gay with me to visit the National Director of the SLM Guyana Branch who was staying with relatives in Miami for a few weeks. We drove from Madison, Georgia, to Miami, Florida, rather than travel by air.)

Now, on this trip to Las Cruces, Anna Gay traveled with me, and we used a different mode of travel part of the way. We drove from Madison to Houston, Texas, where we spent some time with Anna Gay's brother and his family. We also visited with personal supporters, good friends who we had met while living in New Jersey.

After our visits with family and friends, Anna Gay and I continued our travel from Houston to Las Cruces, New Mexico, by my favorite mode of transportation. It was by train! We rode the Amtrak Sunset Limited from Houston to El Paso, then drove a rented car from El Paso to the SLM Branch office in Las Cruces where we spent a week with the director, staff, and the local board of directors. Our goal was to listen to ministry concerns and challenges, to encourage our co-workers, and to offer suggestions, and to convey directives and instructions concerning the Branch.

The segment of our journey by rail was great. We left Houston late at night and reached El Paso the next afternoon. The

Sunset Limited was notorious for running late, but that was all right with me. The more time spent on the train, the better! There was plenty of room in the coach, and we were able to use two full sets of seats which helped us get some sleep during the night. It was daylight by the time our train reached the Rio Grande River. We crossed a very high trestle that spanned a beautiful rugged canyon, and we saw many freight trains traveling both east and west. We really enjoyed our return trip, and saw a lot of new country in the state of Texas as we passed rivers and jagged rock formations. We saw sand, sand, sand, and more sand dotted with wild flowers and cactus. We viewed all this from the comfort of our Amtrak coach. Even Anna Gay liked the train! Train travel has got to be the best!

In Houston, we retrieved our vehicle, spent a day with Anna Gay's brother and family, then retraced our driving on the jampacked interstate highways back to Madison. I sure did miss the luxury of care-free train travel, but savored the many lingering memories (the sounds, the smells, and the sights). During these days I was very thankful that my vision was quite good in spite of several situations that required medical treatments.

However, my journey through the Myopic Zone certainly has had its frustrations, challenges, and adjustments. Through the various eye procedures, God has given me peace, comfort, and healing.

Late December 1987, was an unusually warm, sunny day for wintertime in Georgia, and I took our family to fish in a nearby lake. We were really enjoying ourselves, especially the men (Philip and me), whose job it was to put the slimy worms on the hooks for the women (Anna Gay, Gaylene, and Holly)! The fish were not too cooperative, but we still were having a good time.

All of a sudden, I noticed inky, black dots starting to cover the vision of my right eye. My contact lenses were all right, but something was happening in my eye, and I was concerned. We quickly packed up our fishing gear and headed for home.

The ophthalmologist in Athens, Georgia, examined my eye and found a tear in the retina. He immediately set up an appointment with a retina surgeon at Piedmont Hospital in Atlanta. My dad met us in Athens and took our kids home, and Anna Gay and I drove from Athens to Atlanta. I could not see to drive, so this challenge was up to Anna Gay, and she did very well.

The retina surgeon assessed my right eye, and without delay on December 28, 1987, did cryosurgery to keep the retina from detaching. This was a very painful procedure, but the Lord helped with this and with the healing process. The doctor checked my eye the next day, and confirmed the retina was still attached.

Now, I could not use the contact lenses, so I had no choice but to once again resort to my super-thick bifocal-lensed eyeglasses. Praise the Lord I could see, just not as well as with the contact lenses.

Unfortunately, in October 1992, I experienced the same vision problem in my left eye when inky, black spots suddenly appeared in my vision. I knew immediately what had to be done. It meant another trip to the ophthalmologist in Athens, then continuing on to Piedmont Hospital in Atlanta for the emergency surgery. Once again the surgery prevented the retina from detaching, and I continued my journey through the Myopic Zone with my trusty eyeglasses with their super-thick bifocal lenses.

My visits to the retina surgeon at Piedmont were rather serious, but there were a few lighter moments. The receptionist was behind a counter in the center of the waiting room, and everyone could not help but hear everything she said. She kept referring to the "witch doctor," or so it sounded. Actually, she was asking the caller "which doctor" did they want to speak with. She should have asked, "Who is your doctor?" Then there would be no misunderstanding that maybe one of the surgeons was a witch doctor!

Eventually, my vision stabilized enough so that I could go back to wearing contact lenses instead of the eyeglasses. I was grateful to be able to make this change. During my annual eye exams, the optician noted that cataracts were forming on both eyes. Also, each year my hard contact lenses had to be made stronger to keep my vision close to 20/20. Without corrective lenses, my nearsighted vision was getting worse and worse.

Finally, in January 1995, I had to say goodbye permanently to the contact lenses. The proper prescription could not be made in the hard contact lenses.

By this time, I was unable to drive at night, and driving in daylight was almost impossible, as well. I could not see well in dim lighting conditions and needed to have almost every light on in the house. Also, by this time, my eyeglasses had to be made with super, super-thick bifocal lenses that literally did look like the bottom of Coke bottles. Then the time came for more drastic measures to be taken. The cataracts had to come off, and lens implants would be put in both eyes. I was more than ready!

Some friends put us in contact with St. Luke's Cataract and Laser Institute in Tarpon Springs, Florida. They gave missionaries a discount, something that we certainly could use. Dr. James Gills was the surgeon who had perfected the techniques of cataract removal and lens implant surgeries.

As we left Madison, Georgia, on our drive to Tarpon Springs, Florida, I insisted to Anna Gay that I could drive part of the way. She didn't agree, and she was right! About two miles down the highway, I pulled to the shoulder and admitted I could not see well enough to drive. I guess that hurt my ego, but I had to face reality. I was the same as legally blind, and I needed help from the Lord to adjust my attitude. I also needed Anna Gay's help and depended on her to get us safely to St. Luke's in Florida. And she did.

The eye exams and measurements at St. Luke's Cataract and Laser Institute were the most intensive and exhaustive that I have ever experienced as the technicians "mapped" my eyes.

On February 22, 2000, surgery was successfully done on my right eye. The cataract was removed and lens model number: AQ5010V, serial number: 3050424 was implanted. The very next day, February 23, surgery was successfully done on my left eye. The cataract was removed and lens model number: AQ5010V, serial number: 3028321 was implanted.

Of course, my eyes were very sensitive to light after the surgeries, but I could tell a distinct difference in my vision. I could see without eyeglasses! My vision was basically 20/20 in both eyes! What a miracle; what a blessing!

During my eye exams the day after my last surgery, Dr. Gills came into the room and exclaimed, "Brother, we are going to sing 'Amazing Grace;' you were blind, but now you can see!" And we did just that. We sang "Amazing Grace." I was greatly impressed with the pre-surgery, surgery, and post-surgery treatments, and the prayer for God's help during the procedures. Later, as we talked with Dr. Gills, he commented, "God has given doctors wisdom and abilities to perform delicate surgeries, but it is God who does the healing." Amen!

I praise the Lord for these surgeries and for the almost perfect vision as a result. I have never had such good vision in my entire life! I could see leaves on trees and individual blades of grass, and I could see true colors (such a blessing for an artist). I could read without corrective lenses. Wow! For the next few years my journey through the Myopic Zone was unimpeded by my vision. Praise the Lord!

A year or so later, which often happens after cataracts are removed, secondary cataracts formed on both eyes, and these were successfully removed by laser treatment. A capsolotomy was done on my right eye in September 2001, and on my left eye in August 2002.

While serving at Source of Light Ministries (SLM), I had opportunities from time-to-time to preach and illustrate the message with a chalk drawing using the same equipment that I was given in Philadelphia while attending Bible college. The chalk rig was still in good shape despite being hauled to Bonaire, then to Guam, then to New Jersey, and then to Georgia. I had found a source for acquiring the bogus paper used on the chalkboard, and I had a good supply of lecturers chalk, as well as the special blocks of fluorescent chalk.

I continued to paint on canvas with oils. However, my painting activities did not get as much attention as Anna Gay and family members would have preferred. Apparently, I had too many interests, too many "irons in the fire."

My ham radio activity did not have as much priority as I would have liked either, but I was able to check into the Amateur Radio Missionary Service (ARMS) net periodically on Saturday mornings. I am glad I could operate within Zone 4 with my call sign WA4DUP. The FCC (Federal Communications Commission) used to issue call sign prefixes (WA4) based on the home (QTH) location of the amateur radio operator. My call sign was first issued when I lived in Kentucky (which is also in Zone 4).

I always enjoyed the fellowship of other Christian hams who participated in the ARMS net on Saturday mornings. My dad faithfully checked into the net, as well, using his call sign WA4ZIZ. He and I communicated a lot while I was on Bonaire, but it was harder to make contact from Guam, many time zones away on the other side of the world in the Western Pacific.

On April 23, 1996, the Lord called my dad home to Heaven, and WA4ZIZ became, what is referred to in amateur radio, a "silent key." No more Morse Code and no more voice transmissions from the transmitter of WA4ZIZ. I really missed my dad. He was my buddy. My step-mom really missed him, and so did all our family members. Dad had suffered from some physical troubles that were accelerated with surgery to remove his gall bladder. Cancer had spread into other organs, and the medical doctors and specialists at the Mayo Clinic in Jacksonville, Florida, did all they could, but to no avail. I'm so glad I know that my dad is no longer suffering but is in the presence of the Lord Jesus Christ.

It was hard, but I had the opportunity of speaking at the memorial service, commemorating my dad's life and his missionary service in the Rural Evangel Mission in Kentucky and Source of Light Ministries (SLM) in Georgia. It was a real privilege to work together with my folks in the SLM ministry in the Headquarters in Madison, Georgia. My dad wore many hats during his years of missionary service, and, in fact, I wore some of those same hats myself. Dad was buried in the cemetery of Bethany Baptist Church, Madison, Georgia.

Several years before, Anna Gay's mom went to be with the Lord on March 29, 1991, while living in Houston, Texas. After we moved from New Jersey to Georgia, we began considering how we might be able to add some space to our pre-manufactured home so we could move Granny Chapman in to live with us. But we were unable to get this project off the ground before Granny Chapman passed away. Our family drove to Houston for the funeral service on April 1. Granny Chapman had been in a nursing home, was unable to attend church, and had no pastor. So I had the privilege of conducting the memorial service in Houston before her body was returned to Huntington, West Virginia, for burial alongside Anna Gay's dad, Andrew Chapman. The graveside service took place on April 5. I praise the Lord for the "blessed hope" that is mine as a child of God. One day, we will be reunited with family members (my mom and dad, my brother Paul, and Anna Gay's mom and dad) who have gone ahead of us to Heaven. "Looking for that blessed hope, and the glorious appearing of the great God and our Savior Jesus Christ" (Titus 2:13).

Not only have I participated in funerals, but I had a most unusual and unexpected opportunity to be a part of a Chinese wedding in Singapore on February 15, 2003. The daughter of Alfred and Florence Lim, Valerie, and her soon-to-be husband asked me to share a Biblical challenge as part of their wedding ceremony, and I accepted. What an opportunity this was for Anna Gay and me to be on hand for this important event. The bride and groom, and their parents, wanted to have a Chinese wedding with a Christian prospective in a Bible-believing church as a witness and testimony to the many family members and friends who gathered for the wedding. This was held in the Lims' home church, where I had preached on a couple of occasions during previous visits to Singapore in connection with the SLM Singapore Branch that was directed by Florence Lim.

On these trips to Singapore, I had gotten to know Valerie and her brother Clement while staying in the Lims' home. As we got to know each other better, Valerie and Clement began calling me "Uncle Dave," and I liked that! Clement reminded me of myself when I was his age and wearing glasses like him. He was always ready to help me with directions and suggestions for traveling from one place to another. His dad Alfred was a tremendous help, as well.

The Lim family introduced Anna Gay and me to durien, a very interesting fruit mainly grown in neighboring Malaysia. "You either love it, or you hate it," they said. The hard outer crust had to be removed in order to get to the meat of the fruit. And did it ever stink! It had its own distinct flavor that tasted pretty good once you got it past your nose. Anna Gay and I ate it, but not quite as heartily as Clement and Alfred! However, Valerie and Florence were not quite as enthusiastic about durien.

Actually, durien was banned from taxis, subways, trains, planes, and hotels by Singapore law. So that gives you an idea of how pungent and offensive the odor was for this weird fruit. Needless to say, we never did attempt to bring some samples of durien back to the States.

The challenges of our ministry through Source of Light continued to increase, and I realized that some adjustments to my schedule (as well as Anna Gay's) needed to be made. I was able to shift some responsibilities to other staff members but continued to serve as Assistant General Director, Coordinator for the Chinese outreach, Regional Field Director for Asia, Editor of *The Reaper*, and various other administration duties.

I had been asked previously by the SLM Board to assume the position of General Director. After much prayer and consideration, I declined since I felt the mission needed someone a bit younger than myself who could move the ministry forward. On November 20, 2002, I and other SLM leaders interviewed a pastor and his wife concerning the position of General Director, and they agreed to come on board as SLM missionaries. A couple of months later, SLM experienced changes in leadership as Glenn Dix, the current General Director, stepped aside due to age and health issues.

I continued as Assistant General Director and worked along-side Tom Weber, the newly appointed General Director, during the transition period that followed.

It was during this time that I received the "call" from the Board of Neighborhood Gospel Missions (NGM) to consider serving (on loan from SLM) as the Executive Director. Again, after much prayer and consideration, I knew that God was leading me in this new challenge. Anna Gay was in full agreement, as well. Both the SLM Board and the NGM Board approved the arrangement that Anna Gay and I would maintain our status as Source of Light missionaries but, as set forth in the secondment agreement, would serve under Neighborhood Gospel Missions.

This meant we would move from Madison, Georgia, to Lexington, Georgia, to be near the newly acquired property where the Home Office of NGM would be established and where NGM Camp Bethesda would be developed. Making this change in location also meant the need to sell our home on Mission Road in Madison and to find a new place to live in Oglethorpe County.

By this time, all three of our children had married and were on their own, so the relocation primarily affected Anna Gay and me. Later, this would also affect my step-mom, Adele Newell, who was continuing to serve in the Spanish Department in the SLM headquarters in Madison.

Gaylene married Bill Brewer on August 8, 1988; Philip married Angela Miller on March 2, 1996; and Holly married Dan Conner on March 9, 2002.

My journey through the Myopic Zone now required a number of adjustments in missionary service and responsibilities that would affect Anna Gay's work, as well. And we were ready to face these challenges head-on as we depended on the Lord for His wisdom, strength, and guidance.

## 15

# NGM - LEXINGTON, GEORGIA (2005-2011)

*Being confident of this very thing, that he which hath begun a good work in you will perform it until the day of Jesus Christ.* (Philippians 1:6)

Through serving on the Board of Neighborhood Gospel Missions (NGM), I gained more knowledge of this mission organization. NGM was founded in 1971 and was based in Crawfordville, Georgia, about 25 miles south of Lexington, Georgia.

The original name of the mission was Now Generation Ministries (NGM) and was renamed to Neighborhood Gospel Missions (NGM) in July 1994.

In the beginning, the primary ministry of NGM missionaries was to hold Bible classes in Georgia public schools, a ministry very similar to Scripture Memory Mountain Mission in Knott County, Kentucky, not far from where I was raised in Breathitt and Perry counties, Kentucky. In addition to holding Bible classes in the Georgia public schools, NGM had a summer camp ministry using rented facilities in A.H. Stephens State Park located in Crawfordville.

The goal of the mission was to one day establish a more permanent location for its Home Office and camp facilities.

Neighborhood Gospel Missions (NGM) is an independent faith ministry based on the fundamentals of the Word of God, and shall work in harmony with those churches and organizations that agree with its Statement of Faith.

All ministries of NGM are local and church-centered with the purpose of reaching neighborhoods of our world with the Gospel by:

1. Evangelizing the unsaved
2. Discipling believers
3. Networking with local churches

As I began serving on the NGM Board, it seemed like the goal was going to be reached when property near Barnesville, Georgia, was donated to the mission. However, as we began to develop that property, we discovered it was largely classified as wetlands, and it would not be practical to use this for summer camps.

A few years later, the NGM Board learned about the Bethesda Methodist Church located outside Lexington, Georgia, in Oglethorpe County, on Bethesda Church Road. The conference had closed the church several years before and wanted to sell the 3-acre property which included the church, a fellowship hall, and a cemetery. The location was ideal, and the buildings could be used after some renovations.

The Barnesville property was sold, and the proceeds were used to purchase the Bethesda Church and property in Oglethorpe county. Sufficient funds were available to also purchase about 35 acres of timberland adjoining the church property. Now, NGM had a new location for its home base as well as a nice piece of land for a camp and conference center.

It was about this time in early 2004, that I received a "call" from the NGM Board to serve as Executive Director, and serve as an NGM missionary on loan from Source of Light Ministries (SLM).

As Anna Gay and I began praying about this situation, it seemed that there was a good possibility that SLM might be moving its Headquarters away from Madison, Georgia. This would have been a problem for my step-mom Adele who was finding it more difficult to maintain her home in Madison since my dad was not there to help her. I had told my dad we would look after her, and we had already planned to move her in to live with Anna Gay and me.

So, this was the appropriate time to make several changes in our situation. Anna Gay and I needed to sell our home in Madison, find an adequate home in Oglethorpe County for the three of us that was situated close to the NGM property, move to this new location, and begin to establish the NGM facilities. Wow! That was quite a challenge, but we were confident that God would lead us step-by-step, and that is exactly what He did!

It was not easy to leave our children and their families in Morgan County and to leave our SLM co-workers, but by God's grace we made the transition and began a new venture journeying through the Myopic Zone.

We put our house in Madison on the market on June 26, 2004, and sold it on August 31 and had to quickly move out. Since we had no place in Oglethorpe County, we put most of our things in storage. We moved into a very small house on SLM property as a temporary arrangement. There was not any suitable houses available near the NGM property located in what is known as Flatwoods, which meant we would have to build somewhere. It was amazing to see how God led us to a man who lived on Taylor Road, just down the road from Bethesda Church Road. He was a great help and encouragement to us as we became familiar with the Flatwoods area. He put us in touch with a couple who lived close by on Stephens Grove Church Road and owned some property on Taylor Road, and Anna Gay and I met with them on September 3, 2004.

After this couple learned what we were attempting to do, they agreed to sell us a 5-acre tract just a mile from the NGM property. We closed the deal on September 15. It was on this tract, 132 Taylor Road, that we contracted with America's Homeplace to have a house built. I redesigned the floor plan so it would accommodate Anna Gay and me with a separate suite arrangement for Adele which included a sitting room, bedroom, and bathroom. (Actually, she wanted to delay her coming, so it was not until May 18, 2006, that we moved her in with us.)

Building a brand new home from scratch was a brand new experience for me, and it was interesting to work with the building supervisor who had to secure the necessary permits from the Oglethorpe County Zoning and Planning office. Finally, the house was built, and we were ready to occupy it. The plan was for Anna Gay and me to move our stuff in from storage, get situated, then move Adele from her home in Madison to live with us in Flatwoods.

On January 4, 2005, we moved into the house, but we had a problem. We had not a drop of water! Apparently, when the casing was set in the drilled well, it cut off the water supply. On January 5, the well company started a second drilling operation. The next day, they hit water, but it was not a good source. So, on January 7, a third drilling was started and completed at a depth of 220 feet. And, praise the Lord, it was good water with a good flow of 20 gallons-per-minute. The well-drilling work was guaranteed, so we did not have to pay any extra for the second and third drillings.

We had to spend a couple of nights in a motel in Athens (at no cost to us) while all this drilling was going on. What a way to get settled into a new home!

In reality, it took several weeks for us to unpack the load of boxes stacked in the garage. It was an unusually cold, wet winter, and we had red Georgia mud and huge puddles of water everywhere except on the gravel drive from the garage to Taylor Road. Straw had been scattered around the house, and I placed boards from the back deck and front door to the driveway. It was still a royal mess.

A neighbor up the road had guinea hens, and every morning the bunch of them came to our yard. They walked completely around the house looking for who-knows-what. They seemed to be aggravated by the mud and straw that was getting stuck to their feet. They all kept shaking their feet as they marched around and around the house. Later on, the guinea hens were replaced by turkeys. But by this time, we had grass growing around the house, so red mud was not a problem for them. It was fun to watch these birds every morning while eating our breakfast.

Now, we are being visited by armadillos who sneak around after dark, digging and rooting all around the back yard, and making a real mess. I have taken shots at them with my rifle if I saw them at dusk or dawn. Now, this is real country living, and we love the wooded area behind our house in spite of unwelcome critters like armadillos, snakes, coyotes, skunks, fire ants, and opossums. Frequently, we see deer come out of the woods into the yard. What a beautiful sight! No, I do not shoot deer!

But some of our friends do. For several years, a friend from Morgan County has called us on the phone to tell us he had killed a deer, and it was being prepared for us at a processing plant in nearby Crawford, Georgia. We enjoy venison very much, and Anna Gay knows how to prepare it, and it is delicious. We are grateful for this annual gift from our friend and his wife.

Of course, our purpose for moving to Flatwoods in Oglethorpe County was to establish the Home Office for Neighborhood Gospel Missions (NGM) in the former Bethesda Methodist Church. First, Anna Gay and I had to clear away debris and rubble that had been left when the church doors were closed several years before. The fellowship hall was in terrible shape since the roof had been leaking for years, causing ceiling damage to insulation and Sheetrock. The water heater needed to be replaced along with kitchen cabinets. The gas heaters were unusable; water lines were cracked; the well pump had been stolen; gas lines had been cut; and electrical power lines had been removed. In other words, things were a real mess in both buildings.

And so we started with the church building which was to serve as the NGM Home Office. New power lines had to be installed. On June 22, 2005, the well was re-drilled and sanitized, and a new pump was installed. When water pressure was applied to the water lines, they split apart. All new plumbing was required! Cracked and broken windows were replaced. Gas heaters were removed, and later the oversize church pews were sold. The building had to be thoroughly cleaned; hornets and honey bees had to be removed; window air conditioning units and fans were put in place; and wall paneling was repaired.

About this time, NGM learned about a medical facility in Athens, Georgia, that was relocating to a new building. The existing furniture was being offered to charitable organizations. Well, NGM certainly qualified, and it was so neat to see how God used this to equip our Home Office. From this business, NGM received 30 very nice wooden cloth-covered arm chairs (from their waiting room), 3 large wooden desks, 2 computer tables, 3 filing cabinets, a display shelf unit, several bookshelf units, several secretarial chairs, and a large bulletin board. What a blessing! What perfect timing! God's timing is always the right time, and I have seen this time-and-time again in my journey through the Myopic Zone!

With the purchase of the former Bethesda Methodist Church, NGM now had a place to call home. The plan is to use the Bethesda Church building and the fellowship hall as the headquarters for Neighborhood Gospel Missions. In order to do this, renovation work was needed in both buildings.

First, enough work was done in the church so that regular office hours commenced on September 1, 2005. At that time the staff consisted of myself and Anna Gay Newell, Source of Light missionaries on loan to NGM. Also, Kathy Norman joined the staff as a NGM Volunteer. In November 2006, Mary Lou McPherson began helping in the office as a NGM Volunteer. Other folks came to the office at various times to help, accomplishing a variety of tasks which included stamping the NGM address on Bible study lessons and folding them for mailing, addressing lessons for mailing and applying postage, and doing computer inputting and other secretarial work. The NGM Discipleship Ministries Department handled the Bible correspondence lesson outreach using English and Spanish materials from Source of Light Ministries in Madison, Georgia.

Our goal was to establish a fully functional administrative team of full-time and part-time NGM missionaries, and NGM Volunteers.

Current staff at NGM Camp Bethesda (September 2005): Dave Newell: NGM Executive Director, Office Manager, and Construction Coordinator; Anna Gay Newell: Discipleship Ministries Director, Spanish Lesson Coordinator and Grader, and Secretary; Kathy Norman: English Lesson Coordinator and Grader; Mary Lou McPherson: Discipleship Ministries Assistant.

Also, my step-mom, Adele Newell, was part of the NGM Home Office staff while she lived with us. For many years, she had worked with Hispanic students at Source of Light (SLM) who were studying the Spanish Bible study lessons, and her SLM ministry was incorporated into our NGM Discipleship Ministries Department. When she moved to a retirement center in Greensboro, Georgia, in October 2006, Anna Gay began handling all of the NGM Spanish ministry, something she has enjoyed doing since that time. In the meantime, Source of Light now has personnel who have the ability to once again work with Hispanic students.

This was the very first time that NGM had its own Home Office, and I was privileged to be appointed the first NGM Executive Director. Up to this point, the NGM Board was doing what it could to keep the mission and its missionaries functioning, and this certainly had its limitations. But now things were changing, and it was exciting to see the Lord working in every part of the new developments at NGM Camp Bethesda.

I am very glad that the NGM Board made the decision to maintain the name "Bethesda" to continue the heritage that had been started many, many years before when the Bethesda Methodist Church was established.

Another goal was to introduce the ministry of NGM to local churches in Oglethorpe County and surrounding counties and to explain what was planned for NGM at the former Bethesda Church property. Some of the churches Anna Gay and I visited were really happy to learn of this new venture, especially to know that the youth in their churches would have access to summer camps. Our plan was to use NGM Camp Bethesda for other activities throughout the year such as weekend retreats for young people and adults, missions conferences, and retreats for mission organizations. We look forward to the time when NGM can conduct several weeks of smaller camps, a much better arrangement than putting more than 300 campers and staff together for one week like we are having to do at the rented facility in Lizella, Georgia. (Presently, NGM conducts two camps simultaneously, one for Teens and the other for Preteens. Each group has its own programs and meal times.)

Anna Gay and I, and the Board members had many opportunities to explain to others what was planned for NGM Camp Bethesda. One morning, I was sweeping the front porch of the church (office) when a car with three people pulled into the parking lot. "Are you the caretaker?" one lady asked. I sort of nodded in the affirmative, introduced myself, and explained what NGM was doing there. They were pleased to hear that the church and property was going to be used for the Lord's work. They gave me a donation for the mission and proceeded to the cemetery to visit graves of their relatives.

On another occasion, a neighbor from Buffalo Mill Road (the dirt road across from the NGM driveway) had come to Bethesda Church Road to pick up her children from the school bus stop. She had "heard" NGM was establishing a "reformatory for delinquent boys." I was able to "set the record straight," and assure her we were establishing a church camp. (Actually, what better way to reach delinquent youth than through a summer camp ministry!)

We would have further opportunities to explain to our neighbors and county officials the goals of NGM as we plowed through the newly established county codes and guidelines that were now required by the Zoning and Planning Board and the Oglethorpe County Board of Commissioners.

NGM Board President Rev. Butch Lee and I and others spent many hours planning, discussing, and praying for the Lord's direction and help in our meetings with the county officials as we followed the required guidelines to move the project forward of developing NGM Camp Bethesda with new construction.

In the meantime, we still had to renovate the existing buildings. After opening the office, we had to contend with honey bees, hornets, and lady bugs that had made the church building their home for many years. On October 17, 2005, a beekeeper came to determine what we needed to do about removing the bees. I kept my distance while he smoked the bees and tore away part of an inside wall to expose a huge colony of bees on hives that resembled massive lungs. They were dripping with honey. What a sticky mess! We had honey running down the inside and outside wall and dripping on the carpet. Unfortunately, the honey was not edible.

We extracted the gooey mess, hoping to capture the queen bee in the process. Apparently, this did not happen since the bee colony returned to the same spot in the Spring of 2006 and began rigorously manufacturing more honey than ever. Finally, on October 15, 2007, our beekeeper friend returned, and this time we attacked the bees from the outside wall rather than making a mess on the inside.

After removing more globs of hives and honey, the bees got the message that they needed to do their work somewhere else. After repairing the outside section of wall, we covered the whole area, as well as the rest of the building with vinyl siding. And the bees have not returned.

As we kept on working inside the office during all this buzzing bee business; we felt somewhat like the folks repairing the damaged walls in Jerusalem. They had tools in one hand and weapons in the other. We had our tools (computer keyboards, pens, and pencils) in one hand and our weapons (bug spray and fly swatters) in the other hand. We have no idea how many scores of bees and hornets we killed while trying to do our work. Before we were able to get central heating, we wore gloves while grading the lessons. We often laughed about the picture we made with gloves on, flyswatter in one hand, and a pen in the other hand! You don't see that everyday! Ezra and Nehemiah would have been proud of us.

In October 2006, the fellowship hall building was moved from across the field to a position directly behind the church building. A connecting room was built to join the two buildings together, making a larger area for the NGM office. The entire fellowship hall building had to be renovated before it could be used as the office annex. The old dry wall and floor covering had to be removed, interior walls constructed, insulation installed, and electrical circuits rewired. On November 18 and December 16, 2006, work teams from one of our supporting churches located in Waxhaw, North Carolina, installed insulation and Sheetrock on the ceilings and walls. On February 3, 2007, another work team came from a church in Winder, Georgia, and added plywood to the floor, installed light fixtures, and painted the interior walls with primer.

Meanwhile, other things were happening at NGM Camp Bethesda. After negotiating with the timber company for a year and a half, NGM was finally able to secure the timber rights on the 35-acre tract it had purchased a few years before. On January 6, 2007, the timber work was begun to clear-cut most of the pine trees on the property. After the trees were cut, stumps were removed, the grounds and roads were graded, building sites for the two dorms and multipurpose building were prepared, and the ground was seeded with grass. The proceeds from the timber were used to remove the stumps and rocks, and grade the property. In the process, because of the topographical layout of the land, we had to build an earthen dam to serve as a silt pond and fishing lake. The camp grounds now includes Lake Bethesda which has also been stocked with fish, thanks to two friends of NGM.

I was very thankful for the physical strength that God gave me during the days of renovations in the church and fellowship hall buildings. I enjoyed working with my hands and helping with the manual work. It was also challenging to do some of the electrical wiring work. It was a blessing that I did not have to wear glasses and have to contend with them steaming up and sliding halfway down my nose when I perspired (which I have always done profusely). However, I began to notice when exerting energy, I seemed to be getting short-winded rather easily.

This matter really got my attention on September 8, 2006, when I helped a friend carry two large wooden bookcases into the office annex. They were pretty heavy, and I could hardly catch my breath after moving them inside. I sort of chalked it up as old age catching up with me, and that I was showing my 65 years of age.

Perhaps a break would do both Anna Gay and me some good. And that is just what happened a month later, thanks to some very close friends who lived in the vicinity of Gainesville, Georgia. They planned a trip to Canada and invited Anna Gay and me to travel with them and her parents. They had one stipulation: "We will cover all expenses, and you will not pay anything. This will be to commemorate your 40 years of missionary service, and it will be our privilege to do this for you and Anna Gay."

Wow! How could we refuse such generosity? And to top this off, a good bit of our travel would be by train! Yes, we would ride the iron rails on VIA Rail Canada passenger trains.

On October 12, 2006, we met our friends at the Atlanta Hartsfield-Jackson Airport. There, the six of us flew on Delta Airlines to Buffalo, New York. An early snow storm caused the airport to shut down just 30 minutes after our flight safely landed. Our friends rented a van, and we drove from Buffalo to Niagara Falls, Canada.

After three nights, we drove from Niagara Falls to Toronto where we spent a night. Our friends learned that Anna Gay liked ice hockey. They were able to purchase last-minute tickets, and we watched the Toronto Maple Leafs play another Canadian hockey team. That was neat!

The next day we traveled from Toronto to Montreal by train. After spending the night in Montreal, we returned to the rail station where we boarded an overnight VIA Rail Canada passenger train to travel to our next destination: Halifax. What a great way to travel! Each couple had a private compartment with seats that made into beds during the overnight hours. We also enjoyed riding some of the way in the upper level of an observation car. This offered a great view of the sunrise as our train surged northeast toward the Maritimes. It was also fun to ride in the rear observation car and talk with the conductor.

During our two-day stay in Halifax, we toured New Brunswick and drove over to tour Prince Edward Island. From Halifax, we drove back into the United States to Bar Harbor, Maine. After spending the night there, we drove to the airport in Bangor where we were scheduled to fly back to Atlanta, Georgia, on Delta Airlines.

While waiting for our flight, a plane load of military men and women arrived en route to their base in Germany. We were able to speak with many of them, thanking them for their service to our country and handing out Gospel tracts. All who we talked to expressed thanks to us for caring about them and their families they were leaving behind.

We had a good flight from Bangor to Atlanta, and retrieved our vehicles at the airport. Anna Gay and I expressed our profound gratitude for such a wonderful time together and for such a great gift to us. Our friendships were really deepened during our travels together. It certainly was a journey of a lifetime! God was so good in allowing us to do this at just the right time since I was about to go through some major physical challenges the following year in my journey through the Myopic Zone.

While coordinating the new developments at NGM Camp Bethesda, I was able to tackle some administrative duties in the Home Office. The NGM Board had established a few policies and guidelines for the mission and its missionaries, but nothing was in an organized form. I began putting together a NGM Workers' Manual as a foundation on which the mission could function. I also began preparing position descriptions, something that had not been done. It is great to see how the Lord had already prepared me for such a project. One of my responsibilities at Source of Light (SLM) was to chair the Policy Review Committee. We revised and added several policies and guidelines to the SLM Mission Manual. This work also involved revising and updating the entire manual which had not been done in many years. Revising the current position descriptions was also a part of this undertaking.

This work at SLM was a great help in putting together the new manual for Neighborhood Gospel Missions. This work required a lot of thinking, research, writing, and rewriting. This material needed to be input (which was done initially by Anna Gay). Then, all of these pages needed to be proofread, copied, assembled in a notebook binder, and distributed to the NGM Board members, missionaries, and staff. This major project was completed by the end of 2006.

Fortunately, I like to write, and I like to organize. I believe this is a gift that God has given me, and I really enjoyed this work.

The NGM Workers' Handbook consisted of 80 pages of information in five sections.

Section I     Bylaws
Section II    Principles and Practices
Section III   Policies
Section IV    Forms and Documents
Section V     Position Descriptions

One of the goals in developing the NGM Home Office was to also expand the support base for both prayer and financial support. This involved preparing a monthly donor letter to be sent along with the receipt to those who made a contribution to the ministry and its missionaries.

In addition to the monthly donor letter, we wanted to provide ministry updates to NGM constituents so they could pray for specific needs during the establishment of NGM Camp Bethesda. We also wanted to share reports of praise and information about new developments in the mission. And so in 2007, I initiated a newsletter, *The Neighborhood Watch*, to be mailed out quarterly. This involved planning, designing, writing, editing, and preparing articles and information for this newsletter using the computer software called Microsoft Publisher. I could transfer the files to a disk and take it to the local printing company in Crawford for printing. Those folks have been very helpful in this endeavor. (For awhile, at Source of Light, I was setting up *The Reaper* for printing, using a software package called PageMaker.) It is awesome to see how God puts us into learning new things that will be useful in future situations.

On October 2, 2007, during a routine checkup by our doctor in Lexington, Georgia, I was diagnosed with atrial fibrillation. The doctor immediately put me on a blood thinner and referred me to a cardiologist, Dr. Steven Lowman, in Athens, Georgia. An echocardiogram was done a few days later. Then, on November 9, a nuclear stress test showed blockages that might be treatable with stents. I am so thankful that God guided me to Dr. Lowman through a friend who highly recommended him. I was really blessed when Dr. Lowman prayed with me before he did the heart catheterization procedure. I had already committed this matter to the Lord and was at peace, but the doctor's prayer re-enforced my spirit. However, the heart catheterization on November 13 indicated angioplasty could not be done and that open heart surgery was needed. I was immediately admitted to Athens Regional Medical Center.

I sure wasn't prepared for this situation, but God knew all about it. Unexplainably, blood was somehow making its own path around the blockages and was flowing in my heart, but a heart attack was imminent. Dr. Lowman could not understand how I was alive; he thought I should have already been dead from a massive heart attack! I remember how I was experiencing shortness of breath whenever I over-exerted myself. God certainly had His hand on me up to this time when the diagnosis was made by the cardiologist.

Open heart surgery was performed on November 16, 2007. The morning of the surgery, Dr. Lowman came into my room, placed his hand on my chest, and prayed for wisdom for the surgeon and for a good outcome of the surgery. Wow! The surgeon was able to by-pass the blockages by rerouting an internal mammary artery, so no veins had to be taken from my leg. During the surgery, the surgeon also did an ablation procedure on my heart to destroy the abnormal heart tissue causing the arrhythmia. Praise the Lord, this corrected the atrial fibrillation problem, and I did not have to continue taking the blood thinner medications. The next few days in the hospital were rough with drainage tubes and IV lines running everywhere. I was also hooked up to many types of monitoring machines that continuously beeped, whistled, buzzed, chimed, and chirped. But this was music to my ears as I began my slow recovery!

I remember when the two drainage tubes were removed from my chest. These had been poking into my back causing a good bit of discomfort. What a relief to get those out! My granddaughter Bridgett, who was studying surgical technology at Athens Technical College, intently watched this procedure. I think it hurt her more than it did me!

On November 21, Anna Gay was able to bring me home. Instead of moving me from my room to the hospital entrance in a wheelchair, I had to ride in some sort of a cart which also carried my belongings, including a big red heart-shaped pillow that I was supposed to hold against my chest when I had to sneeze or cough to protect my just-closed sternum.

While I was being trundled along in this gangly contraption, Anna Gay went on ahead to get our van and bring it to the hospital entrance. My cart pusher got me safely to the door where we waited. As Anna Gay pulled up, the pusher moved me outside. I gingerly climbed out of the cart clutching my heart-shaped pillow and moved to the middle seat of the van (where I needed to ride according to the strict instructions of the nurse who checked me out of the hospital).

Anna Gay closed the sliding door, and I gingerly got myself situated in the middle seat. All of a sudden I heard and felt a thud! I almost had a heart attack right on the spot! I saw the pusher come running down the incline to retrieve the cart that had crashed into our vehicle. I struggled to get out the other side to see what damage had been done. That runaway cart put some hefty dents and scratches in the side of our van. Oh, me! I could not believe this was happening!

The pusher was just a little perturbed because he had not set the brake on the cart, and he never did actually apologize. So, before we could leave, I had to file an accident complaint and sign some paperwork. I was assured that the hospital would cover the cost of repairing our van. It was an inconvenience to us, but the hospital did pay for the damages.

A security guard witnessed the whole incident and actually called the Athens-Clark County Police. They eventually showed up, assessed the situation, and informed us that there was nothing they could do since only one of the vehicles involved was licensed for highway driving. So the pusher collected his cart, trundled it back inside while I struggled back into the van wondering, "What next!"

Three days after returning home from Athens Regional, I became very sick and nauseated, and I began to vomit. I vomited so harshly all day long that I was hoarse and very weak. I began to vomit green liquid which was a clue to Anna Gay that it might be my gall bladder. I was really feeling lousy, and after consulting with my private nurse, Anna Gay, we decided to head for the emergency room at Athens Regional. I checked into the ER on Sunday, November 25, at 9:00 PM. I was unceremoniously instructed to, "Take a seat, and we will call you back as soon as we can." Thankfully, a thoughtful nurse handed me a plastic basin, "Just in case!"

So I sat in my wheelchair as emergency personnel wheeled in people on stretchers. Others walked or staggered in under their own power. This one had a chest pain; that one had a cut; that other was in a fight; and so it went. These people were ushered right to the back while I sat in my painful, nauseated state clutching the plastic basin and my big red heart-shaped pillow to my very sore chest. By this time, we had waited three hours.

Then it happened! I vomited so hard into the basin I thought the stitches in my chest would pop! Immediately, a nurse appeared, told Anna Gay to follow her, and she hurriedly pushed me back into one of the ER rooms hollering for a doctor to come "Stat!" I thought to myself, "Man, I should have done this hours ago to get faster medical attention." Thankfully, my sternum did not come apart. By this time it was well after midnight. Since I was dehydrated and my electrolytes were out of whack, I was admitted to the hospital on November 26 at 3:00 AM.

Tests were done over the next 24 hours, including an ultrasound on November 27 that showed I had multiple gall stones. My cardiologist conferred with my heart surgeon who conferred with the general surgeon who all conferred with me and Anna Gay. The consensus was that the gall bladder needed to be removed; I had recovered sufficiently from the open heart surgery; and surgery would be scheduled for November 29, 2007.

And so it was done. Praise the Lord, there was no cancer and the 3-hour surgery was finished by 11:00 PM. (Surgery was initially scheduled for 8:00 AM, but was delayed.) I was able to return home late the next afternoon, November 30. This time, I made quite certain that I left my room in a wheelchair and not in a cart!

Now, I found myself recovering from two surgeries concurrently which was fine with me, even though the recovery process took time and was quite painful. But, by God's grace, I was alive and feeling better and stronger by the day. Anna Gay took very good care of me during the next few weeks as I slowly resumed my duties in the Home Office.

Many times I have thought back when Glenn Dix, General Director of Source of Light, had his open heart surgery with complications so severe that he almost died. God had a reason for that, however, I am grateful I did not have to experience those things myself. I was also reminded of an editorial I wrote for the September/October 1994 issue of *The Reaper*, titled "A Heart that is Fixed."

"The Bible has much to say about the heart. It is an amazing organ that is vital to a person's very existence. Even slight heart defects can give cause for concern. Not everyone has a heart problem, and we should be very thankful for hearts that function normally. But, on the other hand, every person in the world *does* have a heart problem as a result of sin. Praise the Lord, this basic problem can be fixed with a single procedure when a person receives the Lord Jesus Christ as personal Savior.

"In several of his Psalms, David mentions a heart that is fixed. "My heart is fixed, O God, my heart is fixed: I will sing and give praise" (Psalm 57:7). In the *natural sense*, the Great Physician is able to heal and fix any damaged organs in the human body, including the intestinal tract, the heart, and the diaphragm.

"God has permitted doctors to gain wonderful knowledge about the human body to the extent that amazing procedures can be performed to repair or fix a damaged or defective organ, such as the heart. God allows the skills of physicians to be used in the healing process that He designed in the body.

"Of even greater importance is the fact that a heart can be repaired in the *spiritual sense* from the deadly damage of sin. Another personal testimony of David is recorded in Psalm 108:1. "O God, my heart is fixed; I will sing and give praise, even with my glory." An ugly, sinful, unrighteous heart can be transformed to one of righteousness that will honor and glorify God. In His prayer of intercession in John 17, Jesus speaks of having God's glory. His same glory is given to everyone whose heart is fixed (cleansed by the blood of the Lamb).

"Then, in the *supernatural sense*, David had the assurance that no matter how adverse the physical circumstances, he could put his confidence in the Lord. This should be and can be true for any person who has had his or her sinful heart fixed. "He shall not be afraid of evil tidings: his heart is fixed, trusting in the Lord. His heart is established, he shall not be afraid . . ." (Psalm 112:7,8).

"Naturally, we are concerned about the condition of our physical hearts, and we sometimes must take medications and even have them fixed through complex surgical procedures. There are much graver consequences, though, when the spiritual condition of a person's heart has not been cleansed from sin."

Anna Gay and I count it a great privilege to be in the Lord's service with mission agencies such as Trans World Radio, Source of Light Ministries, and Neighborhood Gospel Missions that are presenting the plan of salvation and discipling believers in their spiritual growth. A heart that is fixed is one that has been cleansed by the blood of Christ and is being anchored to the Rock that cannot be moved by any evil principality or power.

As we serve with Neighborhood Gospel Missions, the Lord has given us additional opportunities to minister. In 2006, Anna Gay began helping with the Awana program in Victory Baptist Church in neighboring Wilkes County. In 2007, I also began helping with the Awana ministry. Presently, we are both Truth and Training leaders, working with a group of great boys.

In 2007, Anna Gay began ministering to women inmates in the Oglethorpe County Jail, and in 2009, I began ministering to men inmates. It was, and is, a blessing to conduct these weekly Bible studies on Thursday evenings. Some local Gideons continue to minister in the county jail on Mondays and Thursdays. There are four cell blocks in the county jail, one for women inmates and three for men inmates. (When Anna Gay and I were acquiring our gun permits, we had to be fingerprinted. We were taken way back inside the jail where this was done electronically by a deputy.)

I have had opportunities to do other things such as giving a devotional for employees of the printing company in Crawford and conducting a funeral for a local family. On several occasions, I have been asked to lead the music for church services while Anna Gay played the piano. Anna Gay has provided special music with her accordion.

On October 26, 2005, Anna Gay and I were prepared to conduct weekly English classes in the form of a Bible study as an outreach to local Hispanic folks. We planned to do this at Victory Baptist Church while the Awana program and prayer services were being held. This was promoted by the church in the newspaper and through the distribution of flyers announcing the classes. However, by November 16, it became apparent that no one would come. (Perhaps they were afraid this would put them in trouble with law enforcement authorities.)

On March 22, 2007, Anna Gay began taking a 6-week Spanish class at the University of Georgia one evening a week. I did not want her driving to and from Athens after dark so I went with her. While she was in class, I found a quiet spot to do some of my NGM office work.

Later in 2007, I took a one-day class at the University of Georgia that was conducted by the Soil and Water Conservation Commission in order to receive my Level IA certification. The President of the NGM Board also took this class so that we would be qualified to monitor soil disturbance at NGM Camp Bethesda. This daily monitoring is required by the state while preparing the building sites for the multipurpose building, the two dorms, the camp residence, the gravel road, and the earthen dam for the lake. By doing our own monitoring and recording, we saved the monthly fee of $450.00 that we were having to pay to a commercial company. I learned a lot of new information during this class and passed with a respectable grade, better than some of the younger guys. I believe I was the oldest one in the class. It's true, you are never too old to learn. I passed the refresher course on September 13, 2010, to renew my certification with the State of Georgia for another three years.

Speaking of learning, both Anna Gay and I decided to take some music lessons at a music store in Athens. She was playing her mandolin, and I was playing my guitar. We struggled with the classes from June 10, 2008, through September 1, 2009. This proved to be too costly and, especially in my case, too difficult because I just could not get my fingers to work on the correct strings to play good-sounding cords. We still have our instruments, and maybe some day we'll try it again. (Maybe I am too old for this particular challenge.) We'll see.

I am thankful that I could continue my ham radio activities after our move to Oglethorpe County. Eventually, with the help of eight friends, we raised the 30-foot tower with a three-element beam on top. That was quite a job, but we got it safely erected and secured with three guy cables attached to anchors that I had already put into the ground. That in itself was a real job, trying to screw those things into the layer of Georgia clay, called "hard pan." It was great to be operational again using my original call sign WA4DUP. Instead of setting the equipment up inside the house, now I had the ham shack in a utility shed. The only problem with the shed was the lack of insulation, heating, and air. Over a period of time, I was able to install insulation in the walls and ceiling, covering on the bare plywood floor, and a window air conditioning unit. A small space heater worked fairly well during cold weather. But I couldn't handle really cold, freezing weather, and that kept me out of the ham shack.

This shed was big enough to also accommodate the 4-foot by 7-foot train platform I had built into Holly's former bedroom in our house in Morgan County. I had to cut off the six legs before the move and reconnect them in the shed. Over the years, little-by-little, we had collected various HO gauge engines, cars, and track for the family. Of course, I had a particular enthusiasm for this hobby since I was continuing to develop an interest in trains, especially those railroads that operated systems in Kentucky and Georgia.

After moving to Oglethorpe County, I made an acquaintance with a railroad man who worked for the Georgia Woodlands Railroad with headquarters in Washington, Georgia. My new friend arranged for me to visit the railroad facilities, and much to my delight, I was also permitted to ride in the noisy GP9 diesel locomotive with the engineer while he and my friend switched empty wood chip hoppers with loaded ones. They were making up a train that would travel the 12 miles south from Washington to interchange with the CSX Railroad. Needless to say, that was another one of those once-in-a-lifetime experiences. I had been inside various stationary CSX locomotives in Kentucky and West Virginia, but this was the first time to actually ride in the cab of a locomotive that was moving over the rails!

Another unusual experience which involved both Anna Gay and me occurred on December 22, 2009, just before Christmas. We had the privilege of going into the Lee Arrendale State Prison in Alto, Georgia. Friends from Alto arranged for us to help distribute items to the 1,700 women inmates in that facility. Several churches, businesses, and mission organizations had donated all kinds of items for the inmates, including shampoo, deodorants, soap, toothpaste, tooth brushes, New Testaments, Gospel tracts, books by Dr. James Gills (who performed my cataract and lens implant surgeries), snack foods, and many other things.

What a privilege and blessing for us to tell the individual inmates that God loved them and wish them a Merry Christmas. Anna Gay hugged just about every inmate, and I gave many hugs, as well. There were not too many dry eyes as inmates saw that someone cared enough to share Christmas with them. Anna Gay's eyes teared up many times, as well, and I also had many tears flowing from my myopic, long eyes.

Anna Gay and I returned again to Lee Arrendale State Prison the next year, 2010. And in 2011, once again we returned to the prison. This time we took David and Beth Bentley with us so they, too, could experience this great blessing and opportunity to share God's love. We were able to briefly talk with several of the inmates that Anna Gay had ministered to in her Bible studies on Thursday evenings at the Oglethorpe County Jail.

David and Beth had expressed their desire to be a part of the NGM ministry after coming to the camp with work teams from their home church in Winder, Georgia. They satisfactorily and success-fully completed the required NGM application process for missionary service on January 27, 2009, and were approved as Missionary Appointees. The Bentleys immediately began their deputation ministry of putting together a support team to help them by prayer and financial support. The status of David and Beth was changed to NGM Missionaries on February 15, 2011. David is handling various maintenance details and coordinating Work Day activities and new construction projects. Beth is handling my secretarial work and maintaining the mission bookkeeping responsibilities. The Bentleys are also helping in the NGM Discipleship Ministries Department. As an added ministry, David and Beth joined Anna Gay and me in going into the Oglethorpe County Jail each week to conduct Bible studies with the inmates.

Exciting things were happening at NGM Camp Bethesda, maybe not at the pace we had anticipated, but, nevertheless, progress was being made. On October 23, 2008, the NGM Board President and I met with the Oglethorpe County Zoning and Planning Board to present revised comprehensive site plans and associated documents. On December 1, 2008, our request for rezoning to develop the camp and conference center was considered in a public hearing by the Oglethorpe County Commissioners. Several folks and pastors from the community were on hand to give their support, and two local pastors spoke on behalf of NGM. One person expressed concerns about our development of the camp, and these were appropriately addressed in the meeting. One week later, the Commissioners voted unanimously to approve our request. Praise the Lord, NGM had the green light to proceed with new construction.

## Accomplishments in 2009

New construction was finally started on the steel 60-foot by 80-foot multipurpose building, and other things started to happen.

| | |
|---|---|
| April 6 | Grading work began on the building sites. |
| April 21 | Grading work was completed. |
| April 28 | The building permit for the multipurpose building was issued. |
| May 28 | The steel materials were delivered. |
| June 1 | Digging for the footers, foundation, and floor, and the rough-in plumbing was started. |
| June 11 | Concrete was poured for the foundation and floor, and rough-in plumbing work was completed. |
| June 23 | The steel construction was begun by setting the columns and attaching the beams for the roof. |
| July 2 | The steel framework for the building was completed. |
| September 9 | The concrete floor was poured on the 26-foot by 60-foot second floor. |
| | The roof, side walls, doors and windows, and the inside and outside stairways were completed. |

## Accomplishments in 2010

New construction and other projects were started and completed at the camp.

| | |
|---|---|
| March 19 | The security fence around the NGM property was completed. |
| | The multipurpose building parking lot was graded and gravel spread. |
| August 23 | Grading for the camp residence building was completed. |
| August 30 | Rough-in plumbing was done on the residence. |
| October 2 | Framing was done in the multipurpose building on the ground floor bathrooms, the back wall of the kitchen, and the second floor in the dorm areas. |

| November 12 | The electrical service entrances were complete in the multipurpose building. |
| December 29 | The electric company installed underground cables from the transformer to the multipurpose building. |

### Accomplishments in 2011

New construction continued and other things were happening at NGM Camp Bethesda.

| March | We had our annual Open House and Fellowship Meal at NGM. |
| April | Electrical power lines were run from the multipurpose building to the residence building site. |
| May | A farm tractor, bush hog, and building materials were donated. |
| July | NGM conducted its Summer Camps for Teens and Preteens when many life-changing decisions were made by the campers. |
| September | More work was done inside the multipurpose building; a Chevy truck, a power mower, and power lift were donated to NGM. |
| October | Four large diseased trees were successfully cut down. |
| November | Work was done inside the multipurpose building in main hall, bathrooms, and upstairs rooms. Paint was started on the four-board fence along the county road. |
| December | Painting continued on the four-board fence. Plumbing work was done inside the multipurpose building. |

From January through September 2011, NGM Discipleship Ministries reported 3,854 lessons received, 4,787 lessons sent, 254 certificates mailed, and 9 decisions for salvation.

As we face the challenges of the New Year 2012, Anna Gay and I are finding it necessary to slow down in our time spent in the NGM office, to begin down-sizing our "stuff," and to refocus our ministry activities. This means relocating to a smaller place that is maintenance-free. But we do not plan to retire.

Our desire is to continue to serve in the ministry of Neighborhood Gospel Missions and to see the camp and conference center completed at NGM Camp Bethesda to the point that it can be used for God's glory. I believe we have many more years to serve our Lord should He tarry His return. My (our) journey through the Myopic Zone will continue until then. As long as there is one lost soul, we will never be without a job.

## 16

# GOD'S FAITHFULNESS  (Eternally)

---

*It is of the Lord's mercies that we are not consumed, because his compassions fail not. They are new every morning: great is thy faithfulness. The Lord is my portion, saith my soul; therefore will I hope in him. The Lord is good unto them that wait for him, to the soul that seeketh him.* (Lamentations 3:22-25)

These verses confirm in my heart that God's faithfulness has been present in my life and travel through the Myopic Zone. Through all my experiences in my exciting journey, I praise God for the privilege of serving Him. There have been many storms, many good times and bad times, many challenges and frustrations, and many joys and blessings. And through it all, I thank my heavenly Father, "Great is thy faithfulness!"

At least two Memorial Days have been very special. On Memorial Day, May 30, 1966, Anna Gay and I arrived on the island of Bonaire, Netherlands Antilles, to begin our first term of missionary service with Trans World Radio. On Memorial Day, May 30, 1975, Anna Gay and I, along with Gaylene and Philip, arrived on the island of Guam in the Western Pacific to continue our missionary service with Trans World Radio and to assist in building the new broadcasting facilities there.

I have experienced God's faithfulness in so many ways in my missionary service. God has given Anna Gay and me a tremendous group of partners who have faithfully shared in our ministries through their prayer support, encouraging cards and letters, and financial monthly support. We thank God for every church and individual who has shared in our missionary venture through the Myopic Zone. Many have been with us from the very beginning when we were appointed to serve with Trans World Radio in November 1965.

Since moving to Georgia in 1987, God has given us a variety of opportunities to minister in addition to our duties in Source of Light Ministries and Neighborhood Gospel Missions.

### January 1989 - December 1995

Anna Gay conducted weekly Bible studies with the women inmates in the Morgan County Jail.

### November 1990 - October 1992

Anna Gay and I conducted Sunday morning worship services at a nursing home in Madison. I led the service and gave a devotional message. Anna Gay played the piano and her accordion.

### August 1992 - May 1993

I served as Chaplain for the Morgan County Middle School PTO (Parent-Teacher Organization).

### July 1995 - Present

Anna Gay began helping in NGM summer camps as the Camp Nurse. She also began conducting weekly Bible studies with the women inmates in the Oglethorpe County Jail. I began conducting weekly Bible studies with the men inmates in the Oglethorpe County Jail.

### October 2000

I was named "Alumnus of the Year 2000" by Philadelphia College of Bible (now Philadelphia Biblical University). Anna Gay and I were special guests of the University when I was honored along with a couple of other alumni students during the annual Homecoming events. I praise the Lord for this recognition, and the honor certainly is a result of God's faithfulness.

### February 2002 - Present

I was invited to serve on the Board of Directors of Neighborhood Gospel Missions.

### July 2005 - Present

I began helping in the kitchen during NGM summer camps. Anna Gay and I began helping as Awana Truth and Training leaders in a local church.

While journeying through the Myopic Zone, I was able to wear the very same pair of hard contact lenses with the very same prescription for 13 years. Maybe a record for the Guinness Book of Records? However, I came close to losing one or both contacts at various times during those 13 years.

Late one evening, one of my contacts popped out of my eye in front of the bathroom sink. I looked on the counter, in the sink, and on the floor (and even in the toilet), but could not find it after an hour-long search. Anna Gay and the kids could not find it either; it was lost!

The next morning, I searched again but to no avail. Then, I checked the trash container that had a plastic bag in it. And there it was! My lost contact was stuck just inside the edge of the plastic bag! No, it did not go down the drain. No, it did not fall on the floor. No, it was not in the bottom of the trash bag. It was right on the edge where I could easily find it when I looked in just the right place. It was perfectly safe!

I was immediately reminded of the verse in Colossians 3:3, "For ye are dead, and your life is hid with Christ in God." This is double protection with Jesus Christ holding me in His hand, and God the Father has His hand over Christ's hand. I am totally safe; my new life in Christ is totally secure.

My contact lens experienced double protection. It was in the plastic bag that was in the trash container. Even in seemingly insignificant circumstances, the faithfulness of my heavenly Father is so evident even in the case of my lost contact lens.

I experienced God's faithfulness in at least three situations where guardian angels helped in difficult and potentially dangerous situations in my journey through the Myopic Zone.

While enrolled in Philadelphia College of Bible, I was able to get home to Kentucky only for Christmas breaks and for the summers. After Christmas 1991, I traveled back to Philadelphia by way of Chambersburg, Pennsylvania. I was traveling with Miss Hester Treher, the missionary co-worker who my folks were working with in Perry County. Miss Treher and I were riding in her car and taking turns with the long drive north from Heiner, Kentucky.

It was a very dark, late night, and I was driving. My eyes were heavy; I had my window down a bit; Miss Treher was asleep in the passenger seat. I did not realize I had drifted off the road and onto the shoulder until the steering wheel was suddenly jerked to the left, putting the car back on the roadway. Boy, did I wake up in a hurry! Miss Treher woke up, too! I did not turn that wheel, but somebody did! We were spared a very serious, deadly accident, and we thanked God for protecting us. And Miss Treher took over the driving duties at this point, as well.

Several years later while Anna Gay and I were serving on Guam with Trans World Radio, our family of four had an opportunity to take a short vacation trip in 1977 to the Philippines, Hong Kong, and Taiwan. We stayed in missionary guest apartments in each country. We were pretty much on our own as we explored and investigated the new sights and cultures in these countries. While staying in Taipei, Taiwan, I had the bright idea of taking the family on a train ride. I had discovered we could travel on a passenger train to a city south of Taipei, cross over to the northbound track, and catch a passenger train back to Taipei. Boy, this would be great, but for some reason, I could not purchase round-trip tickets in the Taipei train station. No problem, I would allow adequate time at the southern station to purchase the tickets before the northbound train arrived.

We enjoyed our travel out of the congestion of Taipei and into the rural areas of the country. We actually saw some steam engines that had not yet been retired in favor of diesel locomotives.

Our train arrived at the predetermined station right on schedule. Our family trooped across the bridge over the tracks to the northbound side, and I found the ticket agent inside the station. Unfortunately, I did not speak Chinese, and the agent did not speak English. I tried to point out what I wanted to do and that I needed four one-way tickets back to Taipei. I was getting very frustrated as I kept trying to communicate, knowing that our northbound train would be arriving soon. The ticket agent was equally frustrated! The line of impatient people behind me was growing, and they were becoming frustrated as they had to wait to buy their tickets.

As I tried again, a voice behind me asked in perfect English, "Can I be of some assistance?" There stood a young Chinese man! I answered, "Yes sir, you sure can," and explained to him what I needed. The young man spoke in Chinese to the agent, who nodded, produced and stamped four tickets, and handed them to me. I paid the proper amount in Taiwan currency, and turned to thank the young man. But he was gone; he had disappeared into thin air! I am convinced that he was an angel dispatched to help us just in our time of need.

A very few minutes later, our train arrived, and we boarded, happy to be returning to Taipei. No one knew where we were, and that was an error on my part. But we made it back to the Taipei train station and took a taxi back to our apartment. What a most unforgettable experience that was!

In early 2003, I was once again traveling in Asia in connection with the SLM Chinese Bible study lessons to coordinate the translation, printing, and distribution work. This time I had arranged to meet up with a "tent maker" missionary on Hainan Island in the South China Sea.

My evening flight from Hong Kong to Haikou City on February 28, 2003, was uneventful. I passed through immigration and customs with my suitcase (with Chinese Bible study lessons and other Bible reference materials tucked away inside) and once again, found myself in China. (This was the same location where the United States reconnaissance plane was forced to land by the Chinese Air Force several years ago.)

I made my way into the greeting area with the other passengers on my flight. Waves and smiles greeted everyone, except me. My contact was not there! Not to worry, I thought, he is probably tied up in traffic since the airport was located about a 45-minute drive from downtown Haikou City.

After two hours, the international arrivals terminal was nearly empty. As the overhead lighting was dimmed and then shut off, I made my way to the domestic arrivals terminal right next door. I could not communicate with my contact because I purposely did not want to have his telephone number or home address on my person for security reasons. I only knew that he had made reservations for me in the Hot Springs Hotel.

I walked up to an information counter and asked the attendant if she spoke English. She simply shrugged her shoulders and gave me a big smile. Well, no help here. I felt I needed to get to the hotel and out of the airport before it got too late. It was already almost three hours since my arrival at 7:00 PM, and I was growing a bit more concerned about my predicament.

Then I spotted several young men who were talking on a cell phone. Maybe they can help, so I approached them and showed them the name of the hotel and telephone number that I had copied on a slip of paper. I could not get them to understand what I was trying to do and who I needed to call since none of them spoke English. I was trying not to show my frustration at this point.

Then, I heard a voice behind me ask in English, "Can I help you?" I turned to see that a young Chinese lady had come up to our group. I sighed in relief and replied, "Yes Ma'am, you sure can!" She took the slip of paper from me and asked to borrow the cell phone that one of the young men was holding. She called the hotel and, speaking in Chinese, gave my name to confirm my reservation there. She was told that the hotel had no reservations in my name.

"Now what!" I thought. But then she called another hotel and told me they had a room available. I told her to make sure it was a standard room which would be the most economical, and she confirmed that it was a standard room.

After finishing the phone call, she handed the cell phone back to its owner and thanked him for its use. She then pointed to a bus in the parking lot, told me to get on it, and it would take me to the hotel where I supposedly now had a reservation.

"Don't worry," she said, "I'll be right there with you." That was a relief! So, I dragged my suitcase, attaché case, camera, and jacket over to the bus that was fast filling up with passengers. I found a seat half-way back but kept a very close eye on my "personal guide" who had seated herself in the front of the bus. And we headed into the blackness of night on our way to Haikou City. After about an hour's drive through rural areas and into the suburbs, we began moving more slowly through dimly lit streets.

The bus pulled into a secluded parking lot behind a hotel. The passengers piled off the bus and headed into the back entrance. I followed, lugging my stuff. The young lady was waiting for me but told me this is not where I would be staying. Instead, she said, "Follow me," and led me through the lobby and out the front door. She pointed to a building about a block away and said, "There it is." I followed her down the darkened street thinking about this strange journey I was taking through the Myopic Zone.

At the hotel (Hotel Intercontinental) she spoke to the desk clerk in Chinese, and then she told me everything was in order. I filled out the registration form, paid for the room, and turned to thank the young lady. But she was gone! Nowhere to be seen! The bellhop already had my suitcase and was heading for the elevator. I quickly followed, thanking the Lord for sending His angel to help.

To my amazement, my "standard room" was actually a suite complete with a sitting room with a huge TV, a large bedroom with another TV, a very large kitchen, and a big bathroom. Wow! All of this, and I was charged the price of a standard room. By this time it was a few minutes to 12 midnight.

My first course of action was to call the SLM headquarters and speak with Anna Gay. The time in Georgia was just about 12 noon. Anna Gay "just so happened" to be walking past the reception-ist area when my call was received. I explained my predicament and told her where to find a telephone number for my contact's home church in Alabama. I instructed Anna Gay to have someone there get in touch with my contact in Haikou and tell him where I was and that

I would go nowhere until I heard from him. Then, I again committed all this to the Lord, trusting Him that all would work out according to His plan. By this time I was really exhausted, so I climbed into bed and dropped off to sleep.

My contact called my room at 7:30 the next morning and profusely apologized for his mistake. He had put the wrong arrival date in his pocket calendar. He and his son met me a bit later for breakfast. Before leaving the hotel, he opened the drapes in the front sitting room and pointed across the boulevard. There it was, the other Hot Springs Hotel where I was supposed to be! The hotel where I was trying to go was completely on the other side of the city, many miles away. What a problem that would have been had I gone there! After breakfast, I moved to the correct Hot Springs Hotel.

But here I was because of God's amazing grace and His wonderful provision of assistance from a complete stranger the night before at the airport. What an awesome, faithful God we serve!

When the way looks impassable or obstacles seem to be insurmountable, God intervenes and changes the whole landscape. I have seen this so many times in my journey through the Myopic Zone.

On March 5, 2004, I was completing my travels in Asia with a flight from Hong Kong to Los Angeles, California, then on to Atlanta. When I began my journey in mid-February, the travel agent had told me that I was wait-listed on this last leg of my trip but said "not to worry" because she was confident my Hong Kong reservations would be confirmed with "no problem." Well, she was wrong!

I called the airline several times from the YMCA where I was staying in Kowloon, Hong Kong. I was still wait-listed. I committed this "problem" to the Lord, checked out of the YMCA early the morning of my supposedly scheduled flight, traveled to the airport by bus, and checked in at the airline counter plenty early with my stuff.

The agent confirmed I was still wait-listed but signed me in and told me someone would call me if I was cleared for the flight. Some other passengers were in the same precarious predicament. But the airline agent took my suitcase and checked it through to Atlanta; I paid the departure tax; and cleared myself through immigration.

Now, all I could do is wait. I waited and watched as passengers began moving away out of sight toward the boarding gate. A few who were also wait-listed had been called to the counter, were issued boarding passes, and headed for the departure lounge. I continued to wait, and wonder "what if" I couldn't get on this flight. It would mean spending the rest of the day and all night in the airport. By this time, I and a couple of others were the only ones left in the now quiet check-in area.

My thoughts and prayers were suddenly interrupted when I heard an agent urgently calling my name as a machine was spitting out a boarding pass. This was thrust into my hand with instructions, "I think there is one seat left on the plane! You need to hurry, because they are ready to close the boarding gate! I hope you get there in time! Good luck!"

I quickly thanked the agent, grabbed the boarding pass, collected my coat, attaché case, and camera, and ran as fast as I could down the corridor toward the boarding gate. I just barely made it, as the attendant immediately closed the gate after I slipped through.

I had to step through the half-closed door to board the Boeing 747 jumbo jet. As I stumbled down the aisle toward the coach class seating, a stewardess grabbed my arm and said, "No. No. No. You need to go up the stairs, and hurry!" I thought, "How could this be. I've never flown in a jumbo jet upstairs in business class. This is not really happening, is it? Amazing!"

But it was happening! There was my nice, wide, comfortable, plenty-of-leg-room, aisle seat with a number that matched my boarding pass number. As I flopped into the seat, the young lady in the window seat glanced up from her book, smiled, said "Hello," and went back to her reading. And I was thanking the Lord and trying to catch my breath, all at the same time. God was good! Everything turned out great; I was on schedule and heading back home to my family in Madison, Georgia. This certainly was not luck; it was the hand of my heavenly Father!

A couple of years previously, I was traveling with the TWR Guam Field Director in Asia in connection with the shortwave programming. Our journey took us from Guam to Japan, to Hong Kong, to Taiwan, and back to Guam. As we received our boarding passes at the Taipei airport in Taiwan, I noticed they seemed different, a bit more fancy than usual.

For some reason, we were "bumped up" to first class. What an unexpected treat that was! I had never flown first class, but I sure did like it! Once again, God had provided "exceeding abundantly above all that we ask or think . . ." (Ephesians 3:20). This reaches all the way from the love of Christ and the strengthening of the inner man by the Holy Spirit to airline travel on missionary trips, from the deeply spiritual to the most mundane such as the assignment of an airline seat. Praise the Lord!

I sure did enjoy flying and was never overly concerned about boarding an aircraft, although some flights did have unexpected turbulence as well as on-board emergencies of one type or another. As I began every flight, I reminded my heavenly Father of His promise: "The eternal God is thy refuge, and underneath are the everlasting arms . . ." (Deuteronomy 33:27). God was holding the plane in the air, and that was a great comfort to me.

I cannot say in all honesty that my missionary service has been smooth flying all the way. Rather, there have been many rather unpleasant situations that I have had to face while serving with Trans World Radio, Source of Light Ministries, and Neighborhood Gospel Missions. Missionaries are human beings, believe it or not, and working with fellow-missionaries in the States and overseas has always had its challenges.

I have had my fair share of differences with co-workers, from "seasoned" leadership to "greenhorn" missionaries. I have had to confront fellow-workers in all levels of responsibilities. Confrontation is not the most pleasant thing to do, but it is often necessary, and it is Scriptural, as well. It can be done in a peaceable and positive manner rather than in a harsh way.

Having served in all levels of administration has certainly had its challenges. Some "old-timers" have difficulty thinking "outside the box." This is necessary, however, in moving missions forward. It does not mean changing the "message," but it could mean changing the "method" in how we do certain things. While building the Trans World Radio station on Guam, I tried to avoid the "This is how we did it on Bonaire!" mentality as much as possible (and as much as was practical).

On various occasions, due to an error in my judgment or a misunderstanding, I have had to apologize to fellow-workers and ask for their forgiveness. It has not always been easy, but it has been the right thing to do.

Sometimes in my journey through the Myopic Zone, I felt it necessary to confide in a fellow-worker concerning a particular matter. In a few instances, I have been extremely hurt and disappointed when I learned that my "friend" had broken this confidence by sharing my concerns with others, further complicating the situation with which I was dealing. Unfortunately, this can and does happen with "friends" who mean well. I am so glad that I can confide in One who is a true and faithful Friend!

Two times, due to unacceptable behaviors and attitudes, I had the very unpleasant task of dismissing two national Source of Light missionaries who were directing overseas Branches. This was really difficult but had to be done. Since I was the Field Director, I had to travel to the Branches to meet with the individuals and their national Boards and personally deal with the situations.

On a few occasions, I have had fellow-missionaries shout at me and falsely accuse me of lying. Due to some frustrating situations in the past, I have come close to just giving up and quitting. But then, I remembered, I am ultimately serving my heavenly Father, and I want to please Him as a faithful servant. "Moreover it is required in stewards that a man be found faithful" (1 Corinthians 4:2). I am responsible to mission agencies and their leadership to carry out the duties assigned to me. And I am responsible to work with others, especially co-workers.

Many, many times I have claimed the promise found in Isaiah 26:3: "Thou wilt keep him in perfect peace, whose mind is stayed on thee: because he trusteth in thee." What a promise! What a comfort! What an encouragement!

Over the years, I have found myself in some rather unusual and uncomfortable situations. I have learned that God has given me the gift of a mediator and a peacemaker, and Anna Gay has these same gifts, as well. "And the fruit of righteousness is sown in peace of them that make peace" (James 3:18). Jesus said in Matthew 5:9, "Blessed are the peacemakers: for they shall be called the children of God." I also have had many opportunities to be a listener and an encourager, as well.

It is my desire to serve the Lord with all my soul, spirit, and body no matter what the circumstance. In retrospect, would I have done some things differently in my journey through the Myopic Zone? You better believe I would have! Do I regret serving as a missionary in the Lord's Army? No, sir, not at all! It has been a great privilege! It has been a marvelous journey and is a great evidence of the faithfulness of my heavenly Father!

My journey through the Myopic Zone since moving to Lexington, Georgia, in 2005 to serve with Neighborhood Gospel Missions has had many surprises, twists, turns, and bumps, as well as countless blessings and joyful experiences. God is good; He is good all the time no matter what the circumstances. In His time, NGM Camp Bethesda will be a beautiful camp and conference center.

I had no idea that in mid-2010 I would be diagnosed with a macula hole in my right eye. On June 10, surgery (vitrectomy) was done at Athens Regional Medical Center to remove the vitreous gel that was pulling on the macula. The after-affect was a total detachment of the retina resulting in emergency surgery on June 24 when a scleral buckle (a permanent synthetic band) was placed round the eye to keep the retina attached.

However, fluid began leaking from a tear under the retina, and a third surgery was done on July 6 to correct this problem. The surgery was not successful, and fluid continued to leak, threatening to detach the retina. A fourth surgery was done on July 31 to apply stitches to seal the tear and to replace the gas bubble with silicone oil.

A check on September 14 by the retina surgeon showed the retina was still attached, but swelling persisted in my eye, and the pressure was very, very low. The vision in my right eye was not normal even though it was not as bloodshot, and was not watering as much. By this time, Anna Gay had instilled hundreds and hundreds of drops to help the healing process.

Checkups on October 15 and December 3 were not very promising. Swelling persisted in my right eye, but the retina remained attached. The vision in my right eye was distorted, but I could see colors and objects fairly well. The double vision situation was much improved by this time. The three drops, four times a day routine was still in effect. By this time, Anna Gay had instilled 1,053 drops in my eye.

Then, on January 13, 2011, it happened! I did not see a patch of ice as I stepped out of the truck. My feet flew out from under me, and I hit the gravel driveway hard! I felt a snap and a pull in my right shoulder and arm. Man, did that hurt! Thankfully, it was not broken. However, I could not move my arm without intense pain, so I tried to take it easy. It seemed like it was badly bruised or sprained.

Now, I was dealing with two medical issues: a banged up shoulder and arm, and a defective eyeball, but the retina problem had to have priority at this point. Checks on January 18, February 18, and March 22 indicated another surgery (the fifth) was needed at Athens Regional to again try to alleviate the swelling problem and to remove the silicone oil. The surgery was performed on March 24, and a post-op was done the next day. The surgeon was very concerned because the entire eye had collapsed. (He said my shriveled eye resembled a raisin when it should be formed like a grape.) The retina had detached again!

Emergency surgery was done on March 25 to reattach the retina, to restore pressure, and to reinsert silicon oil to help keep the retina attached and the eye formed. This was the sixth surgery in addition to many painful and unpleasant procedures done in the doctor's office which included laser treatments, needles in the eye, and ultrasound tests.

By this time my eye really was beat up after six surgeries and 35 office visits, and the chance of it remaining collapsed was very real. So, another surgery was scheduled without delay at Athens Regional for Saturday, April 2. However, it could not be done because a critical piece of equipment had malfunctioned and would not be repaired in time. This meant I experienced a "cancel-ectomy."

Surgery was rescheduled for Monday, April 4. I was prepped and ready for the surgeon. He came into my room with a funny look on his face and explained the surgery could not be performed because there was no silicone oil in the hospital. The doctor was very apologetic and very displeased with the hospital staff for the over-sight. (A special courier was dispatched to Emory in Atlanta to secure the needed silicone oil.) This meant I would experience another "cancel-ectomy."

The seventh surgery in my right eye was actually done the next morning on April 5, 2011. The results were very disappointing even though the retina remained attached with the silicone oil in my eye. But I had committed all of this to the Lord, and He gave me peace about my eye situation.

While all of this was going on, I was having my arm and shoulder injury evaluated by the medical team at Athens Orthopedic in March and April. The diagnosis was a torn rotator cuff that would require surgery. By this time I was well-used to the term "surgery" and was ready to get it done, but not until I was released by my retina surgeon after the April 5 eye surgery.

On April 26, surgery was done at St. Mary's Hospital in Athens, Georgia, to repair my damaged shoulder. I was told recovery from this surgery would be slow and painful and would require several weeks of physical therapy. This all proved to be very true. For many weeks, I could only sleep at night in a recliner.

My shoulder was well bandaged with a bulky harness attachment that was needed for applying icy water to the wound area. I also had a cumbersome cushioned-type sling to hold my arm stationary against my right side. My shirt was not large enough to cover all this, but the discharge nurse said, "No problem, you can wear the hospital gown home." And I did! Can you imagine that!?

Because of my eye surgeries and my shoulder injury over the past many months, I had to sleep in a recliner instead of the bed. But now I had a different problem. The recliner handle was on the right side, and I could not use my right arm. "How am I supposed to work the recliner?" I wondered. The answer was obvious, "Find a recliner with a handle on the left side!" So, on the way home from St. Mary's Hospital, we stopped at a furniture store. I thought it best for me to stay in the van since I was dressed in my hospital gown, and I really didn't feel too swift, either, after taking pain medications following the surgery.

Anna Gay discovered that recliners were not made with handles on the left side. The only option was to purchase one with electric controls, which she did. Just a day or so earlier, we received a special gift which covered the entire cost for the recliner. God is good all the time, and we thanked Him for this wonderful provision. I call this special chair my "electric chair!"

We both use the electric chair at various times throughout late afternoons and early evenings. I am so thankful I don't need to use this recliner during the night now that my shoulder has healed and the 21 sessions of physical therapy are finished. I have normal mobility once again. Praise the Lord!

My eye is a different story. On August 11, 2011, a retina surgeon from Emory University checked my eye and told us that nothing more can be done. I am legally blind in my right eye. Even though we had suspected this was the case, it was still difficult to accept. Recently, my retina surgeon found a complication with the cornea in this eye but plans to just wait a bit before doing anything. He does want to keep a close check on my left eye, my good eye. The past year and a half has been difficult with surgeries, follow-up trips to the surgeons, and therapy, but I can say that God's grace has been more than sufficient. Many folks have been and are praying for Anna Gay and me, and we certainly feel and see the power of prayer.

Praise the Lord, at this time my left eye is healthy and is trying to compensate for the loss of vision in my right eye. My depth perception is out of whack, but I am working on that matter. Anna Gay is doing practically all of the driving now, but I can drive during the daytime but only in light traffic. Presently, I am finding it very difficult to do physical maintenance-type projects at the mission and at the house.

Little did I realize that this would be my current condition at the end of 2011 when I wrote my letter to the NGM Board in September 2009, notifying them of my intention to step aside as Executive Director, effective December 31, 2010. I felt it was an appropriate time to turn those responsibilities over to someone younger who could continue to move the NGM ministry forward. I plan to continue to be a part of NGM in other areas of ministry. I had no idea that since making that decision, I would experience multiple eye surgeries and torn rotator cuff surgery. Until the Lord provides a replacement, I have agreed to serve as Acting Executive Director as long as we are living in Flatwoods just down the road from NGM Camp Bethesda.

On July 31, 2011, I was privileged to bring the Homecoming message at Neace Memorial Church in Ned, Kentucky. I was a charter member, having been raised there when my parents began their missionary service in the hills of Kentucky in 1951. It was more than 60 years since I had been back to that church in Breathitt County. I surely did enjoy renewing acquaintances with former school friends and neighbors. It was fun to reminisce about shooting marbles, exploring the mountains, and riding up the creek beds in a wagon pulled by a team of mules. This was also the first time to be preaching since experiencing my medical limitations, and what a blessing! Then several weeks later, Anna Gay and I were able to participate in the annual missions conference at Grace Gospel Church in Huntington, West Virginia. We also visited other supporting churches in the area. It was great to be "out and about" even with my eye situation. Anna Gay stays by my right side and helps me navigate in crowds, something I find a bit disconcerting. She really is my "right hand gal" and what a wonderful helpmeet she is!

I am looking forward to the time when NGM Camp Bethesda will be filled with laughter and singing as boys and girls, and men and women come for summer camps and weekend retreats. This will happen in God's perfect timing. His plan is always perfect in our lives and in our ministries. There is nothing greater than to be in the very center of His will, and this is where I desire to be!

# END NOTES

It has been my goal to at least complete the first draft of this autobiography by year's end 2011. I now have literally 84 hours to accomplish this task, and I believe I am going to make the deadline.

In the last church service of the year at Victory Baptist Church, (December 28, 2011) where we help with the Awana program, the preacher spoke from Psalm 77. He reminded us that we need to focus on the goodness of God and not on our particular circumstances. What a great way to conclude 2011, or any other year. And what a great way to enter 2012, or any other new year.

While recounting my experiences in my travels through the Myopic Zone, I have truly been blessed and encouraged by reflecting on the goodness of my Father. He tells us in His Word, "In everything give thanks; for this is the will of God in Christ Jesus concerning you" (1 Thessalonians 5:18). We are also told that "all things work together for good." "Everything" and "all things" will not always be good in our thinking, but God knows all about our situations, and He is in control. He has a plan for the good of His children that ultimately will bring honor and glory to His name. Praise the Lord!

Because of going through seemingly unpleasant situations and circumstances, I have been able to encourage others. Here are just two examples. While visiting missionary friends in Argentina, Anna Gay and I sensed discouragement on their part, and God used us to encourage them in their ministry. On another occasion, while traveling in Taiwan, we met a missionary who was experiencing eye trouble and was unsure what to do. I was able to relate to her retina condition, and she was grateful for my advice to have this checked without delay. Within twenty-four hours, she was on a flight to the United States for an appointment with a retina surgeon who gave her the proper medical treatment that was needed to save her sight.

There is no better place to be than in the center of God's perfect will, and that is where I desire to be until I come to the end of my journey through the Myopic Zone.

At this juncture, it is time to make some adjustments in my ministry and missionary service. Neither Anna Gay nor I desire to retire but rather to refocus our responsibilities in Neighborhood Gospel Missions (NGM) and in Source of Light Ministries (SLM).

Due to our ages and physical limitations, we both know some changes need to be made. Anna Gay has been a wonderful helpmeet, and I am blessed to have her by my side throughout our missionary adventures. We reached the 45-year mark of our missionary service on May 30, 2011, only by God's grace.

The vision in my right eye is basically non-existent, and I am continuing to learn how to compensate for my lack of depth perception. Anna Gay must do most of the driving now, but I take the wheel when I can do so safely.

I know God can do a miracle and restore sight to my eye, if it is His will, and I pray to that end. I am thankful that the retina remains attached and that the eye is maintaining its shape, even though the pressure is well below normal. The silicone oil will remain in my eye indefinitely. I pray my left eye will remain healthy as it now compensates for the lack of vision in my right eye.

I desire to see the fulfillment of the NGM dream when summer camps will be held in Flatwoods, Oglethorpe County, Georgia, at NGM Camp Bethesda. It has been a real privilege and blessing to have served with three great mission organizations: Trans World Radio (1966-1987), Source of Light Ministries (1987-2004), and Neighborhood Gospel Missions (2005-the present).

The words of Jesus are certainly true. "And he said unto them, Verily I say unto you, there is no man that hath left house, or parents, or brethren, or wife, or children, for the kingdom of God's sake, who shall not receive manifold more in this present time, and in the world to come life everlasting" (Luke 18: 29-30).

"To God be the glory; great things He hath done!" Amen, and amen!